FORZA
SANKT
PAULI

FORZA SANKT PAULI

Nick Davidson

For more information, contact:
nick@outside-left.com.

First paperback edition February 2024

Book design and photography by Nick Davidson

978-1-80541-443-8 (paperback)
978-1-80541-444-5 (ebook)

www.outside-left.com

In memory of

Les Rae & Scott Chrystal
YNWA

Also by Nick Davidson
Team Shirts to Ticket Stubs: A Visual History of Watford Football Club 1977–2002
Pirates, Punks & Politics: FC St. Pauli – Falling in Love with a Radical Football Club

Also by Nick Davidson & Shaun Hunt
Modern Football is Rubbish
Modern Football is Still Rubbish

QR Codes

At the start of each chapter in this book you will find a QR code. Scanning this will give you access to additional materials relating to each chapter.

Resources include Nick's photographs from the games he has written about. In addition, there are links to a variety of resources held by FC St. Pauli-Museum that allow the reader to develop a deeper understanding of various aspects of FC St. Pauli's history. These include links to videos (all available with English subtitles) as well as items of historical significance that are held in the museum's online archive. The links will also allow for updates on particular topics as they continue to evolve.

The online content is kindly hosted by FC St. Pauli-Museum.

Contents

Cover Image: Park Fiction

This is a book about football, but I am not sure it is a *football book*. St. Pauli is about so much more than football. The district and the football team have a symbiotic relationship based on more than just sport. As such, I wanted to choose a cover photo that represented more than the football club.

Park Fiction is an outdoor community space overlooking the River Elbe and Hamburg's docks on its opposite bank. It is also a space born out of struggle. The existence of the park itself is a victory of collective community action over commercial interests. Back in the late 1990s, developers were seeking to build on the land overlooking the waterfront. It was valuable real estate. Fortunately, there is a long history of resistance to the redevelopment of the area, going back to the squatting of the buildings on the Hafenstraße. The same mix of squatters, activists and artists banded together to resist the building on the land that is now Park Fiction. The idea was to develop an open green space with views of the harbour that allowed people to meet, socialise and play music or create collective art.

The park opened in 2005. Since then, it has been an increasingly popular meeting point. Park Fiction is probably most famous for its palm tree island developed from a sketch by a boy called Yusef in 1997. The two central palm trees allow for a hammock to be strung between them. A third which sits to the side (and features on the cover of this book) is a copy of a similar palm tree that features on the carousel ride at the Hamburger Dom funfair.

I chose this to be the main image on the cover to emphasise the point that St. Pauli is about so much more than the football club. The club and the district are indelibly interconnected. It might be the case that St. Pauli through the football club and the

1

iconic Totenkopf (skull and crossbones) branding have come to represent activism and political resistance around the globe, but it mustn't be forgotten that this only became possible because of the unique reciprocal relationship between the football club and the punks, squatters and activists from the district that was forged back in the mid-1980s and continues to this day.

The story of Park Fiction is also ongoing. The theme of this book is that of continuing struggle. St. Pauli isn't something forever preserved in amber in the 1980s – the struggles are ever-present and continue to evolve and respond to events happening around them.

On 14 January 2022, the *Hamburger Morgenpost* ran a front-page story *Place of Violence – Why there is trouble about Park Fiction* criticising the park. It was basically a NIMBY story by local residents complaining about noise and antisocial behaviour. A week later, activists organised a solidarity event in the park to counter these allegations and demand a way forward for Park Fiction that didn't include an increased police presence and more rules and regulations. St. Pauli – as a district and a club – isn't an idyll or a utopia, in St. Pauli the fight is always ongoing.

Chapter 1:
Forza Sankt Pauli

"You can tell these bastards: 'F*ck off!' This will not happen. We will be the role-model for them. Their idea to organise football, to organise life is over. It is over. They can forget it. With their money, with all the bullshit they are doing there. So, we will be the role-model for them and – at St. Pauli – we will go on with everything we do."
– Ewald Lienen, June 2021

This is a quote from Ewald Lienen, the much-loved former FC St. Pauli manager, technical director and club ambassador. He was responding specifically to the plans for a European Super League but more generally against the greed of the big clubs and their continued financial domination of European football. Lienen – always outspoken and always political – was speaking during a *YouTube* broadcast that was primarily aimed at English speaking St. Pauli fans in the United States. There is absolutely no chance anything was lost in translation. Ewald meant every word.

This exchange underlines just how different FC St. Pauli is as a football club. Yes, the club still has to exist within the corporate structure of professional sport, but it sure as hell doesn't always play by the rules. Football convention dictates that managers, chairmen and technical directors can swear like troopers behind closed doors, but when they step into the spotlight, the media training kicks in and the bland, sanitised responses proliferate. Not with Ewald.

At St. Pauli, the club's official standpoint often (although not always) aligns with its supporters, rather than toeing the corporate line. As we shall see throughout this book, the club is not afraid to speak out both against the commercialisation of the modern game and – perhaps even more importantly – against issues affecting wider society.

Much has been written about St. Pauli's transformation from a run-of-the-mill, lower league football club into a politically active 'kult-club' – a process that began in the 1980s. Hopefully, some of you will have picked this up after reading my previous book about FC St. Pauli, *Pirates, Punks & Politics*. That book covered the entire 110-year-plus history of the club, but it had a specific focus on the period that saw a new breed of football fan flock to the Millerntor. In the mid-1980s, an alternative type of supporter descended on the stadium decorated in the famous Totenkopf (skull and crossbones) bringing with them an anti-fascist, DIY ideology born out of Hamburg's punk and squatter scene.

For a while, I was in the fortunate position of being the author of the only English language book about FC St. Pauli. It subsequently granted me great access to the club and allowed me to enjoy some incredible opportunities and experiences: from being able to meet and interview Ewald Lienen and club President Oke Göttlich; to going on tour with the first team to the United States in 2018 and 2019. Writing the book allowed me to live out many of my footballing dreams and that is something I am forever grateful for. I owe the club and the FC St. Pauli-Museum (to whom my book royalties continue to be donated) an enormous debt of gratitude.

However, being the only English language source material on such a unique football club was also a little unnerving. Here I am, a life-long football fan from the home counties with no journalistic training, offering my viewpoint on the most alternative, radical

professional team in world football. I don't know everything
– *far from it*. And I am conscious that my take on all things St.
Pauli remains that of a relative outsider. With that in mind, I was
delighted when in October 2020, Carles Viñas and Natxo Parra
published the excellent *St. Pauli: Another Football is Possible*. Their
book is a detailed analysis of the club and the culture that surrounds
it – and is an absorbing read (and slightly more academic than my
book, by virtue of the footnotes alone!) The authors thoroughly
deserved their shortlisting for *The Telegraph Sports Book Awards
2021 – Football Book of the Year*.

With *Forza Sankt Pauli*, my aim is not to go over old ground,
or to duplicate the work of either *Pirates, Punks & Politics* or *St.
Pauli: Another Football is Possible*. I want this book to focus on the
here and now. This book assumes the reader already understands
the emergence of St. Pauli as an antifascist club in the 1980s.
Instead of dwelling on the events of the previous century, it aims
to look at the challenges the club and wider society faced during
this last turbulent decade. FC St. Pauli isn't something trapped
in that period of time between the 1980s and the dawn of a new
millennium. The club and its fan-base have continued to grow and
evolve in the years that followed its emergence as a 'kult-club'.

The club is a living-organism, one that adapts and responds to
the challenges that society continues to face. We live in uncertain
times. Even the political scientist, Francis Fukuyama has rowed
back on his 1989 essay, *The End of History*. As we move through
the 21st Century, Fukuyama's assertation that the collapse of the
Communist Bloc in the late 1980s and early '90s heralded the
primacy of Western liberal democracy as the definitive form of
governance seems increasingly shaky.

I am not sure how many people saw this collapse of Western
democracy coming from within rather than from external ideologies
or power-blocs, but as we move through the 2020s, it increasingly
seems that the system is decaying from the inside. Under capitalism,
wealth distribution continues to be concentrated amongst a

powerful few; we live in an era of obscene wealth for the '1%' and increasing inequality for everyone else. The system no longer seems sustainable. Something must give. We now live in an age where many of these Western democracies are keen to build walls – either metaphorical or physical – to keep out those 'undesirables' from the global south. These same Western elites are more than happy to fight their proxy wars on foreign soil but are unwilling to help the hundreds of thousands of homeless or stateless refugees that these conflicts create. Add to this a climate crisis that threatens to engulf the entire planet in a battle for survival against the elements (and that will further encourage the hording of resources) and you have a world balanced on a powder-keg of uncertainty.

What has all this got to do with football you might ask? Well, football doesn't exist in a vacuum. It reflects and amplifies the world around it; football is not – and has never been – apolitical. And, as the democratic process becomes eroded by tighter controls on voter registration, and whilst the mainstream media continues to do the bidding of global billionaires, football is increasingly becoming a place where alternative political ideologies can gain exposure and traction. FC St. Pauli have always been ahead of the curve on this. But as the decade continues, sport in general – and football in particular – has become an avenue for supporters, athletes and whole communities to speak up against the increasing injustice that dominates the neo-liberal political system.

This might seem like an over-simplification, it might seem like hyperbole, but there is a lineage in sporting political resistance that began with John Carlos and Tommie Smith raising a gloved fist on the medal podium at the Olympic Games in Mexico in 1968 (Dave Zirin & John Carlos' *The John Carlos Story: The Sports Moment That Changed The World* is essential reading here), through to Colin Kaepernick and the Black Lives Matter protests. Protests that have seen footballers (of different codes) 'take a knee' in the most commercial leagues on the planet: the NFL and the Premier League.

Sports have become a vital platform for protesting inequality and injustice. As we shall see in the following chapters, FC St. Pauli remains at the epicentre of this movement.

The last 'match' entry for *Pirates, Punks & Politics* ended with the night game on Friday 25 October 2013, against SV Sandhausen. The game was an unremarkable 0:0 draw, but what followed was an impressive show of solidarity. Thousands of fans streamed out of the Millerntor Stadion onto the streets of St. Pauli in a protest march organised to support the 300-or-so refugees who had arrived in Hamburg from Libya via the Italian island of Lampedusa. That the people of St. Pauli rallied round to offer help, accommodation and support to these refugees was heart-warming but also no real surprise. What none of us realised at the time was that the arrival of these young men was to be a forerunner for a much more widespread movement of peoples from the war zones of Syria, Iraq, Somalia, Eritrea and Afghanistan (along with displaced people from groups targeted for their ethnicity in the Balkan states).

By the summer of 2015, the refugee 'crisis' had engulfed all of Europe. Whilst our British government created a hostile environment for refugees and asylum seekers, allowing a pitifully small number of refugees fleeing conflict into the country, Germany stepped up. As we shall see in subsequent chapters, the support structures that had begun to coalesce around those first Lampedusa refugees, expanded and developed to support the thousands of displaced people that arrived at Hamburg Central Station throughout the summer of 2015. It is also worth noting, after having conversations with some of those volunteers, that they object to the phrase, "The Refugee Crisis." The language around this seems to imply that the refugees are the agents of this 'crisis' rather than the unwilling victims of decades of Western foreign policy coupled with religious and ethnic cleansing by their own nation states. By labelling it a 'crisis' it subtly (or not so subtly) implies that it is the refugees themselves that are the problem, that their presence on European (or US) soil is an inconvenience to the host countries, a drain on their resources. It absolutely fails to recognise that these people seeking refuge are doing so because they are fleeing immediate danger, escaping war zones or conflicts that are often the result of disastrous foreign policy interventions. It lays the blame on the wrong people. It distracts from the realisation that the West has placed financial greed above compassion for their fellow human beings.

The mass movement of refugees that reached its peak in 2015 seemed to trigger repercussions that would impact the political and social landscape for the remainder of the decade.

In a gamble to win a majority in the 2015 General Election, David Cameron made a promise to grant a referendum to the British people on their membership of the European Union. It was a sop to Nigel Farage's UK Independence Party, and it led the country further down a slippery slope of xenophobia, racism and the demonisation of migrants. It was a political gamble that would divide a nation.

A year later, on 23 May 2016, after a long and bitter campaign led by, amongst others, Boris Johnson, Britain voted to leave the EU. The country was split 52% to 48% in favour of Vote Leave. Brexit would come to epitomise a nation's insecurities. Rather than tackling the problems of the future, the Leave campaign had sold the nation (or just over half of it) a lie. It was a lie based on an imagined, whitewashed past of church bells, village greens, sunlit uplands and a time when Britannia still ruled the waves. It was a lie told with such balls that it was writ large on the side of a bloody bus. Yes, there was, and is, a left-wing case for leaving the European Union, but that wasn't the vision the country was sold.

Leaving the European Union wasn't quite as straightforward as the politicians had hoped. The country went to the polls again in 2017 and couldn't even decide on a majority government. Theresa May took up residence in 10 Downing Street, but she was only able to do so thanks to a 'confidence-and-supply' agreement with the Democratic Unionist Party of Northern Ireland. It would cost the Tories at least £1 billion in additional funding agreements. It did nothing to quell the disquiet from both sides of the political divide. Brexit was dragging and it forced Theresa May's hand. In May 2019 she resigned as Prime Minister and was replaced after a short leadership contest by Boris Johnson. To the surprise of no one, Johnson appointed Vote Leave's arch-strategist, Dominic Cummings as his senior advisor.

This further lurch to the right, compounded with the Labour Party's murky position on Brexit, saw Johnson win the Tories an 80-seat majority in a snap election called for December 2019. Opposition leader, Jeremy Corbyn had run the Conservatives close in 2017, with his manifesto of 'radical' left-wing policies. But an indecisive message on Brexit coupled with a three year-long coordinated smear campaign by the establishment and the media, paved the way for Boris Johnson's victory. The country was now being governed by one of the most right-wing, opportunistic governments in living memory. Theresa May had begun the process of the hostile environment for foreigners during her time as Home Secretary, but every day in those first months of the Johnson regime the xenophobic rhetoric seemed to be turned up a notch.

This shift of the Overton window to the right wasn't a phenomenon exclusive to British politics. In Germany, the *Alternative für Deutschland* (AfD; Alternative for Germany) were making significant gains at local and national level. They too fed off a climate of xenophobia and fear that was partly a backlash to Angela Merkel's government and their policy for giving unprecedented numbers of refugees settled status in Germany. Since 2014, over 1.4 million people had applied for asylum in Germany, around 43% of the total number of applications in the entire EU. This number was still dwarfed by the number of refugees living in camps in Turkey or countries in the Middle East like Jordan. But Germany's decision to take 1.4 million asylum seekers certainly shames the response of the United Kingdom who processed a paltry 97,000 asylum applications in the years between 2015 and

2017. But the AfD capitalised on this, adapting their policies to stoke the fires of xenophobia and islamophobia. The party used this fearmongering to take seats in the Bundestag securing 12.6% of the vote in the 2017 federal elections. This translated into 94 seats and, alarmingly, made them the third largest party in the Bundestag. In the 2021 federal elections, AfD's percentage had dipped slightly but solidified at around 10% of the total vote, giving them 83 seats in the Bundestag.

November 2016 saw perhaps the most visible and worrying manifestation of right-wing popularism: the election of Donald Trump as the 45th President of the United States of America. It was the election result that sent the world reeling. Nobody had really believed that Trump would take office, but he was swept to power on a ticket of anti-establishment rhetoric and xenophobia. The world's most powerful nation had elected a reality TV star and prolific tweeter of nonsense as its Commander-in-Chief. Here was a head of state that made his policy announcements off-the-cuff on social media, and whose cornerstone policy for 'Making America Great Again' was building a wall between the US and Mexico and housing migrant families in cages in border prisons. It was going to be a long and dangerous four years.

Perhaps more damaging than all the policy decisions made by these new, popularist right-wing governments was the legitimacy that these regimes provided those people harbouring racist, sexist and homophobic opinions. It felt like any modest progress made since the 1960s had evaporated almost overnight. These abhorrent viewpoints had found legitimacy. Social media was awash with regressive vitriol and the hate wasn't confined to the online world. In the US, Britain and Germany there was a substantial increase in the number of violent assaults on foreigners. Trump may now be out of office but the outpouring of misogyny and racism that he legitimised still runs through society like the words on a stick of rock. Trump has left the Oval Office but in June 2022, the Supreme Court overturned the 1973 Roe v Wade case that had made abortion legal in the United States. The Supreme Court ruling effectively ended the constitutional right to an abortion, handing individual states the powers to outlaw abortion. In Texas, the Senate Bill 8 which was passed in September 2021 (pre-dating the Supreme Court's 2022 ruling) is a horrific piece of legislature that bans abortions as early as six weeks into a pregnancy. This law includes cases where women are victims of rape or incest. It is hardly a coincidence that these law changes were passed on the back of Donald Trump's administration – a man with such scant regard for the sovereignty of women over their own bodies – presiding over the country for four years. This was the man who proclaimed he "grabbed women by the pussy".

This potted history of the last decade is not new information for anyone with even the faintest interest in politics. But it does provide some backdrop and context to the history of FC St. Pauli over a similar timeframe. My feeling is that so much has happened since I completed *Pirates, Punks & Politics* in late 2013 that the story needs to be updated.

For me this is a very different book to write. Most of my research for *Pirates, Punks & Politics* was done through secondary sources. First, I hoovered up any information or articles that I could find on the club that were written in English. After that, I spent a lot of hours putting German-language materials through Google translate. I was incredibly fortunate to meet Christoph Nagel author of *St. Pauli. Das Buch.,* a heavyweight tome and, perhaps, the definitive book documenting the history of the club. Christoph showed the patience of a saint as we traded emails that both cleared up many of my misunderstandings and gave me extra details on specific people or events. *Pirates, Punks & Politics* was very much a history book in the traditional sense. Most of the events I was documenting had happened years before I even became aware of the club's existence. My own personal experiences were shared via chapters on the games I had attended, but these were very much the tales of a wide-eyed foreigner experiencing a footballing-awakening in another land. Also, as many people pointed out in the reviews, my 'match entries' were hardly punk rock! Most of the time, aside from describing the match, I usually spent an incredibly long time on a train and then went to bed early. This wasn't some '90s lads mag recount of weekends on the piss complete with stories of waking up naked in a dingy room on a back street off the Reeperbahn. The hedonism was dialled right down, and I spent most of my evenings in Hamburg checking and rechecking train timetables.

The crucial difference between this book on St. Pauli and my last is that I feel I lived through – and to some small extent participated in – the events I am going to be describing. I witnessed them unfold in real time. I am also fortunate enough to have got to know a lot of people closely connected to the club during my regular trips to Hamburg. So, even when I wasn't there, I felt like I was getting 'live' feedback from the events unfolding. It makes this book very different to write. Primarily, I am not scouring secondary sources for information. Instead, I am recalling events that I remember happening and returning to messages and conversations from the time for clarification. There is, of course, more of a risk that the history in this book is much more subjective – born of my personal interpretation. The period is also much more recent, meaning that the dust has yet to completely settle, thereby adding a layer of time and distance that is often valuable when unpicking historical events. I have tried to remain objective throughout this book, but I am aware that my own prejudice and perspective will colour my judgement. On the plus side, as I got to know more people in Hamburg, I did manage to stay up a bit later and have a few drinks. However, if any of you are still looking for exaggerated tales of drunken debauchery, you will remain largely disappointed.

That said, history continues to unfold, and we are, perhaps, better placed to analyse events that we have lived through than of those that we can only evaluate through secondary sources. I don't want this book to be a hagiography of the club. St. Pauli – the club and the fans – are not perfect, nor do they claim to be. I have been the beneficiary of some incredible opportunities provided by the club, but I don't think that makes me completely uncritical. History is ongoing and events and participants in those events are re-evaluated all the time. My intention is not to add a layer of gloss to the ongoing 'Mythos of St. Pauli'. Instead, it is to bring the story of the club up to date whilst objectively reflecting on the events I have witnessed. As I attempt a second book on St. Pauli, I am also increasingly conscious that I am another middle-aged, middle-class, white male offering his viewpoint. My voice has been amplified enough and I believe that the stage needs to be shared by St. Pauli fans of different generations, ethnicities, and genders. As we move forward in the history of this special club, it is vital that these voices gain prominence. It is vital that a light is shone on neglected areas of FC St. Pauli's history, whether that be documenting the history of women's football at the club or the work that has gone into researching and recording the experiences of those involved with St. Pauli during National Socialism.

It is the club and its supporters' response to the recent historical events that form the basis of this book. It will examine 'The Refugee Crisis' of 2015 and the welcome and support provided by St. Pauli fans and residents. The exponential growth of St. Pauli fan groups in the United States in the immediate aftermath of Trump's election and the subsequent tours of the country by the St. Pauli squad will be unpicked and evaluated. In an interview with club president Oke Göttlich, we will explore the tightrope that the club walks – balancing being a global brand whilst staying true to its activist roots. Also, re-evaluating how the club doesn't always get it right and that a state of harmony doesn't always exist between the board and the fan base, something exemplified by the five-year kit deal with US manufacturer, Under Armour. A discussion with former Commercial Director, Bernd von Geldern will explore the club's decision to part company with Under Armour and produce their own kit, placing an emphasis on sustainability and ethical trade.

St. Pauli also continues to speak up against the continuing monetisation of football. For example, in 2018 the club submitted a motion to the German Football League (DFL) that renewed the league's commitment to the 50+1 rule of ownership, something that seems especially poignant in a footballing landscape dominated by billionaire owners and the threat to the future of the game posed by the forces pushing for a European Super League.

There will also be chapters that focus on two St. Pauli icons: former manager Ewald Lienen and former player Deniz Naki. In a fan culture that places primacy of the collective over that of the individual, it is rare for individuals to rise to prominence. But in the case of Lienen and Naki an in-depth analysis of their popularity is necessary and important. Both men come to embody the activism and spirt of FC St. Pauli in a manner that goes beyond and outlasts anything they achieved for the club on the pitch. These two men are, in many ways, the embodiment of St. Pauli in the modern era. Yet, as we shall discover, Naki's story – like that of St. Pauli itself – is far from straightforward.

Then, in line with the seismic shift that occurred in the global game, the focus of the book (and my attendance at matches) pivots towards FC St. Pauli 1. Frauen. It documents the inception and rise of the women's department at FC St. Pauli from their origins in the 1970s, rebirth almost two decades later, right through to the team's historic first appearance in the German national cup competition in August 2023.

Much of this chapter has been taken up outlining the events of the last decade that have shaped society and the global political landscape. But all of them can be linked back to FC St. Pauli. Indeed, all these forces converged and descended on Hamburg in July 2017 when the city hosted the G20 summit. Whilst Trump, May, Merkel, Erdoğan and others discussed trade deals inside the fortified compound of Hamburg Messe, the city outside burned. Three days of protests boiled over as police brutally intimidated and suppressed activists. Hundreds of people were arrested or taken into custody. The trials of those who were arrested rumble on to this day. The G20 summit took place barely a kilometre from FC St. Pauli's Millerntor Stadion, placing the club at the epicentre of the protests. The club didn't stand idly by: it remained true to its anti-establishment beliefs. During the day, the Millerntor acted as an 'alternative media centre' providing a voice for outlets critical of the political circus that was occurring a stone's throw from the stadium. At night, the stadium acted as a place of refuge for protestors who were offered a place to sleep, food and sanitary facilities safe from the violent police operation that was going on around them. For me, one of the most poignant and worrying moments came during those long July evenings, when friends holed-up in the 1910 e.V. Wine Bar in the stadium relayed descriptions of the thousands of police officers and armoured vehicles that were amassed on the adjacent Heiligengeistfeld awaiting orders. Describing the plumes of smoke spiralling upward into a darkening sky constantly criss-crossed by police helicopters – it felt like a scene from a war zone or a dystopian novel. Those of us not in the city worried incessantly for the safety of our Hamburg friends.

The G20 in Hamburg was a powerful example of how politics and sport can never be separated. As Ewald Lienen said, "everything is political" and St. Pauli remains at the centre of this convergence of sport and politics. Nothing brought that as clearly and powerfully into focus as Trump & Co. trying to forge out their future just a few hundred yards from the Millerntor. During those violent few days of protest in 2017, FC St. Pauli as a club and its supporters were the embodiment of Ewald Lienen's quote at the start of this chapter: *"You can tell these bastards: 'F*ck off!' This will not happen."* If the fightback against global politics' sharp right-turn didn't begin in Hamburg that weekend, it certainly gathered momentum. That's what this book is about: a football club's response to the events going on around it, fighting back against this decade's lurch to the right.

Chapter 2:
Voran Sankt Pauli (Match)

FC St. Pauli 1 RB Leipzig 0
Bundesliga 2
13:30, Sunday 3 May 2015, Millerntor Stadion

An overcast afternoon in early May. Against my better judgement, I found myself back in Watford. Having parked miles from the ground, I was walking to the last, decisive game of the 2014/15 EFL Championship season. I had ummed-and-ahhed about attending this game all week. FC St. Pauli of Hamburg are my club now, but with the weight of nostalgia tugging heavily at my heartstrings, I had decided I couldn't miss out on witnessing Watford – the club of my youth – winning the biggest trophy in their history. It was my chance to see them lifting the old First Division Championship trophy, that glorious piece of silverware held aloft throughout my childhood by a succession of Liverpool captains. Of course, with the advent of the Premier League and the subsequent rebranding of every level of the national game, the proud old trophy had been relegated to the EFL Championship, but it would still be a far bigger prize than anything the Hornets had won before in over a century of existence. My inner child told me I couldn't miss such a momentous occasion, and when the opportunity arose to stand with two old mates from college at the back of the Rookery, I decided to take it.

I'd wandered past the Town Hall pond, scene of many a promotion celebration in the golden years of the 1970s & '80s and had made it about halfway down the High Street when I noticed a small crowd of people singing. They were surrounding a befuddled haystack of a man – all unruly hair and ill-fitting blue suit. Then, my brain decoded the chant: *"Boris is a Hornet! Boris is a Hornet!"*

There he was in all his confused buffoonery: The Mayor of London, Alexander Boris de Pfeffel Johnson – a Watford scarf draped awkwardly around his neck. You'd think after all the Conservatives had done to football fans over the previous thirty-years (from the lies and the cover-up born out of the Hillsborough disaster to the selling of the game's soul to the Murdoch empire via an aborted attempt at introducing ID cards) that this clown would've been set upon and chased out of town by a baying mob. But no. Here he was – a politician with no interest in Watford FC or even football in general – being mobbed by delighted Watford fans singing his name and posing for selfies. I did my bit and tried to substitute 'Hornet' for something cruder and more appropriate, but I was soon moved on by an irate PR lady, who was simultaneously on the phone to someone saying, "We need to get Boris out of this situation. *Now!*"

To put this encounter into its political context, this wasn't some random Saturday stroll by the Mayor of London pushing his Oyster Card to the very limits of the underground system. Five days later was the 2015 General Election. The parliamentary constituency of Watford had been something of a three-way marginal in previous elections and Tory Central Office were obviously intent on wheeling out the big guns to solidify support for their incumbent MP, Richard Harrington. Spoiler alert: it worked; Harrington was returned to Parliament with a – much-increased – 9,794 majority.

But Boris Johnson's circus stopover in Hertfordshire was representative of something more sinister that was beginning to fester in the second decade of the 21st Century: Right-wing authoritarianism, fronted by the cult of the strongman, popularist leader.

Putin had been in power in Russia for fifteen years by this point. He had recently been joined in office by President Erdoğan in Turkey and would subsequently be followed by the likes of Bolsonaro in Brazil. We were witnessing a seismic shift to the right in global politics. Then, of course, came the rise to power of a pair of flaxen-haired truth twisters on either side of the Atlantic. In May 2015, Boris Johnson was still four years away from ousting Theresa May to become leader of the Conservative Party and it was still almost two years until Donald Trump would set foot in the White House – but the storm clouds were gathering, change was coming.

You could write a book itself charting the popularity of the right-wing authoritarian political leader but, in some small way, Boris Johnson surrounded by football supporters chanting his name on Watford High Street encapsulates everything succinctly. Here were football fans swarming around a man with a outwardly affable persona, but who was manipulating his popularity for personal gain. Johnson – like Trump and Farage – was feeding off a groundswell of racism, sexism and xenophobia that was being whipped up by a right-wing media keen to blame the failings of late capitalism on the vulnerable. This in turn masked the reality of those in positions of power hording wealth and resources amongst themselves. You could argue it is a lot to pin on a chance encounter with an ego-maniac politician on a high street walkabout, but those Watford fans surrounding the future Prime Minister just seemed to confirm the way society was heading. Bluster and confidence taking precedence over policy and integrity. Maybe, my politics was colouring my judgement but, I felt betrayed by it all. My decision to attend this title-deciding fixture started to feel flawed.

I won't dwell too long on the Watford match – because this remains a book about FC St. Pauli – but suffice to say, the Hornets didn't win the silverware. Everything was going to plan, right up until the 91st minute. Watford were leading 1:0 and the Championship trophy was on its way to Vicarage Road. Then, something baffling happened. A lone pitch invader – a *Watford* fan – caused a prolonged stoppage in play, that was only ended when he was escorted off the pitch by Hornets' captain, Troy Deeney. It was enough to break the home side's concentration and allow Sheffield Wednesday to equalise. This was a hammer blow; however, it was the events that followed that really broke my heart.

Prior to the last gasp Wednesday equalizer – and in anticipation of victory – Watford fans had clambered over the perimeter walls and were lurking behind the advertising hoardings ready to invade the pitch. At the Rookery End, hundreds had gone even further and were encroaching onto the playing surface. The stewards stood idly by. Then, with 90 seconds of stoppage-time remaining, Watford forced a corner – a corner that represented the last hope of scoring a winner and thus salvaging the Championship title. Trouble is there were so many *Watford* fans on the perimeter of the pitch by the corner flag that Dániel Tőzsér – a *Watford* player – couldn't take a run up to deliver one of the most vital corners in the club's history. Utter idiots.

Looking at the photos, it was a bunch of pissed wannabe hooligans in their second-generation casual clobber who didn't give a toss about history or achievement. They just wanted to take selfies on the pitch and repeatedly chant, *We are Premier League!* The corner was cleared, the ref blew his whistle, and everyone got their pointless pitch invasion. Not quite everyone. Granted there were also plenty of people inside the stadium who were absolutely gutted that the team had come within 90 seconds of winning the biggest trophy in its history. I sure as hell felt the disappointment and I was only a lapsed fan. I really felt for my mates Chris and Nick and the hundreds of other supporters of our generation who were genuinely distraught at conceding the title to AFC Bournemouth in such dramatic fashion.

It was a stark reminder of why I had turned my back on English football. These days, so many fans think being 'Premier League' is the be-all and end-all to football. It isn't. We all know from previous encounters that the Premiership can be a dismal, depressing experience for a small club but, in today's world, making it to the Premier League 'party' is all that matters. Even if, on arrival, your team will only ever be ignored, ridiculed and patronised.

If I didn't know St. Pauli, I'd put it down to my age. History matters to those of us old enough to remember life before the Premier League. No need to be gutted though, when you can be on the pitch with your mates letting off smoke bombs and singing – you've guessed it – *We are Premier League!* over and over again.

Walking back through town after the game – with Boris Johnson long since ushered back aboard the Tory Battle Bus – the pubs were packed. The air was quasi-celebratory. Promotion had been achieved and celebrated a week previously, today the Championship title had been lost. Yet people were in the pond, it all felt a bit false – a bit 'this is what we are supposed to do'.

That Saturday night, I had pretty much had enough of football. The feeling hadn't really evaporated when my alarm went off at 4:15am for the weekend's main event.

It was dawn on a dreary Sunday morning, and I was on my way to Hamburg, something that normally filled me with joy. But my mood hadn't really improved as I drove down the M40 to the airport through pouring rain. I'd not seen a single goal in my three previous trips to watch FC St. Pauli that season, not much of a surprise as goals had been hard to come by. A couple of weeks previously, I was in Karlsruhe for a depressing 3-0 defeat. We were facing relegation to 3. Liga unless we started winning games soon. So it was more in hope than expectation that I decided to make the trip to Hamburg for the Leipzig game.

Of course, the trip to St. Pauli ended up providing me with footballing redemption. As it does almost every time I make the journey to the Millerntor. Those of you who read *Pirates, Punks*

& Politics will probably recall that my fear of flying often led to me making the long (and expensive) trip to Hamburg by train. In the intervening years, a redundancy, the global financial crash and the years of austerity that followed meant I had to conquer my fear of flying in order to take the much cheaper and quicker flight to Hamburg. Writing this in 2023 with the impending climate catastrophe, I realise that I probably have an environmental decision to make when it comes to my trips to watch St. Pauli, but more of that in a later chapter.

Just two hours after taxiing along the runway at Heathrow, I was stepping off the S-Bahn train at the Reeperbahn. It was enough to lift the cloud from over my head. There is something about being back in the unique district of St. Pauli that makes me feel at home. Just wandering the sticker and graffiti covered streets in the early morning sunshine was reminding me of why I make the trip – and I wasn't even in sight of the Millerntor Stadion at this point. I didn't need to be, FC St. Pauli and the district the club represents are entwined in the very fabric of each other. You can't walk more than five yards without setting eyes on a St. Pauli sticker, a flag hanging from a balcony or someone wandering around in a Totenkopf hoodie. It was like an antidote to the bland election propaganda we'd had rammed down our throats over the past few weeks back in England. Being in St. Pauli is like plugging in and recharging your political batteries. It might not provide answers, but it provides hope.

This was the penultimate game of the 2. Bundesliga season and one FC St. Pauli had to win to stand a realistic chance of avoiding the drop into the third tier of German football. Additionally, I was curious as to how the fans of RasenBallsport Leipzig would be received at the Millerntor. The 'RasenBallsport' being a bit of clever word play on behalf of owners Red Bull to circumvent the DFB's rules on club names. The German Football Association forbids clubs to be named after corporate entities (Bayer Leverkusen being the historical exception to the rule).

There is a rumour that when the Red Bull organisation were first looking at investing in German football they met representatives of the FC St. Pauli to discuss a deal. Given that St. Pauli's fanbase had been active participants in the demonstrations against Red Bull swallowing up and rebranding SV Austria Salzburg, it seemed an unlikely union. It was certainly a partnership that never got as far as a membership vote. In the end, Red Bull reached an agreement with Oberliga side SSV Markranstädt to buy its place in the fifth tier of German football. Markranstädt is located on the outskirts of Leipzig, a city with a proud football history. VfB Leipzig were the first national champions of Germany as far back as 1903. But post-unification, no team from the city had played in the Bundesliga since the relegation of VfB Leipzig in 1994. Despite the lineage of VfB Leipzig continuing through into the present day in the form of 1. FC Lokomotive Leipzig and the existence of BSG Chemie Leipzig, the city of Leipzig was a huge potential market for football that was waiting to be tapped. Red Bull recognised that opportunity.

RB Leipzig are a franchise, pure and simple, like their (almost) namesakes in Salzburg and New York. Think MK Dons, only with more money to throw at branding (and players). In many ways, Red Bull are the logical conclusion of what happens to football when fans no longer care about history, only about success. They are the epitome of what happens when money is placed at the centre of everything they do.

In May 2015, RB Leipzig were just passing through St. Pauli and 2. Bundesliga en route to their ultimate destination: The Champions League. Two years on, RB Leipzig would complete their mission by taking part in the 2017/18 UEFA Champions League; fast-forward another three years and they would be losing out to another bank-rolled member of the new European elite, Paris St. Germain, in the semi-finals of the competition. In 2022, they would lift the DFB Pokal (German FA Cup) for the first time.

St. Pauli are the polar opposite of RB Leipzig. Whereas the visitors found a clever way of subverting Germany's 50+1 ownership model that prevents clubs from being swallowed up by foreign investment, FC St. Pauli remains a club that belongs to its members – all 36,500 of them (as of August 2023). The club belongs to the people; it belongs to the district of St. Pauli.

For the pre-match choreo, Ultrà Sankt Pauli opted for a couple of pointed banners. They read, *This is football, here are dramas* a line from the Thees Uhlmann song *Das hier ist Fußball* and also a reference to the organic fan culture that has grown over the years at the Millerntor, and that has not been corrupted and eroded by the arrival of cash-rich benefactors. And my favourite banner, a message for both Red Bull players and fans alike, lifted from Wu Tang Clan, *Cash rules everything around you!*

The banners were enough to make a point but not so much as to detract us from getting behind the team, because today the team needed us. They had a relegation battle to fight.

Just like the day before in Watford, there were fans drinking pre-match, but that horrible laddish atmosphere was completely absent. It was simply like-minded people drinking in the sun. If Boris Johnson was yesterday's portent of what was to come, then I got an inkling that things were going to be okay today when I walked into the Fanräume and *Out On The Floor* by Dobie Gray was blaring out. I love Dobie Gray's music, it holds a special place in my heart, but I never dreamt I'd hear it at *football*. But then again, this is the Millerntor, anything is possible. They might be a punk club, but they are not afraid to throw a bit of Northern Soul into the mix as well.

Inside the stadium, the Millerntor had out done itself. The Gegengerade was awash with brown, white and red flags. There was a confetti storm in both the Gegengerade and the Südkurve. And following on from the confetti was some great rainbow pyro by USP. Yes, pyro is illegal. Yes, the club will get fined for it, but it was done safely and sensibly and – when used appropriately – the smoke and flares add so much to the atmosphere. That sensible usage needs to be legalised. Here the DFB have a chance to take the lead in the safe use of pyrotechnics in football stadiums. Sadly, although they are a considerably more progressive football association than the English FA, even they are not quite ready to give pyro the green light. But that's a fight for another day. Legal or not, the result was spectacular. This was how to welcome our team prior to a relegation scrap.

The players played their part. They even broke my goalless streak, Lennart Thy putting St. Pauli ahead right on the stroke of half-time. And, just like the day before at Vicarage Road, the score was 1-0 to the home side as the clock edged ever closer to 90 minutes. But instead of the crowd going quiet with nerves (or some idiot invading the pitch) it just got louder. It was immense. Full-back Sebastian Schachten commented after the game that it was the loudest he'd heard the Millerntor. He wasn't wrong.

But football always throws up that one last chance for the opposition. However, unlike yesterday, that last opposition chance was brilliantly turned round the post by St. Pauli keeper, Robin Himmelmann. The celebrations – real earned *victory* celebrations – could begin. Yes, the context was entirely different – it was a euphoria fuelled by relief – but it felt way more genuine than a load of lads on the pitch chanting *We are Premier League!* after conceding a last-gasp equalizer.

St. Pauli weren't mathematically safe, just yet. The win had helped, but the season would go right down to the wire and the last game of the season – a 525-kilometer trek to promotion-hunting Darmstadt. It wasn't going to be easy.

This had been a weekend that allowed for comparison and reflection. As I stood on the terraces of the Millerntor, beer in hand, I realized that I had no regrets. I had made the right choice. FC St. Pauli was the football future I wanted. It was time to leave my childhood team behind for good. There was no going back. Only forward. *Voran Sankt Pauli.*

Chapter 3:
The Sonderzug Trilogy (Matches)

They say things come in threes and my story of the Sonderzug (direct translation: 'special train') is a trilogy. But how on earth do you describe the Sonderzug experience to someone who has never been?

St. Pauli photographer, Stefan Groenveld in his photoblog, 'The Sonderzug Files' acknowledged the fact that it is impossible to fully explain Sonderzug, ending his piece with the quote, "Who does not feel it, cannot understand it." And in a sense that statement holds true: if you've not experienced the 'special train' it's hard to comprehend it, especially if you are from The British Isles.

To be absolutely clear, the concept of the Sonderzug wouldn't be allowed in modern-day Britain. If you were to put a load of British football fans on a train packed with hundreds of crates of beer and no police presence whatsoever, it wouldn't make it 10 minutes out of the station. Not without the bar being looted, the train being smashed up, and some idiot pulling the emergency stop cord.

That's not to say it hasn't happened in Britain. In the early 1970s, Football League officials (with a little help from British

Rail) dreamed up the concept of 'The League Liner'. In 1973, the first 'Liner' set sail from Burnley station taking fans to their away game in London against Queens Park Rangers. It offered 'genuine First-Class travel' for football fans, a hitherto unthinkable concept. It was an attempt by the authorities to try and combat the amount of vandalism that was occurring on the regular 'football specials' of the era ('football specials' were trains comprised of battered old rolling-stock that were used to transport fans to games). The idea seems naïve by modern standards, but it isn't too different from what happened with the launch of the Premier League some twenty years later. Essentially, the idea was to price out troublemaking, working class fans in a bid to attract a more affluent, civilised football supporter. Also, in true sexist 1970s fashion the Football League also thought they could attract more 'wives' and 'girlfriends' under the guise of a shopping trip to London. According to an article on 'The League Liner' published in *The Guardian* in February 2013, Jack Butterfield, part of the committee responsible for launching the train service, said, "Even if they (women) are not interested in football they can be guaranteed five hours in London for a shopping spree."

That's not to say 'The League Liner' wasn't a fun concept. They were dubbed 'disco trains' in the press. There's archive footage on *YouTube* that shows teenagers in high-waisted trousers grooving to the sounds of the '70s in a fully equipped disco carriage. Sadly, the train was removed from British Rail's fleet in 1976 after complaints that supporters had vandalised the carriages. Which brings us full circle: British football fans wouldn't be trusted with anything like the Sonderzug these days. But – in Germany – supporter-run 'special trains' are a feature of the fan culture. At St. Pauli the concept has been pushed to the very limits of the imagination.

So, how do you describe the Sonderzug experience? I am not sure I can do it justice but, this is the best I can do with words. If you really want to know, you'll have to get lucky with finding a ticket for next year's train. Please excuse the hyperbole:

Sonderzug is a post-apocalyptic Hogwarts Express, populated not by wizards and witches, but crammed full of punks, anarchists, ultras, skins and (social) romantics – all members of St. Pauli's leftfield football fan scene. It hurtles through the dawn towards the Armageddon of the last away game of the season, fuelled by the Astra being drunk by everyone stupid enough not to have hunkered down in their compartment to grab a few hours rest. It's Astra that seeps from every pore of those brave souls dancing in the disco carriage at 08:00 and it is spilt Astra that forms a tacky bond between your trainers and the carriage floor as you make your way to the bar. Fans bang the roof in time to cheesy Eurotrash anthems that they wouldn't be seen dead dancing to outside of this train carriage, occasionally bursting into a defiant round of football songs. It's not even 10:00. Sonderzug is Mad Max *on rails. It's the dystopian future-football movie that nobody has thought to make (although they've come close with film/series* Snowpiercer *which just lacked a weekly stop-over at some far-flung football fixture). It's completely insane, yet it feels like the most wonderful place in the world.*

I promise you, my – heavily clichéd – words still don't do it justice.

But I'm getting ahead of myself, we need to take this one Sonderzug at a time... I have been fortunate enough to experience two of my three trips on the special train with my best mate, Shaun. And for all three journeys I was also travelling with the lovely people from Yorkshire St. Pauli. Together, we've all been able to share the crazy experiences of early morning drinking tempered by afternoon hangovers. And, through experience, we have just about learnt how to pace ourselves and survive to the end.

A slight warning: this chapter contains more alcohol consumption than the whole of *Pirates, Punks & Politics*. However, I remain a lightweight when it comes to drinking and I am still convinced that reading about people's drunken exploits is actually pretty dull! But here goes...

Sonderzug Lite
FC Köln 4 FC St. Pauli 0
Bundesliga 2
15:30, Sunday 4 May 2014, Rhein-Energie-Stadion

Shaun and I were up early on the morning of our first ever Sonderzug – excited and ever-so-slightly nervous, unsure of what the next 18-hours would bring. On the advice of Scott from Yorkshire St. Pauli (a veteran of the previous year's trip) we loaded up with snacks at the 24-hour supermarket. Apparently, this was one of those trips where alcohol was the necessity and food a mere afterthought. At our age, we knew we needed to keep half an eye on our blood sugar.

Then it was on to Altona station, the starting point for our adventure. It is worth pointing out it wasn't even 06:00. Not long after navigating our way through the station's maze of concourses, we caught our first glimpse of the Sonderzug – a hulking (and slightly rusting) 15-carriage beast, last used as a stunt-double for the Hogwarts Express. It was a mighty impressive sight – its maroon-coloured coaches stretching the entire length of the platform, seemingly disappearing over the horizon.

The beer was being loaded on and hundreds of fans were making their way down the platform to find their allotted carriage. That they were dressed variously as Super Mario, Batman, Catwoman and The Undertaker didn't raise an eyebrow. It is another St. Pauli tradition that this epic trip is made in some sort of fancy dress.

It is worth recognising the incredible amount of effort that the Fanladen crew go to make this event happen every year – the logistics are mind-blowing. Then, imagine everyone adhering to their allotted seat or compartment on a train full of English football fans? Imagine crate upon crate of beer being left unguarded yet remaining untouched on a train full of English football fans? Imagine Catwoman not being subjected to a load of sexist and derogatory nonsense on a train full of English football fans? You get the picture. Sonderzug is different.

Throw into the mix, that said beer was being loaded onto the train by members of St. Pauli's Supervisory Board (who also put in a shift behind the bar) and it's a total mind-bender for your average British fan. A member of the club's board loading beer onto a train? Interacting with supporters? Running the bar? For free? At 06:00 on a Sunday morning? Don't be daft... Even better, they just saw it as totally normal behaviour to want to help. It is shared community responsibility, pure and simple.

We located our carriage, slid open the door to our compartment and sat down. After waiting for at least five minutes for the trolley selling chocolate frogs to come round, we upped sticks and headed for the party wagon. It took a while to snake our way along the corridor, as already there were impromptu gatherings breaking out all along the train – an eclectic mix of specially decorated and themed carriages, full of friends beginning to party.

Eventually, we made it to the bar and official party wagon. It was relatively quiet, but the music was already blasting out a mixture of Ska, '80s rock and, somewhat ironically, the HSV club anthem. Despite my growing (and deserved) reputation as a lightweight, I knew that this could possibly be a once-in-a-lifetime experience and made the bold decision of starting on the Astra at 08:00. It's funny, 'cos after a couple of bottles, time kind of ceases to matter and it seems totally reasonable to get another drink in.

It's a novel experience dancing in a moving train carriage and I did spend some time wondering how those platformed-shoed 1970s youngsters on 'The League Liner' coped moonstomping as the train navigated the notoriously rickety British Rail tracks of the time. One thing worth noting is that for the Sonderzug, Deutsche Bahn deliberately slow the train down, although this has less to do with concern for the stability of those in the disco carriage and more to do with giving priority to regular train services. As such, the journey from Hamburg to Köln was going to take around six hours instead of the usual four.

I'm pretty sure we peaked about 10:00. Somewhere between a fantastic Ska version of the Billy Bragg's *A New England* and *I Just Can't Get Enough* by Depeche Mode. In terms of beer drinking, it was all downhill from there. We arrived at Köln Messe/Deutz station at around 12:30. From here we made our way onto the S-Bahn under a moderate police escort. However, our journey on the S-Bahn to the stadium was done in tandem with the sort of police cavalcade usually reserved for American Presidents. The driver kept having to stop the train to wait for the assortment of riot vans, police cars and motorcycle out-riders to catch up – as hilariously – they kept getting stuck at the traffic lights on the road that ran parallel to the track. On arrival at the station, the temperature went up a few notches as a couple (and it was only a couple) of Köln youths engaged in some macho posturing which in turn upset a few of the excitable youngsters in the away support. These young St. Pauli fans tried to slip the police blockade and exchange 'pleasantries' with their rivals.

We too gave the police escort the slip on the way to the ground, but not for an 'off' with some Köln fans. Instead, we recognised that after six hours drinking beer on a train, we needed a rest. Our group chose a nice patch of grass in the park by the stadium and had a picnic, a beer and – in Shaun and my case – a well-deserved nap. St. Pauli and Köln fans mingled freely, without a hint of bother. Whether the semi-formal 'fan-friendship' of previous years was still in place is very much up for debate – although a banner in the Köln section near us appeared to indicate it was.

After a brief nap, it was time to head into the stadium. I'd been a couple of times before (en route to various St. Pauli games) and always liked it as a ground. Our pizza slice of an away section was bathed in sunshine and was being occupied by a bedraggled set of fans nursing fuzzy heads from the first leg of the Sonderzug.

Köln were champions and we had nothing to play for except the mystical 'Golden Pineapple'. I kept hearing this phrase being used but had no idea what it was about until I looked it up on the internet. The 'Golden Pineapple' is a fictitious trophy awarded to the winner of a match that has absolutely no significance. As a result, it is normally contested on the final day of the season between two teams with nothing to play for. This was the penultimate game of the 2013/14 campaign, but Köln were already champions and St. Pauli mathematically safe from relegation. That said, the result was a forgone conclusion. Köln underlined their status as the best team in 2. Liga by romping home 4:0, the only bright spot for the visitors being the introduction of the soon-to-retire Fabian Boll from the substitute's bench.

The main drama occurred in the guest-bloc with one fan fainting in the heat and others, I think, injuring themselves in a fall. They were treated by a team of medics which subdued the atmosphere as the fans allowed the first aiders to go about their job in peace. At the final whistle, Boll and the team came over to shake the hands of the fans down the front on the terrace.

For Shaun and I, the day had been all about experiencing the Sonderzug. It had been an honour to be a part of the legendary party train and to share the experience with so many good folk.

Being perennial lightweights, and due to the fact that Shaun has to work Bank Holidays, we were jumping off in Köln to catch the red-eye back to Stansted, but it had been an absolute blast. Pissed on a train by 09.00. Dancing to *Panic* by The Smiths in a carriage rammed with fancy-dress loons by 10.00 and crashed out on the grass in front of the stadium by 13.00 – all in half-a-day's work for us Sonderzug lightweights. Of course, for everyone else, the party was just getting started. The disco carriage would be in full-swing for the entire six-hour crawl back to Hamburg.

We left the Köln fans to their celebrations, said our farewells to the YSP massive, slung our trendy Hoxton-boutique Gola man-bags over our weary shoulders and headed for our hotel in the city centre. A quiet meal in Köln, wrapped in a blanket looking every bit like the dishevelled veterans of six-hours drinking on a train, then it was up early for the return flight to Stansted. We were back in

Britain by 07:00 the next morning. Shaun was back at his desk by 10:00.

Sonderzug Fick Dich 3.Liga:
Darmstadt 1 FC St. Pauli 0
Bundesliga 2
15:30, Sunday 24 May 2015, Stadion am Böllenfalltor

A year later we were back in Altona readying ourselves for our second Sonderzug. We had travelled from London to Hamburg with Scott and Luke from Yorkshire St. Pauli. This wasn't a problem, in fact it was great to share the journey to Hamburg with them. We learned from each other: I went all *Tomorrow's World* and took them for a ride in Heathrow's futuristic Pod transporter; they opened my eyes to the tantalizing world of WH Smith 'Meal Deals'. But deep down, I was worried about being unmasked as the grumpiest man in European football. Shaun, my regular companion for these trips, is a dab-hand at managing my highs and lows, but with no fancy dress superhero costumes to hide behind on this year's Sonderzug, I was sure I was going to be rumbled by the others as a bit of a misery.

Then there was the realisation that last year we only attempted *Sonderzug Lite* – we had a blast on the trip down to Köln, but this was safe in the knowledge that we weren't going back on the train, we were flying back to Britain from the Rhineland. Principally, this was on the grounds of Shaun having to work the next day, but let's be honest, it was as much about me being a total lightweight on the alcohol front. Really, we were veterans of half a Sonderzug or Sonderzug 0.5. Which begged the question, how the hell were we going to survive a whole one?

Meticulous planning, that's how. No late night for us, we left that to the rest of Yorkshire St. Pauli. Instead, it was a nice meal and a mojito in our favourite restaurant in Sternschanze followed by an early night. Well, after we'd completed Phase 2 of our Sonderzug preparation: a trip to the supermarket. Yep, we picked up a trick or too last year. Too much beer equalled too much time queuing for the toilet. So, instead, we bought a couple of bottles of readymix vodka at €3.90 a pop, energy-beer (no really, it contained guarana as the vital active ingredient) and some regular energy drinks (energy being the recurring theme). Oh, and food supplies. There's no limit to the amount of alcohol a bag of home-brand tortilla chips can absorb. Sorted.

We were up with the proverbial lark at 05:00 (notice all my times are in 24-hour, as this felt like a military operation) and at Altona station in time to rendezvous with the rest of Yorkshire St. Pauli and Heinz, the keeper of the tickets.

Then, it was full steam ahead for Darmstadt. We located the allotted Yorkshire St. Pauli compartment and then made for the disco carriage in search of some feel-good Balearic trance served with a dash of Nana Mouskouri. There was no way we were going to manage the entire six-hour trip down to Darmstadt in the party wagon, so soon we filtered our way back to the relative sanity of our compartment. I managed a tactical nap, which I knew would come in handy later. I was woken at various points by our German pal, Christian bursting into song or swearing, in English, in his work-in-progress cock-er-nee accent. The consensus was that the atmosphere on the way down was subdued, not surprising given what was riding on the outcome of the game.

Relegation, a nailed-on certainty a few weeks previously, was now avoidable with a win at Darmstadt, but that wasn't going to be easy, given victory for the home side guaranteed them promotion to the Bundesliga. No 'Golden Pineapples' this year – it was all up for grabs. I'm not sure any of us really understood the various permutations of results that could see us stay up or go down. There was a crumb of comfort, however: all our relegation rivals had tough away games ahead of them too. There was also a chance a draw or a narrow defeat might also be enough.

Whilst the atmosphere wasn't quite as raucous as normal en route to Darmstadt, the six or so hours did provide a fantastic opportunity to catch up with friends I've met over the years at St. Pauli. It was a metaphorical shot in the arm to talk to so many great people. It remains my favourite thing about the St. Pauli fan experience – everyone will stop, chat, hug and catch up, even if the last time you saw them was on the Sonderzug the previous season. It felt especially poignant this year. I'd been really struggling since the general election, a couple of weeks earlier, on 7 May. Where I live, it is true-blue Tory country (with a worryingly large amount of UKIP thrown in). I found it genuinely hard to look people in the eye going round Tesco, knowing that most of them voted Conservative or worse. As a public sector worker, I've spent the last five years being battered with cuts, pay-freezes and criticism. I've seen far worse going on in other essential services like social care and the NHS. The 2015 election should've been a time to stick two-fingers up at austerity and put the mildly less offensive Labour Party in government. Instead, the country showed itself to be populated by selfish bastards, who don't give a toss about anyone else but themselves. To return a majority Conservative government after five years of being screwed into the ground felt like the end of days (little did I know, back then, that this was only *the start*).

Anyway, that's what made being aboard the Sonderzug so special. At last, I was with people who just 'get it'. Sure, as a diverse left-wing fanbase we disagree over how to achieve things, but broadly speaking we all want the same thing: a better, fairer society for everyone. I felt that talking to people on the train. Whether they were connected to the Fanladen, Supervisory Board, the 1910 e.V. Museum or FC Lampedusa. These were good people, who believe in a fairer world. Post-election, I had too many arguments online and de-friended too many closet Tories. It felt good to be amongst people who cared.

As we rolled into Darmstadt, we were even given a warm welcome by the local police who'd rigged up a sound system at the station that was blasting out *Das Herz von St. Pauli*. This was a complete opposite to the Köln police's approach a year earlier. It was also nice to catch up briefly with Svenja who'd made her way to Darmstadt independently as she was unable to get a ticket for the Sonderzug. As I mentioned previously, I love the way you just bump into people at St. Pauli games. It even happened the night before in Altona, when we were wandering down the road looking for our hotel. There, walking towards us, was our friend, Thomas, on his way back from a martial arts class. Sometimes, you have to check yourself and think: is this just a place we visit a few times a year? Because it feels so much like home.

A short walk through an enchanted forest (if by enchanted you mean people wading through the undergrowth to find somewhere secluded to go for a piss), and we were at the delightfully dilapidated Stadion am Böllenfalltor. We climbed a few concrete steps and found ourselves on a bank of terracing that wraps itself around the ground. Even filling up with fans, it was an impressive sight, a throwback to different times. The terracing swept around both ends, although not at the height and depth of St. Pauli's new Gegengerade. There were old school floodlights fitted as standard, but even more impressive was the life-size Subbuteo TV Tower (a must-have accessory for us children of the 1970s and '80s) located behind the goal in front of us. However, as always, changes were afoot. With promotion would come the need for stadium renovation, with the amount of terracing reduced and seating increased.

The crowd built steadily, as the stragglers from the Sonderzug were joined by other St. Pauli fans who had made the 525km journey to Darmstadt independently. The atmosphere *felt* loud. However, one disadvantage of an open-air terrace is that the only direction the noise travels is up. But armed with balloons, confetti, and glitter, even if the noise wasn't heard, the colour and atmosphere was certainly transmitted from the stands to the pitch. The Darmstadt fans did their bit too, after all this was a huge afternoon for them as well. Positioned in a forest of flags, I didn't even realise the game had kicked off. In fact, the entire game was like a stop-motion animation, you'd be watching one part of the pitch, a giant flag would pass across your line of vision and when the action returned the ball would be somewhere else entirely. Given the looming threat of relegation, it was probably the best possible way of watching.

St. Pauli made it to half-time 0-0 and other results seemed to be going our way. But all that changed when a Darmstadt free kick sneaked past Robin Himmelmann in the St. Pauli goal. The home fans were delirious, but in the guest bloc things started to get a little tense. It felt like there was no way we were going to equalise, so the attention really turned to the action elsewhere. To cut a long story short, relegation rivals, Erzgebirge Aue pulled it back from 2:0 to 2:2 in Heidenheim causing a fair degree of anguish for us St. Pauli fans. Obviously, any mobile phone reception had long since collapsed under the weight of fans trying to find out the score. And, despite the retro stadium vibes, nobody had the foresight to bring a transistor radio. Another goal from Aue and we could be relegated.

The final whistle went in our game. Our fate was out of our hands. The Darmstadt fans poured from the terraces onto the pitch to celebrate promotion to the Bundesliga.

Eventually, the news filtered through from the ether that Erzgebirge Aue hadn't found a winner, other games had gone our way, and we were completely safe from relegation. The players and manager, Ewald Lienen, made their way over to the St. Pauli fans who also poured onto the pitch to celebrate. Without sight of an actual league table, I couldn't really believe it, but we were safe! We also found out that the players and coaching staff had been in the same predicament as we were: they couldn't get the score confirmed on their phones and had to wait for someone in the press box with an ASDL link to the outside world to confirm our safety.

The celebrations on the pitch continued for some time. Meanwhile, word got round that several of the players would be coming back with us on the Sonderzug. It was time to party!

This was where the combination of pacing ourselves on the way down and our bountiful supply of energy drinks came into their own. We were ready! It was straight to the disco carriage where we remained, toilet stops aside, for the next six and a half hours. It was an incredible experience. We were high fiving the fans and players out of the train window as they made their way along the platform in dribs and drabs.

We danced. We sang. We hugged *everyone*. We ploughed through the vodka and moved onto celebratory 'champagne' (which was really a very drinkable sparkling wine). There was singing along to both the Duisburg club anthem (or was it Bochum?) and the song, *HSV is My Wife* apparently performed by Mozart (this was confusing on multiple levels). There was crowd surfing with another of our Hamburg friends, Maarten, spending much of the journey home being passed up and down the carriage by a forest of outstretched arms.

Over the course of the trip home, I remember hugging Stefan from the Fanladen and profusely thanking him and his team for doing all this for us. I recall jumping on an unsuspecting Sönke Goldbeck of the St. Pauli Supervisory Board. I was so relieved for all of them, as I knew they'd been saved from having to make some horrible decisions if we'd been relegated. The financial drop-off from television rights alone between 2. Liga and 3. Liga would've posed significant financial headaches for the club, especially after taking out loans to finance the redevelopment of the Millerntor Stadion.

Then – in one of those mystical moments – the carriage cleared. Maarten (who must've been on a crowd-surfing break at this point) introduced me to Ewald Lienen, St. Pauli manager and the architect of our escape. Here he was, the first team manager, in the middle of the party wagon, on the special train! Of course, he spoke to me in his perfect English. I thanked him repeatedly in my slurred vernacular. He then thanked *me!* I told him to stop thanking me! We embraced. You get the picture. It was incredible. Although, undoubtedly, more so for me than him.

The sun set, the music got heavier then lighter, we danced on. Shaun was a man possessed, raving like it was 1990. He fell over. And fell over again. In the rare moments he wasn't dancing or fist bumping relative strangers, he was queuing for the toilet. Well, that's what he thought he was doing. He was actually waiting patiently outside the door for the DJ booth. He carried on queuing, despite numerous proclamations and lots of us pointing at the sign on the door that said, 'DJ booth'. He wasn't going anywhere, after all, as he kept on insisting, he "was next in the queue!"

Of course, it had to come to an end. The train limped back into Altona station at about 01:00 in the morning. However, there was still time for some comedy comedown moments. Shaun managed to step off the train not onto the concrete but into the gap between the train and platform. I had always wondered why train announcements would remind passengers to 'Mind the Gap' when the doors opened at every stop. Here was living proof. Shaun ended up being sort of wedged in the gap up to his knees. He was also being held upright by Yorkshire St. Pauli's Fuzz, who was conceding about ten stone to Shaun in weight alone. Fortunately, he emerged laughing and unscathed.

Even better than that, he managed to trip me up on the short walk back to our accommodation which resulted in me bleeding all over the hotel room, something I only realised I'd done on waking up in the early hours of Monday morning. I turned the light on and was greeted by a trail of blood that wouldn't have looked out of place in a low budget horror movie. It turned out I'd taken a chunk out of my elbow, and it hadn't stopped bleeding.

However, if you cast your mind back to my two confessions at the start of this recount of our trip to Darmstadt, I'd done pretty well. I had managed to pace myself for the return leg, thoroughly enjoying myself on the way back with my bottles of budget vodka mix. However, my exposure as the most miserable man in Europe came to fruition when the alarm went off at 05:00 for our 06:50 flight home. In my defence, it isn't easy mobilising a hungover

Shaun first thing in the morning. Especially when all he does is giggle – and your elbow won't stop bleeding. Anyhow, we made it. We met up with Scott and Luke at the airport and, before we knew it, we were back at Heathrow accessing our cache of Wagon Wheels that we had stashed in the boot of the car.

I'd done it – a whole entire Sonderzug! Not only that, but also one where we had somehow avoided relegation and partied with the team on the way home. It was a truly unforgettable experience, probably my favourite ever St. Pauli trip.

Sonderzug Drei/Dry
VfL Bochum 1 FC St. Pauli 3

Bundesliga 2

15:30, Sunday 21 May 2017, Ruhrstadion

I took a well-earned rest from the special train in 2016. Sometimes, like with the Glastonbury Festival, a fallow year is good for recharging the batteries.

The trip to Bochum was to be my third Sonderzug. This time, with Shaun unable to attend and with me having a manic work schedule looming the following week, I decided to attempt the impossible: *Sonderzug Dry*. Shorn of Shaun and alcohol, my third trip on the party train was going to require a degree of mental strength and resilience. On the upside, I'd at least have a fighting chance of remembering the game. Although, that's not always a positive when it comes to St. Pauli. Sometimes I think St. Pauli fans drink to forget the football.

Everyone was relatively awake and on-the-ball at Altona station the next morning. Granted the 07:39 departure from Platform 9 ¾ was much more civilized than we'd been used to in previous years. This year, the passengers on the Hogwarts Express were dressed almost exclusively in the garish polyester football kits of yesteryear. It was like riding the train with a thousand Jorge Campos in an acid-casualty, day-glo nightmare.

There was confusion early on, as we were all bumped down a coach, due to some generosity on behalf of DBahn, who'd given our train an extra carriage. Finally, we found our compartment and settled down for some Sonderzug chat about the relative merits of foods preserved in brine. We also enjoyed Luke's decade-defying Wikipedia inspired 'pop-quiz'. Having spent all my previous trips in the disco-carriage, I was pleasantly surprised that they piped the usual selection of cheesy 80s Euro-pop anthems direct into your compartment via the train speaker system.

Again, so much of the Sonderzug is about chatting to people you only ever see on the Sonderzug! It's a lovely experience, interspersed with random folk popping their heads into your compartment and offering you homemade snacks from Tupperware containers. Even queuing for the toilet can be a cathartic experience: I was stood waiting when a bloke started chatting to me in German. When he realised I didn't understand him, he reached into his pocket and gave me a fist full of stickers. Fortunately, I had some Yorkshire St. Pauli stickers to give to him in return. That's how it works: language can fail you, but stickers don't.

After traversing the length of the train to reach the part of it that had some contact with the platform, we disembarked into a warm and muggy Bochum afternoon. There we met up with the rest of the YSP contingent who hadn't been lucky enough to win Sonderzug tickets in the ballot. I thought they might be in a somewhat better state than many of those on the party train, but it soon became clear that they were utterly hammered too. Turns out it's never too early to drink on a train, even if it is just a regular Deutsche Bahn service between Hamburg and Bochum.

After a longish uphill walk, we finally reached Bochum's Ruhrstadion. It has more than a touch of concrete brutalism about its exterior, not to mention an impressive set of floodlights. It didn't take too long to get into the ground, despite the tight security.

The atmosphere was loud right from the start – at the end of the game St. Pauli defender Jan Philipp Kalla called it an extra home game. Even when we conceded an early goal it was noisy. Sometimes the Sonderzug can have the reverse effect on the atmosphere: a morning of drinking taking its toll and subduing the crowd. Not this time. We'd equalised before half-time with a goal from Lennart Thy. The interval was spent with *I Just Can't Get Enough* bouncing back and forth between the fans in different sections, whilst we were singing a version of 2-Unlimited's *No Limit* aka the Hakan Suker song (*Hakan, ha-ha, Hakan, ha-ha, HAKAN SUKER!*) in tribute to the bloke a few steps below us, exquisitely dressed in a yellow and red polyester homage to the man himself. This wasn't just a shirt with 'Suker' on the back. This was an all-over photo print tribute to the Turkish striker. But no matter how loud we sang the bloke just wouldn't look round.

The second half was a bit of a blur, made memorable by a fine headed goal from our giant defender Lasse Sobiech and an incredible goal-line clearance from Kalla. A second goal from Thy that put the game to bed. It had been a really good performance. Of course, it was really all about the post-match celebrations. The team got a huge ovation, but it was nothing compared to the reception reserved for Ewald Lienen. We were dead-and-buried at Christmas, cut adrift at the bottom of the table and heading for the third division. Yet here we were finishing the season in seventh place. It had been a remarkable turn-around: a credit to the players, credit to Lienen and credit to the club for not taking the well-trodden path of sacking the manager. And – as pointed out by Ewald himself on the pitch at the end of the game – credit to Olaf Janßen, the St. Pauli assistant manager who arrived during the winter break. I was glad to be there to say 'goodbye' to Ewald – he had become my favourite St. Pauli manager and, perhaps, the first since Holger Stanislawski to really connect with the fans.

We ambled back to the station. I'd swapped my ticket for the Sonderzug home with another member of Yorkshire St. Pauli. Instead, I was scheduled to head back to Hamburg via Hannover on the ICE. However, the mysterious extra carriage laid on by DBahn did us a huge favour: there was room aboard the party train for everyone, arranged by Stefan from the Fanladen. It should've been relatively straightforward getting us all on the train but keeping errant Yorkshire St. Pauli members in one place is akin to herding cats. Charlie and Chris had wandered off in search of an off-licence. A frantic phone call later and they were legging it up the steps to the platform – making it with seconds to spare before the train lurched into life.

The journey back was as just as you'd expect the Sonderzug to be: the disco carriage in full swing, people staggering around in various stages of drunkenness. Despite this there were enough sober people around to happily pass the four hours back to Hamburg, filling the time with some great conversations about the meaning of life, politics and football.

Sonderzug Drei/Dry was certainly different. Nobody had queued for hours outside the door to the DJ booth thinking it was the toilet (Shaun); nobody fell down the gap between the train and the platform as we disembarked (Shaun); nobody tripped me up on the walk back to the hotel (Shaun); but it was still as brilliantly surreal as always. No matter how many times you experience it, the concept of a train full of St. Pauli fans, a disco carriage and an endless supply of beer never ceases to blow your mind.

And what Sonderzug doesn't finish with four of us sat in a sauna at our Airbnb at 01:00 in the morning plotting to overthrow Yorkshire St. Pauli's Svengali-figure, Scott and replace him with Gary from Glasgow St. Pauli? Gary being taller, more handsome, more organised and with superior fanclub merch. What's not to like? Don't worry, this wasn't some factional leftist coup. Scott was present *and* in broad agreement with the proposal.

Three Sonderzugs: all different, but all utterly brilliant in their own way. I count myself very fortunate to have been able to experience these trips. And, unless the British football authorities make the unlikely decision to bring back their 'League Liner', it is not something football fans in Britain will ever get to experience. Plus, our rail network is crap.

Chapter 4:
Refugees United: FC Lampedusa St. Pauli

Refugee. Just the word refugee. It's loaded. It necessitates opinion, either positive or pejorative. For many, the word evokes empathy and compassion – and solidarity with those who have suffered enormous physical and emotional distress and hardships. For others, it triggers hate, fear and insecurity. It is a division that is constantly amplified in either direction across both social and mainstream media.

Yet, these emotional responses are abstract; they are not connected to individuals. In the same way it is impossible to truly comprehend the scale of this movement of people through numbers alone: Germany registered 964,574 asylum claims in the first 11 months of 2015. That's nearly one million people.

How can you comprehend a million people? Even breaking it down doesn't help. At its height, in the summer of 2015, around 1,000 refugees were arriving at Hamburg Hauptbahnhof every day.

The numbers, like the word refugee, don't help us connect – we need something more. Something personal. Something that makes us register that – beyond the semantics and statistics – there are people, individuals and families caught up in the crisis. It's why individual stories of tragedy or triumph resonate.

It's why one photo of the little Syrian boy, Alan Kurdi, washed up on the beach stopped the world in its tracks in September 2015. Tens of thousands of others have suffered the same fate in the Mediterranean over the last few summers with much less attention from the media or interest from the public. Yet that one photo got to all of us. It humanized and contextualised a much wider tragedy through the shocking and heart-breaking image of one little boy.

It's also why the Olympic Refugee team was greeted so warmly in Rio in 2016 and in Tokyo in 2021. Again, the powerful personal story of swimmer Yusra Mardini captured the hearts of millions of people around the globe. (I would recommend reading *Butterfly: From Refugee to Olympian, My Story of Rescue, Hope and Triumph* by Yusra Mardini.) As a 14-year-old, Yusra had represented Syria in international competition. But the war in Syria destroyed everything. In August 2015, Yusra and her older sister, Sara, left their home in Damascus and fled the country. Like thousands of refugees both before and after them, they paid smugglers a small fortune and boarded an overcrowded dinghy bound for Greece. The engine failed. Yusra and Sara pushed, pulled and cajoled the boat through the Aegean Sea for over three hours until they reached the island of Lesbos.

Even then, the journey was far from over. The two young women endured a traumatic overland trip across Europe before reaching Berlin. There, eventually, the two girls joined a swimming club and Yusra's journey to the 2016 Olympics in Rio de Janeiro began its improbable final phase.

Suddenly, Yusra Mardini's story – the girl who swam for hours pushing her boat to safety – could be heard and contextualized through her achievements in the Olympic pool. Her courage, determination and resilience won the hearts of those watching the games in Rio. It also saw her return to compete in the Covid-delayed game in Tokyo as well as carrying the flag for the IOC

Refugee Olympic Team in the opening ceremony. There is, almost inevitably, a governmental and legal storm cloud hanging over the Mardini's story. Sara, who returned to the island of Lesbos to work helping refugees, is one of 24 humanitarian aid workers facing decades in prison if convicted of ridiculous espionage charges by the Greek government.

It is not right that these individual stories are needed to humanize a much wider catastrophe. We should be able to feel compassion for refugees regardless of being exposed to their backstory, but these personal stories are a starting point in turning the tide of public opinion in support of all refugees.

These examples also highlight the importance that sport can play in breaking down boundaries and assimilating people into their new homes. As Yursa Mardini herself stated, in a video produced by the IOC: "In the water, there is no difference if you are a refugee or a Syrian or German." Sport is universal.

It is why football is important too. People have a connection with football. It transcends languages, borders, religion, class, race and gender. Football connects. On the pitch, it is just you and your teammates playing the game.

There is a Hamburg link to Yusra Mardini's story too – albeit a small one. She now lives in an apartment in the Barmbek district of the city. The Olympian aspect of her story might be unique, but by settling in Hamburg she shares the city with thousands of others who have found a home there since 2015.

Hamburg is a port city on the banks of the river Elbe. This port is often referred to as 'The Gateway to the World'. For more than 800 years it has been a trade and transportation hub. It first prospered as part of the Hanseatic League; it suffered too, most notably during the recession that gripped Western Europe in the 1980s.

But even today, in the era of mechanization and giant container shipping, the port's importance to the city of Hamburg remains. Of course, it wasn't just goods and raw materials that arrived and departed at Hamburg's docks and quays – there were people too. A large proportion of the five million Germans who left their homeland for a new life in the United States between 1850 and 1960 (including those fleeing the Nazis in the 1930s) began their journey from Hamburg's docks. Being a port city, Hamburg has always been cosmopolitan and diverse and, throughout most of its history, tolerant of outsiders.

When we think of the 'refugee crisis' –a widely disputed and derided term that would appear to blame the refugees themselves for the large-scale displacement of people across Europe, where as the responsibility for the 'crisis' lies firmly at the door of disastrous Western foreign policy intervention and corrupt authoritarian regimes – we immediately associate the crisis with the displacement of people, predominantly from Syria, Afghanistan and Iraq that reached a peak in 2015/16.

However, the people of Hamburg had opened their arms to a group of refugees that arrived in the city some two years earlier. In March 2013, St. Pauli fans alongside Hamburg residents and activists began to campaign and support a group of refugees who had fled the civil war in Libya and became known collectively as the 'Lampedusa Refugees.'

This group of young men, predominantly from countries in West Africa, fled Libya after the collapse of the Gaddafi regime and the end of the civil war. Many of them had lived and worked in Libya – as bricklayers, electricians and decorators – sending money home to their families. However, at the end of the civil war in 2011, they were accused of being mercenaries working for Gaddafi and fled the country in boats. Many were rescued or picked up by coastguards and taken to the Italian island of Lampedusa where they were held in a refugee camp.

Lampedusa is a small island in the Mediterranean almost equidistant between Tunisia and Sicily. Crucially, it is the first significant island north of Libya that is within the European Union. The island of Lampedusa and the story of the large number of refugees that have arrived on its shores has been documented in both print and film. The 2016 Italian documentary, *Fire at Sea*, is a moving watch; whilst Emma Jane Kirby's book, *The Optician of Lampedusa* tells the true story of Carmine Menna, his wife Rosaria and their own harrowing involvement in the rescue of 47 souls pulled from the water off the island's coast.

In 2011 – and throughout the mass movement of refugees in the years that followed – the island of Lampedusa was a starting point for many people to begin the asylum process; not that this process was ever quick or straightforward.

Eventually, after two years, in 2013, the Italian government issued around 500 of the initial Lampedusa refugees with residency permits for the Schengen Area and gave them either 500 Euros or a train ticket to a destination of their choosing elsewhere in Europe.

In March 2013, a group of approximately 300 refugees arrived in Hamburg. Initially, they were given shelter under the City of Hamburg's 'winter programme' – however, when this support expired in April 2013, the men found themselves homeless.

In the summer of 2013 activists, church leaders and residents continued to do what they could to support the Lampedusa refugees. On 3 October 2013, the plight of refugees escaping by boat from Libya once again made headline news, following a tragic accident that saw 390 people drown off the coast of Lampedusa – when a boat sank carrying refugees from Somalia and Eritrea that had left the port of Misrata in Libya.

From that point on, in Hamburg, there were weekly demonstrations in support of the Lampedusa refugees, who themselves were experiencing renewed victimisation by police who were stopping, searching and frequently arresting them for being on the streets without the correct papers. In response to this crackdown by police, the St. Pauli church opened its doors to refugees offering them a sanctuary – a safe place to sleep.

In the week leading up to FC St. Pauli's home match against SV Sandhausen on Friday 24 October 2013, there had been nightly disturbances on the streets of Hamburg between police and activists protesting about the harassment of the Lampedusa refugees. Tensions in the St. Pauli district had been running high. A huge demonstration was planned to coincide with the final whistle of the game against SV Sandhausen. A march through the city, starting at Millerntorplatz outside the stadium and ending at the St. Pauli church, in solidarity with refugees is not something that would happen at most football clubs. At the end of the game, a dour 0-0 draw, thousands of fans filed out of the stadium and began to congregate outside it.

Activists, worried about trouble, handed out slips of paper with the telephone number of solicitors written on it – in case anyone was arrested by police. Slowly, the march began to snake through the streets of St. Pauli. However, the police – to their credit – took a low-key approach to the protest, perhaps a result of this being an officially registered demonstration. It took two hours for the protestors to make their way from the stadium to the church, with an estimated 8-10,000 people taking part in the action (making it one of the largest demonstrations in the district since the days of the Hafenstraße protests in the 1980s). Many of the participants came directly from the stadium to the streets. It was a decisive show of solidarity with the refugees from Lampedusa, one that contributed to a relative softening of the racial profiling of refugees by the Hamburg police.

A bond had been created between the supporters of FC St. Pauli and the Lampedusa refugees. The formation of FC Lampedusa represents perhaps the best example of St. Pauli fans' commitment to supporting refugees through football.

It was down to the incredible dedication and hard work of a small but committed group of women – all St. Pauli fans – that eventually led to the FC Lampedusa being adopted by FC St. Pauli and becoming the first 'refugee team' formally associated with a professional football club.

The formation of FC Lampedusa is a testament to the compassion of the women who founded the club. In Hamburg during 2013, there were many groups working hard to ensure that the refugees' basic needs were met. Shelter, food, accommodation – all these things were vitally important, alongside legal support for accessing documentation and fighting against police victimisation and the constant threat of deportation. But one of FC Lampedusa's coaches, Georgie, was also a social worker and spent a lot of time meeting and talking to refugees. She took the time to ask them what they enjoyed doing in their spare time (which was reasonably plentiful, as their refugee status prevented them from working legally). 'Football' was the common response. However, without the correct paperwork, these young men were barred from playing for any of Hamburg's established amateur clubs or in organised leagues. In football – as in life – they were stuck in a bureaucratic loop: No papers, no right to stay. No papers, no right to work. No papers, no right to play football.

FC Lampedusa was established to give the refugees an opportunity to play proper, organised football. As Georgie stated: "It was mainly about giving people the opportunity to play soccer because in regular leagues they wouldn't be allowed to play without proper papers."

The coaches at FC Lampedusa – most of whom have played and coached in the women's football department of FC St. Pauli for many years – were upfront about the political element of the project. This is their mission statement:

> "FC Lampedusa Hamburg wants to create awareness and draw attention to the evils of European refugee policy and the situation of refugees in Hamburg, in Germany and in the wider European Community."

Their mission statement continues:

> "FC Lampedusa Hamburg welcomes all refugees and migrants over the age of 16, regardless of their nationality,

ethnicity, religion, sexual orientation, other identities, abilities or whatever. It doesn't matter how our players came to Hamburg, how long they will stay or whether they have official documentation or not. No papers are needed to be a member of our team – with FC Lampedusa Hamburg everyone can play football. We aim to make sport in general – but especially football – open to everybody. It is our mission to ensure anybody can play in official league competitions regardless of whether they have official papers or not. We want the football authorities to realise that football is for everyone."

By 2017, most of the original FC Lampedusa players (drawn from the 300 'Lampedusa' refugees) had moved on – either voluntarily to other parts of Germany or elsewhere in Europe, or else deported by the government.

However, in the interim, world events intervened. By 2015, ongoing instability and war in the Middle East created the largest European humanitarian crisis since World War II.

Since FC Lampedusa's foundation in 2013, well over 100 different players have worn the yellow-and-red striped shirts of FC Lampedusa, the ever-changing make-up of the players reflecting both the scale and scope of the refugee crisis that enveloped Europe in 2015 – with players coming from Syria, Iraq, Afghanistan, Somalia, Eritrea and the Balkans. The turnover of players also reflects the transitory nature of being a refugee or asylum seeker in Europe. For some players, Hamburg was only a temporary home before they decided to move on freely to join friends or relatives in other parts of Europe. Others, often those fleeing from designated 'safe-countries' like Bosnia or Kosovo are deported with little or no warning (something that is heart-breaking for the coaches and team-mates alike). However, at any one time, despite these constantly shifting sands, FC Lampedusa has had between 20-40 young players on its roster.

Undoubtedly, training and playing for FC Lampedusa are highlights of these young players' week. Matches provide them with something to look forward to and an opportunity to socialize and, of course, to let off steam and play some football.

"When I came to Hamburg and started playing for FC Lampedusa my life changed in a big way." These are the words of FC Lampedusa player, Mooto who fled Mogadishu due to the war. In Hamburg – in stark contrast to the future he faced in Somalia – Mooto as he says "has a chance." It is that chance or opportunity that gives hope to these young people with so much of their life ahead of them. The coaching staff and fellow players of FC Lampedusa help to make real that hope.

In November 2016, FC Lampedusa were invited to Barcelona to accept the 'City-to-City Barcelona FAS Award' – in recognition of FC Lampedusa's commitment to supporting refugees in Hamburg. The coaches took 11 players with them, a trip that was months in the planning and the result of hundreds of emails exchanged between the club, the City-to-City initiative and Hamburg's Foreigners' Registration Office.

But even such recognition of FC Lampedusa's work with refugees doesn't stop the heart-breaking deportations. Despite the frequency with which it happens, the pain of players disappearing with little or no notice will never get easier to cope with or to comprehend. This was especially painful and poignant during the 2016 trip to Barcelona.

Coach Hagar Groeteke spoke of the frustration and absurdity of being at a gala reception with the Mayor of Barcelona, whilst back home in Hamburg a member of the team was deported: "For three years now, you've given your all to a project that has become internationally renowned, wins awards... and then you're brought back to reality in such a terrible way. Over the last three days we were having so much fun, had so many wonderful people around us, shared great conversations and experienced very positive press coverage of our trip. And the City of Hamburg? It puts one of our players, all alone, into a jail – which they don't even want to call a jail and fabricate disgusting terms like 'departure custody' for such a thing."

As if losing a player whilst most of the squad and coaching staff were away accepting an international award wasn't painful enough, on their return to Hamburg two of the FC Lampedusa coaches, Hagar and Nico, had to journey to the deportation centre out near Hamburg Airport to collect the belongings that their player (and friend) had left behind – including a Germany U23 training jacket given to the deportee by FC St. Pauli player Christopher Avevor.

This itself was a harrowing experience for the two women: making their way through the shipping container 'village' that provides accommodation for 850 people housed on the site – ring-fenced inside a former BMW parking lot. During the process of collecting the belongings, they got into conversation with one of the officers at the centre. What she divulged still haunts them to this day. As they walked across the puddle-pocked tarmac between the converted shipping containers, the officer stopped and pointed at a block of containers on the other side of the makeshift street. She said, "And at night, buses come to collect the families with their kids."

The Lampedusa coaches were stunned. "This is the family area, most of them from the Balkans," the officer said quietly. "And then the buses come at night. Thereafter, the families are gone and only the teddy bears are left behind."

There is something deeply disturbing about all this: children disappearing in the night, the teddy bears designed to comfort and pacify them being disinfected and used again with the next group of frightened children. This shouldn't be happening in Germany, it shouldn't be happening anywhere in the world, not in the 21st Century. The coaches' trip to collect the belongings of a much-loved player was a sad enough duty already without being exposed to the horrific ordeal so many other refugees were forced to go through on that repurposed parking lot beyond the airport. Even so, the FC

Lampedusa coaches themselves knew they were the lucky ones – the ones with the correct documentation (in the form of a German passport) and the right to remain within the borders of 'Fortress Europe'. Like all those sympathetic with the cause of refugees and asylum seekers, Hagar and Nico knew their freedom was all down to luck and the accident of birth.

However, moments of positivity and recognition continued to exist alongside the sadness of the deportations. The official adoption of FC Lampedusa (now formally known as FC Lampedusa St. Pauli) by FC St. Pauli in 2016 was not just an acknowledgement of the good work carried out by Lampedusa's dedicated coaching team, it also represented the values of the club and the fans coming full circle.

Many football clubs in Germany have supported refugees – whether it is through coaching sessions at Bayern Munich or free tickets to matches at clubs like Bourissia Dortmund – but none have gone so far as to formally adopt a refugee team. On a practical level, the adoption allows FC Lampedusa access to pitches to train and play matches; it also allows for the provision of kit and equipment, but crucially it aligns the club behind the political element of FC Lampedusa. It isn't just about 'supporting' refugees, it is about sending a clear message to the government, not something that most 'normal' football clubs would be keen to highlight, but as FC Lampedusa's coach Kroger states: "Besides football our goal is more political. We want the government to recognise these people and not send them back to the so-called 'safe countries'." This political commitment was further underlined – in a statement issued by FC Lampedusa on the day of its adoption by FC St. Pauli:

> "This amalgamation further confirms FC St. Pauli's position as an anti-racist club and shows that it stands for much more than just professional football. Furthermore, FC Lampedusa Hamburg demands a general right to stay – for all! Football shall be open for all people."

The adoption of a refugee football team by FC St. Pauli is not the only positive action the club has taken in support of refugees in Germany. At the height of the refugee crisis, on 8 September 2015, FC St. Pauli played a friendly match against Borussia Dortmund at the Millerntor Stadion. The club invited 1,000 refugees – more specifically those refugees who had arrived in Hamburg within the previous few days and weeks. The objective was to action the oft-used slogan, 'Refugees Welcome'. Both teams entered the field holding hands with young refugees; the players produced a large banner containing both clubs' crest and the message 'Refugees Welcome'. The club also raised €45,000 in donations to be put towards funding of a search-and-rescue boat in the Mediterranean.

The refugee crisis had dominated news headlines across Europe since the summer of 2015. In Germany, as in the United Kingdom, the media was split between a supportive or a xenophobic narrative with most mainstream publications espousing the latter viewpoint. During the week beginning 14 September 2017, a dispute broke out between FC St. Pauli and one of Germany's most popular tabloid newspapers, *Bild-Zeitung*. The conservative, nationalist newspaper had over the previous summer stoked fear and resentment against refugees and asylum seekers in Germany. Then, in September, the newspaper backed an initiative by the DFL (German Football League) and its shirt sponsor Hermes, for all Bundesliga and Bundesliga 2 & 3 teams to wear a 'We Help' patch on their shirt sleeves, supporting refugees. However, FC St. Pauli refused to participate. This was due to *Bild's* previous editorial stance on the refugee crisis. The club was further angered when *Bild* published a confidential letter between FC St. Pauli and the newspaper, explaining the club's decision. Andreas Rettig, the club's Commercial Director, issued the following statement:

> *"The FC St. Pauli has been active on various levels for a number of weeks, which has been emotionally moving for months, to help the people who have fled to Germany. Our test game against Borussia Dortmund, the private commitment of our players*

as well as various actions of our fans and departments for the refugees in Hamburg are proof of this. Therefore, we do not see the need to participate in the planned, voluntary action of the DFL for all clubs. We have informed all parties concerned in advance. FC St. Pauli stands for a welcome culture, and we act in a way that has been our club for decades. We provide practical and direct assistance wherever it is needed."

As football fans in Germany found out about the dispute they sided with FC St. Pauli, leading to the widespread circulation of the hashtag *#BILDnotwelcome*. Nine German clubs also joined with FC St. Pauli, refusing to support the wearing of patches on their sleeves. SC Freiburg, VfL Bochum, Union Berlin, 1.FC Nürnberg, MSV Duisburg, 1.FC Kaiserslautern and Eintracht Braunschweig refused to wear the patch completely, whilst Fortuna Duusseldorf and 1860 Munich chose to cover the Bild logo on the patch. Fans from other clubs supported FC St. Pauli's stance prominently displaying 'Bild Not Welcome' banners in the stadium on matchday.

This clash between Germany's best-selling newspaper and many of its leading football clubs highlighted football fans' strength of feeling about the refugee crisis and their anger at how it had been portrayed in the mainstream media. It is evidence of how widespread support for refugees and asylum seekers is amongst Germany's progressive fan scene. The strength of support for FC St. Pauli's stance against *Bild*, also shows an understanding of how football fans have been at the forefront of the 'Refugees Welcome' movement, providing a highly visual and high-profile progressive voice – absent from the mainstream media – during the crisis. Of course, FC St. Pauli's prominent role in the support of refugees, can be understood in the context of its position as a progressive, left-wing 'kult-club' – a process that began with the squatters and anarchists of the 1980s and continued through the activism of the fans that has developed over the intervening 30-years.

Without doubt, the fans' experience organising and fighting the far-right on the terraces of the Millerntor and in the streets of Hamburg (and beyond) built the club's reputation in challenging racism. St. Pauli fans have fought hard against all forms of discrimination: racism, sexism and homophobia. As a result, they were quick to identify the 'Lampedusa Refugees' as victims of persecution and oppression from the state and the police. Support structures that were already present in Hamburg through the city's activist communities were able to coalesce and support these new arrivals to the city. As the crisis played out, those support structures were vital in both providing support to the refugees and getting a positive message of solidarity out to the wider public – through campaigning and visual displays of support within the stadium. In turn, this support was replicated by other left-wing fan groups across Germany building a highly visible network of support, under the broad banner of 'Refugees Welcome'.

This football-led social movement has spread across Europe: initially through left-leaning supporters' groups and the anti-fascist 'ALERTA' network of clubs; but most recently receiving support from more orthodox channels.

An Amnesty International initiative called Football Welcomes Refugees working in conjunction with the English Football League celebrated the contribution of refugees to English football over the weekend of 22-23 April 2017. Set against a bitter Brexit campaign, fought prominently over the issue of immigration, it was a bold and positive step by football clubs and supporters in the United Kingdom to recognise the contribution that refugees have made to sport and society.

FC St. Pauli doesn't lay claim to have initiated the support for refugees and asylum seekers among German football fans, but fans of the club were certainly among the first to actively support refugees.

The work is far from complete. Individuals and families still need to be supported in making a new life in Germany – just as those who face deportation due to unsuccessful asylum applications need to be comforted and supported in the challenges that lie ahead. This is perhaps, the most heart-breaking aspect of being actively involved with refugee groups. FC Lampedusa St. Pauli have certainly had to endure many upsetting moments saying goodbye to teammates and their families. Sometimes, if those deportations happen in the middle of the night, they don't even get to say farewell.

Again, it is these harrowing, personal experiences that get lost in wider discussion of the 'refugee crisis'. But even the deportations motivate those close to the cause, a point confirmed by FC Lampedusa's coaching staff after the deportation of a young player and his family back to the Balkans in October, 2016: "This is why we keep on going: to raise awareness, to pool more strength and – with our football family – to play our part in creating a better world where everyone finds him or herself a place to live, that they have chosen. A world where all people can live everywhere they want to, where they feel at home, where they can be whatever they are and where it absolutely does not matter in which corner of this one world, they and/or their parents were born."

FC Lampedusa St. Pauli wasn't just there for the short term – the period between 2015 and 2016 when the mass migration of people fleeing war, terror and oppression was making national and international headlines. As we have seen, FC Lampedusa – as a team and an organisation – pre-date the mass movement of peoples in 2015 and ensuing media hysteria. FC Lampedusa's support for the displaced and vulnerable has continued long after the news media have moved on. Coach Nico Appel summarises this perfectly, "We didn't want to be the sort of people who latch onto this whole refugee thing just to clear our consciences, and then walk away the minute it stops feeling fashionable. No way. Our aim was to set up something long term. Something community-based, something that can bring us all together for a constructive purpose." Their hard work has certainly achieved this.

For those refugees able to build a new life in Hamburg, FC St. Pauli has provided them not only with support, but also somewhere to watch football and – in the case of FC Lampedusa – play football. Perhaps, more than that, football has helped to sow the first seeds of belonging in the place they have chosen to call home – Hamburg.

Justice cannot be done to the remarkable story of FC Lampedusa in one chapter of a book. They've been the subject of numerous television and news reports. They've even featured in their own documentary filmed by *Religion of Sports*. My dream as a writer would be to facilitate the telling of their story through their own voices in a book devoted to them. By rights, they deserve their own film dramatization of their collective story. But none of these forms of media can ever replace spending some time with the squad. I've been fortunate enough to play against them on five different occasions and I've also been lucky enough to travel with them to a tournament. This is where the real story unfolds, sharing time with them. Seeing them not as refugees but as people. And the blockbuster film, how would it conclude? FC Lampedusa coach, Hagar Groeteke has already imagined the ending. She said, "We hope that there is no need for our project anymore." A world without refugees, that would be some Hollywood ending.

Chapter 5:
No Smoke Without Fireworks/
Refugees Welcome (Matches)

VfB Lübeck 0 FC St. Pauli 3
20:45, Friday 19 August 2016, Stadion Lohmühle
DFB Pokal 1ˢᵗ Round

The Baltic coast is nothing like I imagined. With the sun blazing and not enough breeze to tempt the windsurfers to the beach it was anything but 'Baltic'. The 20:45 kick-off time – made for TV, I'm guessing – had the unintended consequence of allowing me to head for the sea. It's about half an hour beyond Lübeck on the train and looked lovely in the sun: monster sized seagulls, funny giant beach chairs 'n' all – like a German version of Eastbourne, with a clientele to match.

By the time I made it back to the 'Lübeck – Home of Marzipan' as the signage proclaimed, the station was filling up with St. Pauli fans and police. Of course, there's history to this game, most directly the trouble at the Schweinske-Cup – an indoor tournament played during the league's winter-break – in January 2012, when a group of about 80-120 VfB Lübeck hooligans (and possibly some HSV fans, although I am not sure it was ever proven) stole flags and attacked FCSP fans, before getting away unchallenged whilst the police waded into the St. Pauli supporters with pepper spray and batons causing injury and distress. It was one of those strange occasions where the perpetrators of the violence get off-the-hook whilst the St. Pauli fans, including many families and, if I remember correctly, FC St. Pauli's security officer, Sven Brux, got attacked by police. It left a sour taste.

Lübeck's ultras stoked the flames in the week before this game by posting on social media that St. Pauli fans and 'groundhoppers' who had tickets for the home section of the ground would not be tolerated. All a bit unnecessary, especially as there are many parts of German stadiums that unofficially, but happily, accommodate mixed groups of fans. Extending the warning to groundhoppers seemed particularly funny – what next: train spotters? Stamp collectors?

In response, Ultrà Sankt Pauli organised a march from Lübeck Hauptbahnhof to the stadium, leaving at 18:30. Despite the big police presence, it was a relaxed affair – a pleasant stroll through Lübeck in the early evening sunshine. A few fireworks and smoke bombs were let off en route, but they just kind of added to the mood, the smoke lingering atmospherically in the trees in the low evening sun.

There was something of a bottleneck as we approached Stadion Lohmühle, I guess as a direct consequence of about 2,000 fans arriving together from the march. It took ages to get into the guest-bloc, the stewards doing their best to process everyone under the watchful gaze of even more police.

The Lohmühle itself was like the 'old' Millerntor's little sibling. Shallow terracing on three sides, broken by a small, seated stand on one side and a much larger 'grandstand' on the other. Curiously, the main stand had a completely empty block of seats. If it was next to the away fans, you could understand it being left empty to aid segregation, but it was between the seated and standing home fans

– strange, maybe a capacity/safety issue? They'd also plonked what looked like temporary seating on half of the away terrace, I guess to accommodate those FCSP fans who like to be seated? Quirks of the stadium aside – and for somebody who regularly pines for the 'old' Millerntor – it was a timely reminder of how far FC St. Pauli has come in the last 10 years. Nostalgia aside, you can actually see the game from the terraces of the new Millerntor, rather than craning your neck on the shallow steps of the Lohmühle (with the obligatory tall bloke stood directly in front of you!)

Before the game kicked-off, there was some fun and games with a bloke who put up his HSV banner in the adjacent bloc before being swiftly told to take it down again by stewards. Then, as we were holding up our black squares of paper for our choreo, the pyro began in the Lübeck end. Pretty impressive it was too: a wall of fire. FCSP fans responded with their own, although from my position in line with the corner flag, it was hard to see if it matched Lübeck's efforts.

There were the usual chants of 'Scheiß St. Pauli' from the home fans; I saw on the internet that the Lübeck ultras even went to the trouble of getting some matching 'Scheiß St. Pauli' t-shirts made for the occasion.

The match itself was pedestrian. St. Pauli seemed lethargic, unable to move the ball quickly, a fact probably not helped by Lübeck keeping the grass long and un-watered. We went ahead early from a Vegar Eggen Hedenstad free kick at the opposite end of the stadium, not that anyone in the away end realised we'd scored for a minute or so. It looked like the keeper had pushed the ball round the post. That, combined with the fact that Lübeck's ultras had obviously silenced any rogue groundhoppers or St. Pauli fans, meant that the goal was greeted with utter silence. It was only when we realised the players were celebrating rather than trying some elaborate new corner routine that we knew we were ahead.

Sören Gonther settled the nerves in the second half, heading home a second and killing off any chance of a Lübeck comeback.

It also highlighted a couple of bits of stupid pyro at both ends of the stadium. Lübeck fans chucked a couple of flares onto the pitch, halting the game for a few moments; whilst earlier someone in the FCSP end had let off a couple of rockets into the sky. This was just stupid. Normal pyro, I'm okay with, as usually the people around nearby are aware of the risks, but with rockets you've got as much chance of knowing where they will land as you have predicting where one of Big John Verhoek's shots will end up. There's just no way of being accurate. One of the rockets fired from the St. Pauli end landed in the section of terracing between home and away fans that was housing fans in wheelchairs and an additional deployment of riot police. Not clever. I thought the police showed good restraint deciding not to act; on another day it could've provoked them into another 'Schweinske-Cup' response. I know it wasn't deliberate, but we have to be careful, we are not a million miles away from Hansa Rostock fans firing rockets into the guest-bloc a few years back. A real strength of the St. Pauli fan scene is self-reflection and self-policing, so I hope those responsible think long and hard about their actions.

The game finished 0:3. We had progressed beyond our traditional first round cup exit. Maybe it had something to do with not wearing the usual, cursed 'Pokal-Trikot'? Although, a prolonged cup-run was going to require us to raise our game considerably.

We then began the slow shuffle out of the stadium and the march back to the station. Time for some more pyro, obviously. The Fanladen or USP guys were at the front keeping everyone at a certain pace with the police a few yards in front, walking slowly backwards. I was along the periphery near the front when, suddenly, it all kicked-off. I couldn't really see what happened, although I have vague recollections of some kid in a white tracksuit, appearing from a side road and trying to kung-fu kick a St. Pauli fan – a stupid move. In seconds, there was a mix of St. Pauli fans and police reacting. It was in those moments of confusion that I thought "fuck this" and managed to slip through the police-cordon and out ahead of the march. I hate being trapped in those situations, plus I'm a runner not a fighter and I'd rather take my chances out-running some dickheads than be pepper-sprayed or hit over the head with a police baton. It was most probably kindergarten stuff. It seemed from my position about 100 metres ahead, that the police were again reasonable in their response and the St. Pauli fans also restrained; and that there wasn't much more trouble after that. Finding my way back to the station was dead easy too, as the police had kindly blocked off all other exits at roundabouts and road junctions with their dogs and vans. I guess it also made me realise how middle-aged I look when the police paid zero attention to a bloke with stupid hair and shorts casually wandering back to the station.

Heralded by sirens and flashing lights, the majority of St. Pauli fans arrived back at the station about 20 minutes after me (which at least gave me a chance to get a head start on the vending machines; there's not a lot open in Lübeck after midnight!) The platform filled up quickly as the fans arrived. If this had been Britain, the shitty privatised train operator would've only had a three-carriage train on, but fair play to DBahn: a big double-decker train pulled in, although even then it was what Jeremy Corbyn would call "ram-packed" – there was nowhere to stand, let alone sit.

The train journey back was subdued, getting into the Hauptbahnhof just after 01:00 but hey, we are in the second round of the DFB Pokal – and that doesn't happen too often. The fireworks were the only real drama and, even then, it was more smoke than fire. And I saw a seagull on a surfboard. Good times.

Anti-Racist Tournament
with FC Lampedusa St. Pauli
Saturday 20 August 2016, 12:00, Prignitz

My weekend travelling on Deutsche Bahn wasn't even halfway done. After a few hours fitful sleep, I found myself waiting outside the Burger King at Hamburg Hauptbahnhof at 07:45 on a Saturday morning. I was there with FC Lampedusa St. Pauli, on our way to an Anti-Racist 7-a-side tournament being held in the district of Prignitz, somewhere between Hamburg and Berlin.

This was a proper trip Ostee – to the old East. Yesterday, at the coast I was told of the beach border at Priwall (not far from Lübeck) where the demarcation line between East and West Germany had been a single chain-link barrier dissecting the beach. Of course, set back slightly from the sand had been a fenced-off compound with a watch tower which nullified the potential for unauthorized border crossings. All that remains of it now is an ivy-clad border tower set a bit further back into the forest and a commemorative rock with 'Nie wieder geteilt' (Never again divided) and the date 3 February 1990 etched into it. But in Lübeck, I had remained on the other side of the arbitrary line in the sand. Today, I was going to be heading to Karstädt in the rural east, where the opposition was to be provided by – among others – a team from the local slaughterhouse.

As detailed in the previous chapter, most of the original 2013 'Lampedusa refugees' from Libya have either moved on voluntarily or been deported but their places on the team have been taken by young men from a variety of backgrounds: Syria, of course, but also Somalia, Eritrea, Afghanistan and the Balkan states. As well as older players, the project has evolved to work with youngsters between the ages of 15 to 18, some who arrived in Hamburg with their families, but many who arrived alone. Training sessions and tournaments not only give these young men a chance to get together and socialize, but also to alleviate the boredom of life in a container (where families are housed) or in a boarding institution (for those unaccompanied minors). These get-togethers take on extra significance in the long school holidays (most of the young refugees have school places and willingly attend) when their travel passes are not paid for by the state, thus drastically reducing their ability to socialize and move around the city. With the players too shy or proud to ask, the Lampedusa Coaching Crew rely on their intuition to find out who might need a few Euros to make it to training the next week.

Outside the Burger King the players started to show up. Most were there on time, but just like any amateur football team meeting up anywhere in the world there were a few late arrivals, but not many. The guys had been looking forward to this trip. There was all the usual banter you get when a group of lads get together, albeit I couldn't understand most of it because it's in German. There were also the ubiquitous selfies and standing around looking at mobile phones (yes, *Daily Mail* readers, even refugees have smartphones these days, as far as I'm aware it's not a crime – more a necessity for keeping in touch with friends and relatives both in Germany and beyond).

The boys were getting pretty used to travelling with FC Lampedusa. They regularly attend tournaments across Germany. They've been to Berlin, Köln and Flensburg (right up on the border with Denmark) and they've twice travelled to Switzerland to play in tournaments organised by their friends, FC Winterthur. For the second of these tournaments, Lampedusa even flew to Zurich – for many of the players their first trip on an airplane. As you'd imagine, taking a team of refugees between different countries in Europe requires a considerable amount of paperwork and patience from the Coaching Crew who had to organise the trip in minute detail, liaising with the local authorities in Hamburg, the German and Swiss embassies, and the airlines. Even for this trip to Prignitz paperwork is required, in fact as we waited for everyone to arrive, I was put in charge of looking after the players' identity papers. Some must even have special written dispensation to leave the Hamburg area. When you start to factor in all this red tape and admin, the admiration for the coaches' – on today's trip, Nico and Hagar – dedication to the project only grows. They don't get paid a penny for this: FC Lampedusa is run entirely by a handful of volunteers.

There was a slight problem before we headed down to the platform to catch our first train of the day. One of the players had brought another young lad with him. His friend, who had skipped a few training sessions, wanted to come too. Nico and Hager firmly and politely told him that he couldn't come; that he knew the rules: you can only be considered for tournaments if you regularly turn up to training. It seemed harsh watching this young lad shuffle away, moments later disappearing into the throng of travellers on the station concourse. The coaches didn't like it much either, but they know that firm rules are important, both to the smooth running of trips like this but also for the players themselves: they like knowing where they stand. They value knowing what is allowed and what isn't. Fair enough. Not many teams or clubs get very far without a set of rules and some discipline.

It was a good two and a half hours on the train to Karstädt and I wondered what our fellow passengers would make of a bunch of refugees getting into their carriage – especially in light of the recent, well-publicised knife attacks committed by refugees on German trains (the scaremongering, sensationalist British media certainly lapped it up). I couldn't have been more surprised. Everyone we encountered on the trip was positive and inquisitive about the project. People in adjacent seats were keen to chat; FC Lampedusa stickers were handed out to passengers. Even the train guards, working their way through a selection of group tickets were positive. Hagar and Nico, the coaches, did say that they make sure at least one of them is wearing their 'Coaching Crew' tracksuit top on trips like this, as the acknowledgement that they are part of an organised team puts fellow passengers' minds at ease. That said, they plan these trips carefully, always making sure that they change trains in relatively busy stations – and avoiding excessive waiting time between connections – as there's still a worryingly large number of people who are openly hostile to refugees. Being in the wrong place at the wrong time can still be dangerous.

As we settled into the first leg of our trip, the whole *refugee* thing began to fade into the background. Anyone who's been part of a sports team that's travelled to away matches together or, indeed, anyone who has been on a school trip could identify with the ebb-and-flow of travelling as a group. There were noisy bits, quiet bits. There were those kids who were at the centre of everything, laughing and joking; there were quiet ones trying to grab some kip; or those just listening to music or reading a book. It was an hour or so in and already I had started to forget they were refugees, each with their own – probably traumatic – backstory, and I started to think of them as players and teammates, living in the *now* and having a laugh.

It's worth mentioning how courteous these guys were too. Even when they were out of their seats chatting to their mates in the aisle, as soon as another passenger came through the carriage, they made sure that they could pass, sending them on their way with a grin or a few friendly words in German. Yeah, German. Most of them hadn't been in the country that long, yet they were all reasonably fluent in German. I've been coming over to Hamburg for nearly ten years, and I can't understand more than a few words let alone speak it. In fact, I was told that one of the running jokes among them is taking the piss out of those players that speak the worst German – frankly, this has got to be the best motivational tool for improving a language: piss taking and peer pressure! I had thought more of them would speak some English, but most of the players only knew a few words, either that or they just didn't want to chat to the bloke with the stupid hair who was tagging along with them for the day (one of my favourite bits of the trip was when one of the players asked the coaches to ask me if my hair was really that colour, or if I'd dyed it!). For me, this determination to improve their German just showed that these youngsters already consider Germany home.

A slight delay to our first train meant we *did* end up changing trains in the middle of nowhere, but the stopover was brief and the other passengers on the platform friendly. We arrived in Karstädt on schedule and were met by a cheery bloke in a St. Pauli t-shirt – one of the tournament organisers. The players piled into a couple of minibuses, and we took a ride with our St. Pauli fan in his car. The tournament was being held pretty much in the middle of nowhere: in a field somewhere between Karstädt and Perleberg. It was in its second year. Last year, it was mostly local teams including those refugees living in and around Perleberg. This year they had extended the invitation to refugee teams from further afield.

In the car from the station, we were briefed on an incident that occurred the previous night. Two people who were camping at the pitches – looking after tents and equipment – were paid a visit by some local fascists. At about 23.30 a red and brown Trabant roared up the country lane, stopping to ask if the guys in the tent had any beer. They replied, "No." The car pulled off again, but stopped a few yards further down the track: a man got out and shouted, "Heil Hitler!" and made some vague threats about returning with sticks. Fortunately, nothing came of it, but it serves as a reminder that refugee-hating fascists are never far from the surface, even in sleepy, rural east Germany. The threat was taken seriously though: the next day, the local police arrived and took details of the incident, as fascist sloganeering and references to Hitler are a criminal offence in Germany.

The tournament was already up-and-running by the time we arrived. The players quickly got changed and ready for action. I had the job of setting up the FCL merch-stall. Much of the money needed to buy equipment for the players, book pitches and pay transport costs comes from the sale of t-shirts and bags. To add to the weight of responsibility on my shoulders, not only did I have travel documents for the players, but I was also now in charge of all their mobile phones and wallets. To keep the players' focus, phones were to be handed in until the tournament was over. Most of them went in my bag, but the keeper, known as 'Neuer' (obviously), wanted me to keep hold of his phone as he was expecting an important call from his social worker. I appreciated the level of trust he'd placed in me. Although, slightly worryingly, this must've meant I still had the look of a schoolteacher about me, even in the bloody holidays.

The tournament schedule was fairly punishing: 7 x 15-minute matches for each team. Stereotypes are so terribly reductive, but there's something to this German punctuality thing. If a game was scheduled to kick-off at 14:08, it kicked off at 14:08.

It's fair to say FC Lampedusa bossed the tournament. The playing surface was rough and uneven, sections of it home to some digger wasps, who buzzed in an out of a network of tiny holes in one corner of the pitch. A couple of the teams were comprised of big burly blokes who worked at the nearby slaughterhouse. None of this fazed the young lads from FC Lampedusa. The football was patchy in places, but they quickly got into their stride, winning match after match. They were given their closest game by a team of refugees from nearby Perleberg. FC Lampedusa were just too quick, skilful and well coached. The squad of 11 players was rotated throughout the tournament, but it didn't matter what combination of players were on the pitch, Lampedusa were in control.

Neuer, in goal, was rarely called into action. He'd recently been given Sevilla keeper, David Soria's gloves at a pre-season friendly, but they hardly got dirty. 'Rooney', a spitting image of a young Wayne, also played in the all-action style of his namesake. Not the ageing Manchester United version but the bustling Everton youth from all those years ago. It would be unfair to single one player out, but FC Lampedusa's striker stood out head and shoulders from the rest. Recently turned 18, he showed more than enough skill and composure to be playing at a much higher level. It got me thinking, how incredible would it be for a player from FC Lampedusa to get a shot with one of FC St. Pauli's youth teams, or even to make it all the way to the first eleven? If individual stories bring this crisis into focus, then – *perhaps* – there's a fairytale right there waiting to be written. But individual talent shouldn't diminish what was clearly a well-drilled, team effort. And like most football teams, especially one comprised of young lads, there's nothing they like more than winning. From my vantage point on the merch stall, I'd already done the maths: the tournament was won by FC Lampedusa before they went into their last match. Not that it made any difference, they won the final game too, making it an impressive 7 wins out of 7. Maximum points and another trophy. After each tournament, a different player gets the trophy for keeps. Until they get their own club house, there's nowhere for the trophies to be displayed. Perhaps it is nicer that way, the threat of sudden deportation is very real for these lads, a small trophy tucked away in a holdall, might just serve as a memento of their time with the team.

Of course, despite the enjoyment of winning, these tournaments are about more than football. They are the chance to meet up with like-minded people and show support and solidarity with refugee groups and stand together to show that racism and fascism will be defeated. The food, drink, music and group photos at the end of the afternoon were testament to that. Here, in a clearing – in a wood – in the middle of nowhere, people from all over came together to play football. That's special. For some of the refugees, it was also a chance to catch up and exchange news and stories with other players from other teams. It's surprising how effectively news is disseminated this way: most of them know someone who knows someone who shared their journey or who originates from a nearby town or city back home. It's another way of keeping in touch, although nowhere near as useful as a mobile phone.

In many ways, FC Lampedusa are lucky. In July 2016, they were formally adopted by FC St. Pauli. They officially became part of the club, just like the array of other amateur sports teams connected to St. Pauli. It's a relationship that should help them enormously. One of the biggest problems about being a refugee team is the problem of booking pitches. Not having players registered to the local Football Association (the players are transient, some stay for just a few weeks, others months and, of course, many don't have the 'correct' documentation) means they can't compete in official league competition, only friendlies. Plus, all the pitches in Hamburg either belong to established clubs or schools. Being part of FC St. Pauli will ease this process considerably. Then, there's equipment:

kit and boots. One of the other teams at the tournament, proudly commented that FC Lampedusa were already wearing official FC St. Pauli socks! There is hope that the club will help out with boots too. Now though, it's usually one of the Coaching Crew who buys the players new boots, the money coming out of their own pocket. In fact, they joke that they probably don't go anywhere without a pair of new football boots in their bag ready to give to someone in the team.

It's great that FC St. Pauli is putting its money (and resources) where their mouth is and is actively supporting FC Lampedusa. It was fabulous for the players to walk out onto the pitch with the teams before the recent friendly between FC St. Pauli and Sevilla FC. You could see how much it meant to the boys to be out there in the Millerntor Stadion receiving the adulation of 20,000 fans. I said earlier that FC Lampedusa are lucky to have the support of a progressive club like St. Pauli. Maybe I was being a bit casual with my words. The relationship isn't about luck at all: it was born from the tireless work of the FC Lampedusa Coaching Crew – a truly dedicated group of women – and the energy and enthusiasm of their players.

There was some nice symbolism with our departure time from Karstädt station for the journey home. The train was scheduled for 19:10. 1910 being the year FC St. Pauli were founded, over a century ago. And, of course, punctuality being a thing, the train left bang on schedule.

Everyone was a bit less bleary-eyed on the journey back to Hamburg. Maybe it was the euphoria of winning, or just the fact that it was early evening rather than early morning. Either way, spirits were much higher. Like earlier, there were still those who kept their own counsel, or sat quietly chatting, but there was also some impromptu dancing to music from phones. The carriage was deserted apart from the team, so they were entitled to have some fun, yet the players always remained mindful of other passengers passing through the train. Once the dancing had subsided, Neuer showed me some photos on his phone (I'd long since returned it to him, although his social worker never called). He was showing me pictures of himself at a dance class he'd attended through school. It turns out his ambition is to be an actor, but dance was another possibility.

I think this was the moment it really hit me. The story isn't about where these guys have come from. It's about where they want to go from here. These aren't refugees. That's just a catch-all term for people without the 'correct' documentation. They're kids. Kids with all the usual dreams and aspirations of anyone their age. They don't want sympathy. They don't want to reflect on how they got here. They just want a better life – a better future. It's why those who came with their families made the journey to Europe. It's also why others were sent on alone, because their parents (if their parents were still alive) knew it was the best chance they could give their kids of a better future. And who doesn't want that for their kids?

The goalkeeper wants to be an actor. The guy who played at left-back might want to be a doctor, an engineer or work in a warehouse. I don't know, I didn't ask him. But it's almost irrelevant. At 16 or 17-years old, these youngsters just need the safety of knowing they *can* dream about the future. They shouldn't be worrying about having the correct papers or going through the complicated process of seeking asylum. They should be having a laugh; coping with the day-to-day shit that comes with being a teenager; they should be dreaming of the future. That's what we want for our kids. And let's face it, they are, but for an accident of birth, our kids. *Not refugees. Our kids.*

I guess that's what I learnt from this trip. Through a medium I can understand – *football* – I realized that FC Lampedusa are just like any football team anywhere. They laugh; they joke. They win; they even lose – occasionally. The only difference is they don't have the right documentation or passports. My mind wanders back to the big-budget FC Lampedusa film that I imagined in at the end of the previous chapter. The more I think of it, the more I realise that these young men wouldn't want that film to be about their past. Most of them are understandably reluctant to discuss their long, traumatic and dangerous journeys to Hamburg. The film should instead focus on the people that they become.

There was one more thing that really hit me. As the train guard announced our return to Hamburg Hauptbahnhof, a buzz of excitement and chatter ran through the team. The noise levels grew, just as you'd expect from any team, group, or family as they neared home after a long trip. And that was precisely it: for most of the players from FC Lampedusa, Hamburg is exactly that – *home*.

For us looking in from the outside at the plight of these young men, a football team provides a scaffold, a familiar context to identify and empathise with those forced to flee their homes and countries. For the players themselves, FC Lampedusa has given them a chance to play the game they love and to socialise with teammates. But more than that: football has sewn the first seeds of belonging – in Hamburg.

It seems appropriate to finish these two chapters the way they began, by looking at the word refugee. Of course, the word necessitates an opinion. Of course, those sympathetic with the undeniable physical and emotional suffering that they have experienced should show solidarity and support for these displaced people. But what I have learnt during the – albeit limited – time I have spent in their company, is that the word 'refugee' isn't what should define them. To permanently saddle them with that label is to limit both our view of them and their potential. All these young people are so much more than refugees. Being a refugee was just a process they had to go through due to the life-threatening situations they found themselves in that forced them to seek refuge elsewhere. These people have hopes, dreams and aspirations that they deserve to fulfil. They are the same as everyone else. They have as much right as all of us to want to grow up to be footballers, actors, doctors, teachers or scientists. It is the job of the people and institutions in their new homeland to enable them to fulfil those dreams. At a base level, the establishment of a football club like FC Lampedusa gives them a platform from which to build the rest of their lives; as well as somewhere to practice and play the game we all love.

Chapter 6:
The Complex Case of Deniz Naki

When Deniz Naki left FC St. Pauli in the summer of 2012, nobody could've foreseen the dramatic twists and turns that life would have in store for him. In his short time at the Millerntor, he had become something of a cult hero. But in the years that followed his departure, Deniz Naki became – perhaps – the most political player to have ever represented FC St. Pauli and also one of the most controversial.

He's got competition of course, from the likes of former Hafenstraße resident and goalkeeper, Volker Ippig – a man whose St. Pauli career was punctuated by a spell in Nicaragua where he helped to construct a health centre, working with activists from the Sandinista National Liberation Front. More recently there was Ultrà Sankt, Pauli's own Bene Pliquett, another keeper. Pliquett was forever immortalized in the photo of him kicking the corner flag in celebration at the Volksparkstadion in the 2011 derby win over HSV. Pliquett was a vocal opponent of right-wing extremism during his time with St. Pauli and was equally at home watching games on the Südkurve with USP as he was keeping goal on the other side of the fence that separates fans from the pitch. A post-football career has seen him work as an estate agent in Majorca (where he saw out his playing days with a short stint in goal for Club Deportivo Atletico Baleares) as well as owning a bar and – more controversially – a sex shop on the Reeperbahn.

But, as we shall find out, few players have had a more complex life – post FC St. Pauli – than Deniz Naki. The ten years that have elapsed since Naki left the Millerntor have been eventful, complicated and – at the time of writing – in a state of flux.

In December 2020, Deniz Naki was arrested in Aachen by the North Rhine-Westphalia State Police on criminal charges that included: blackmail, extortion and drug trafficking. Naki was remanded in custody until his trial began at Aachen Regional Court in April 2021. He was accused – along with three other men – of being part of the Kurdish 'Bahoz' group (an organized crime syndicate) that some in the German media were quick to link with the outlawed Kurdistan Workers' Party (PKK). Naki is alleged to have been the ringleader of the group. He had been under investigation by the authorities since being shot at whilst driving his car near his hometown of Düren in January 2018. The trial was scheduled to last 39 weeks but a strange series of events saw Naki remanded in custody for almost three years. Then, suddenly, in May 2023 Deniz Naki was released with the court declaring that his pre-trial detention was 'no longer proportionate'. There were further irregularities with the case. Over seventy minutes of translated voice recordings obtained from a car that had been bugged by the police had disappeared – the translations would need to be made again before they could be used as evidence. It was all very unusual. Naki himself has remained silent, only posting a photograph of himself in a car with the caption 'freedom' written underneath. At the time of writing (July 2023) it is unclear when the trial will resume. The strange goings on in court have all added fuel to the fire regarding different theories as to Naki's involvement in criminal activity. It is entirely possible that, following a traumatic series of events (that will be explained in more detail below), Naki had fallen into a post-football life of criminality. But it has also been speculated, that charges could've been exaggerated to suit a more political agenda – that Deniz Naki's actions as an activist and outspoken supporter of Kurdish independence has made him some powerful political enemies, not just in Turkey but in Germany too.

The truth is forever clouded by perspective. However, the situation serves as a timely reminder as to why at St. Pauli, so little focus is put on the status of the star-player or celebrity; of why the collective is given precedence over the individual. It's not that hero-worship is discouraged, it is more that the process of footballing heroes is more complex. Footballers are human beings and human beings are multi-faceted, complicated, and flawed. This chapter will look in detail at the active and passionate political activism that ran in parallel with the later stages of his football career. It is a role that made him an icon to many who have championed justice and independence for the Kurdish people, but whether the criminal charges brought against Naki are true or not, an individual's life is far more complex than the unconditional creation of a football legend. At some point, the court will announce its verdict, it will be up to individual St. Pauli fans to decide to what extent they agree. In the meantime, it is prudent to look at some of the key events that happened to Deniz Naki since he departed Hamburg in the summer of 2012.

It's 20 October 2012 FC St. Pauli were visiting SC Paderborn 07 at the Energieteam Arena. The match is over but the impassioned chant *Den–iz Naki! Den–iz Naki!* is belted out by the FC St. Pauli fans in a packed away section. A diminutive figure strides across the pitch towards them – applauding in return. Deniz Naki had come on as a substitute and scored the equalizing goal in a 1-1 draw between the two teams. Only he'd scored for his new club, SC Paderborn. Naki had left the Millerntor that summer, but it made no difference – *still* – the fans were chanting his name.

Naki played just 74 times and scored 14 goals for FC St. Pauli between 2009 and 2012, and yet – in that short space of time – he had become a folk hero at the Millerntor.

Naki was perhaps the ultimate impact player: his short 5ft 7inch frame concealed a burst of pace and bags of trickery that could leave defenders for dead. Trouble was, he struggled to do it over 90-minutes. Looking back at the statistics, 30 of his 74 appearances were as a substitute. He was substituted off a further 36 times (a quick mental calculation shows he only played a full game on eight occasions). His role as an impact sub even bookends his St. Pauli career: he scored both goals in a 2:0 victory in the DFB Pokal at FC 08 Villingen on his debut in 2009, including a goal in the 120th minute. In his final match – coincidentally – against Paderborn in May 2012, he once again came off the bench to score with his final touch as a FC St. Pauli player, in the 90th minute, to complete the scoring in a 5:0 romp.

But the statistics don't even tell half of the story. What Naki meant to FC St. Pauli fans can't be reduced to mere statistics, as anyone who witnessed Naki's tearful farewell in front of the Südkurve after the 5:0 victory over Paderborn would testify. This wasn't about football; it was about identity, belonging and love.

Perhaps, more than anything, St. Pauli fans' love for Deniz Naki is drenched in symbolism. On a dank November evening in 2009, Naki (again from the subs bench) had scored the decisive second goal as St. Pauli defeated fans' bitter political rivals Hansa Rostock 2:0 in a hostile atmosphere at Rostock's Ostseestadion. As he rushed to celebrate, he made a cut-throat gesture to the Hansa Rostock fans signalling the game was over as a contest (for which he received a three-match ban from the DFB). However, it was his actions at full-time that truly cemented his place in St. Pauli folklore. In an already highly-charged atmosphere (St. Pauli fans had been attacked by Hansa Rostock hooligans as their train arrived in Rostock), as the team went to celebrate with the away fans at the end of the game, Naki carefully laid out a totenkopf flag on the playing surface before defiantly ramming one of USP's distinctive brown, white and red flags into the green turf beside it. It was an iconic moment; it didn't just symbolize a victory on the pitch, it also laid down a marker that St. Pauli's antifascism would always defeat the right-wing bullshit spouted by some elements of Rostock's support.

Then there's, perhaps, the second most iconic image of Naki which shows him standing on the roof of the dugout surrounded by jubilant fans and waving a flag after FC St. Pauli secured promotion to the Bundesliga with a 4:1 away win in Fürth in May 2010 (he'd started that particular game and scored the equalizer before being – *you guessed it* – substituted).

It was his passion and connection that made St. Pauli fans fall in love with him. He knew the importance of symbols, connection, and gesture to the club's supporters. He knew the importance of victory over Hansa Rostock – ideologically – as well as in pure football terms. He was only 19 when he joined St. Pauli and hadn't quite turned 23 when he left the club, but in that short space of time he had made an indelible mark at the Millerntor. He understood the club; he understood the district; he understood what the fans believed in. Of course, he wasn't alone in this. In fact, he was probably fortunate to be surrounded by a group of players including Fabian Boll, Ralf Guensch and Bene Pliquett who all, in differing ways, embodied the values of FC St. Pauli. He was also fortunate to be coached by Holger Stanislawski – a former club legend himself – who knew how to get the best out of Naki on the pitch but also knew the importance of Naki's connection to the fans (sadly, neither of these points seemed to be understood by Stanislawski's successor André Schubert).

Naki left football's most political club a modern-day folk hero, remembered for playing with his heart on his sleeve and for his iconic acts of symbolism. However, he wasn't an overtly political figure at this stage. It is far from certain that any St. Pauli fans would've predicted what the future held for Deniz Naki. Over the next few years, Naki transformed his youthful political symbolism into defiant political activism – and he did it all through football.

In 2014, after a season in Paderborn, Naki moved to Turkish Süper Lig club, Gençlerbirliği S. K. in Ankara. Naki is of Alevi-Kurdish heritage, his family heralding from Dersim – a city that was devastated by the Turkish army in response to the Kurdish uprising of 1937 and 1938. Exact numbers vary, but thousands of Kurdish civilians were killed and thousands more forced into exile in an operation that is considered by many as an act of genocide against the Kurdish people. In an ongoing campaign of suppression of non-Turkish culture, Dersim had been renamed Tunceli in 1936 – this is why Naki has a tattoo 'Dersim 62' on his arm, the '62' referencing the area's traffic code. Naki's father had been a Kurdish activist who had been tortured by the State in the late 1970s but had been able to escape to Germany. Naki's father had made sure that Deniz was aware of his Kurdish roots and took him to community events when growing up in Düren, Germany.

Naki made 25 appearances in total for Gençlerbirliği (19 in the 2013/14 campaign and 6 in 2014/15) scoring one goal, but his time in Ankara ended abruptly in November 2014.

If Naki attributes one event to his political awakening it is the siege of Kobane by ISIL forces in October 2014. Kobane had been under Kurdish control since 2012, but during September of 2014, ISIL forces captured villages surrounding the city, triggering a wave of Kurdish refugees back over the border from Syria to Turkey. By 4 October with ISIL forces on the brink of capturing the city it is estimated that 90% of its inhabitants had fled. During this time, Naki made several social media posts supporting the Kurdish fighters in their battle against ISIL in Kobane. Then, on the evening of 2 November 2014, Naki was heading out from a friend's house in Ankara to get some food when he was accosted in the street. Three men swore at him repeatedly and taunted him, "Are you that dirty Kurd, Naki?" They also shouted abuse about Kobane (Naki had previously posted a message on Facebook saying, "Freedom for Kobane" and had posed for a photo on twitter holding a sign reading "#Save our girls from ISIS"). They also referenced his tattoo asking him why he did not refer to Dersim as Tunceli. Before he knew what happened he had been punched by one of the men, sustaining a black eye. He managed to hit back at the assailants before running to safety. The attackers had shouted that this was just a warning, implying worse was to follow.

Despite immediately reporting the attack to his club, officials at Gençlerbirliği were less than supportive, condemning the attackers but also implying that Naki's social media comments had been inflammatory. Naki was quite rightly worried for his safety along with those of his teammates. He pointed out that this time it had just been punches, but next time it could be a knife attack or a gun. As a result, on 4 November Naki and Gençlerbirliği terminated his contract and he returned to Germany. At this point, there was a sizeable debate about Naki returning to the Millerntor permanently. He'd made a cameo appearance at Fabian Boll's testimonial match where hundreds of fans held up 'Naki Back!' placards.

Deniz Naki is the type of footballer who wears his heart on his sleeve – it is one of the many reasons fans love him. Like countless other players, Naki's arms are also adorned with tattoos. For Naki these tattoos are both personal and political – a visual representation of the wider struggle of the Kurdish people. As mentioned above, Naki has received abuse both on-and-off the pitch for his 'Dersim 62' tattoo (a declaration of his ancestry and heritage but viewed by the thugs who attacked him as disrespecting Turkish authority). On his hand, Deniz has a tattoo of Che Guevara, a classic example of left-wing iconography and one shared with Ultrà Sankt Pauli for whom the image is an important part of their identity. However, it is a tattoo on his left forearm that has caused the most controversy for Naki in Turkey. He has the Kurdish word 'AZADI' written in a serif font inscribed, boldly, in capital letters. 'Azadi' means simply 'Freedom' and for Naki it is just that – an expression of a basic human right. For his detractors, it is a call for Kurdish independence

– a further insult to the Turkish state, undermining its national identity. In a country where journalists and academics increasingly find themselves locked up for expressing any anti-government viewpoints, simply having the word 'Freedom' tattooed on your arm is construed as an incendiary political act. It is worth noting the case of another Deniz, Deniz Yücel in this regard – the German-Turkish journalist who worked for *Die Welt* and was imprisoned in Turkey for more than a year on charges of spying before being released in February 2018.

In the immediate aftermath of Naki leaving Gençlerbirliği, the idea of him returning to play football in Turkey appeared remote. It was anticipated that he would pick up a contract playing in Germany. However, in the summer of 2015 Naki signed for Amed S.K. (Amedspor) who play in the Turkish third tier and are based in the city of Diyarbakir – often referred to as the unofficial capital of Northern (Turkish) Kurdistan.

Amed S.K. courted controversy in 2014 by changing their name from Diyarbakır Büyükşehir Belediyespor to Amed S.K. (Amed being the Kurdish name for the city) an action that saw them fined 10,000 Turkish Lira by the Turkish Football Federation. The club also changed their kit to traditional Kurdish colours of red and green. Indeed, the club is viewed by some as the Kurdish national team by proxy. Joining Amed S.K. gave Naki the sporting platform to represent the Kurdish struggle against Turkish oppression, it seemed like a clear political decision for Naki to play for Amed S.K. – he certainly could've earned a better wage by remaining in Germany or playing elsewhere in Europe.

On 31 January 2016, Amed S.K. played against Süper Lig club, Bursaspor away in the last-sixteen of the Turkish cup; the third division side pulled off a shock 2:1 victory. On 66 minutes Naki put Amed S.K. 2:0 up with a coolly taken right-footed drive from the edge of the penalty area, it turned out to be the winning goal. The situation had been tense even before the visitors secured their surprise victory. In 2010, Bursaspor had travelled to Diyarbakır but the game was abandoned after crowd trouble in the ground that spilled out on the streets surrounding the stadium after the game (Diyarbakır were ordered to play nine matches behind closed-doors).

Naki described that the 2016 cup game was as if "Turkey were playing against Kurdistan" – it was especially hostile as no Amedspor fans had been permitted to travel to the game. He said photos of the Bursaspor players wearing military uniforms were circulated amongst fans in the build-up to the match and the visitors from Diyarbakır being referred to as 'terrorists'.

It is fair to say that the game itself was hard-fought; Naki in particular was singled-out for rough treatment by several Bursaspor players – including one particularly brutal knee-high challenge on the halfway line, which somehow only merited a yellow card. Later a player from Bursaspor was dismissed for a particularly cynical challenge on the edge of the penalty area. None of this was particularly surprising, given the history surrounding both the game and Deniz Naki.

Indeed, Naki has acknowledged that his tattoos and the number '62' on the back of his shirt have often marked him out as a target for abuse from opposition fans – and some players – whenever he has played for Amed S.K. in away games.

For Naki, however, the real drama was still to follow. On Facebook, after the match, Deniz Naki made the following statement, "We dedicate this victory as a gift to those who have lost their lives and those wounded in the repression in our land which has lasted for more than 50 days." The Facebook post ended with the declaration, "Her biji Azadi!" which translates from Kurdish as "Long Live Freedom!" It was accompanied by a picture of Naki's 'Azadi' tattoo.

Naki's post was in response to 50 days of curfew that had been imposed by the Turkish army on Diyarbakır, Cizre and other Kurdish towns. The curfew was part of a campaign by the Turkish army aimed at targeting members of the outlawed Kurdistan

Workers' Party (PKK) who had been in conflict with Turkish forces since a ceasefire agreement came to an end in the summer of 2015. Since then, the Turkish army had been carrying out ongoing military action against the PKK. The curfew in Cizre had seen the town of 100,000 people completely sealed off for several weeks – it also resulted in many civilian deaths.

In Cizre, according to a report from the BBC, "Some of the most serious allegations centred on the area around Bostanci Street, where Turkish security forces are accused of killing as many as 100 civilians who were sheltering in three basements."

Naki had previously visited Cizre. In an interview with *Der Übersteiger* fanzine published in March 2016, Naki explained how he had visited families in the area and had helped them out financially. He said that he had tried to do the same in the old walled district of Sur in Diyarbakır but he couldn't get in. Sur had been under curfew since December 2015.

In this context – with the violence so close to home – and with Naki's personal experience of its consequences it easy to see why he dedicated Amed S. K.'s shock cup win to the people who had suffered during the curfew and violence.

Naki's post was picked up immediately by the media. The Turkish Football Federation acted decisively, claiming that Naki had been disseminating "separatist and ideological propaganda" – they banned him for a record 12 games and fined him 19,500 Turkish Lira.

Amed S.K. won only two of the 12 matches they played without the suspended Deniz Naki. Not only were they missing their talisman, but they were forced to play their quarter-final tie against Fenerbahçe behind closed doors. Without any actual fans present in the stadium the club had erected huge murals of supporters from previous matches to inspire the team. There was also a protest by the players at kick-off. Amedspor's players refused to play for the first minute of the game, a move supported by their opponents from Fenerbahçe who passed the ball about amongst

themselves before putting it out for a throw-in. The game finished
3:3 yet, despite, leading twice Amed S.K. were pegged back and had
to settle for a replay in Istanbul which – once again without Naki
– they lost 3-1.

Naki returned to the side in March 2016, scoring on his return
in a 1-1 draw at Tuzlaspor, but his troubles were far from over.

Following on from the victory over Bursaspor, criminal charges
were brought against Deniz Naki for a series of Facebook posts
including a photo that Naki posted of children killed in Palestine
that Naki had mistakenly attributed to the attack on Cizre.

Naki was unrepentant saying, "Would it have been better if
I had posted pictures from Cizre showing corpses?" His stance was
clear, whether it be Palestine or Cizre, innocent children were being
killed. Again, Naki had experienced this firsthand – when visiting
Cizre he had met a family whose child had been killed and they
were unable to perform the burial because of the curfew.

Naki was to stand trial in a Turkish court on 8 November
2016. Friends advised him to return to Germany, but for Naki
this wasn't an option. He held firm in his belief that he had done
nothing wrong. He wasn't promoting terrorist propaganda, his was
a message of peace. He stated, "I did nothing wrong. I want peace,
no matter what nationality or religion people have." Naki knew
what was at stake, since the failed coup against President Erdoğan
in July by those allied to the exiled Fethullah Güllen, an increasing
number of people had been arrested by the regime.

Naki faced the prospect of up to five years in prison if he
were found guilty of spreading terrorist propaganda on behalf of
the PKK. Naki's trial made international news. Two German MPs
from Die Linke, Cansu Özdemir and Jan van Aken attended the
trial in Diyarbakir. Players from FC St. Pauli showed solidarity with
Naki by all wearing shirts with 'Naki 23' prior to a friendly at the
Millerntor against Werder Bremen. Immediately before the trial,
Jan van Aken presented Naki with a St. Pauli shirt signed by the
squad.

The trial lasted just 35 minutes. Naki was acquitted by the judge. Given the climate of fear and repression it was a miraculous result, Jan van Aken believed that international pressure both through the presence of the two German politicians and a wider solidarity in the football community contributed to the outcome. Naki expressed both relief and surprise in an interview with *Spiegel Online*, "I am happy and relieved. The way things have developed in Turkey, I could not have been expected to be acquitted of the charges."

However, the matter was far from closed. The prosecution appealed the decision and in April 2017, at the retrial – overseen by the *same* judge – Naki was found guilty and handed an 18-month suspended jail sentence. Naki was not perturbed; his lawyer indicated that he would appeal the verdict and reiterated that Naki's message had been one of peace.

Naki continued to play for Amed S. K. and remained a target for opposition fans. In the first away game of the 2017/18 season – a 7:0 victory at Mersin İdman Yurdu – Naki was attacked from behind by a spectator as he waited to take a free-kick.

Naki carried on playing regardless, his last game for Amed S.K. came in the 1:0 defeat away to Hatayspor in December 2017, just before events took another, unexpected twist.

Late in the evening, around 23.00, on Sunday 6 January 2018, Naki – who was back in Germany visiting friends – was shot at whilst driving on the A4 motorway near his hometown of Düren. The shots came from a black van driving in the fast-lane and forced Naki's vehicle onto the hard shoulder of the motorway. His car was hit by two bullets. Naki stated, "One bullet hit my car in the middle window, the other landed near a tyre. Luckily, I wasn't hit." Initially, German officials were unwilling to confirm a potential motive for the attack. There was much conjecture that this was a politically motivated assassination attempt.

After the attack, Naki spent two hours at the police station in Düren making a statement. His family and friends then collected

Naki and drove him to Cologne. Naki was then summoned to a police station in Aachen and underwent a further nine hours of questioning without a legal representative – despite Naki repeatedly requesting a lawyer be present. His mobile phone was confiscated and, subsequently, his father, brother and several friends were questioned by police.

Naki says that he was repeatedly asked about his political affiliations, including who he had voted for in the Turkish elections and about his links to the PKK. The nature of the interrogation left many wondering why Naki – the victim of the shooting incident – was being questioned as if he were the perpetrator. As mentioned above, in December 2020, Deniz Naki was arrested and charged with being the ringleader of a criminal gang. The German authorities appear to have concluded that the shooting was not political in motive but, instead, criminal.

Naki was asked in an interview with journalist, Gezal Acer published in *DW* just three days after the attack whether he had felt at risk in Germany before the attack. He replied that he had not, although he had received threats on Facebook from people in Germany that something would happen to him either in Turkey or Germany – but hadn't taken these threats seriously.

On 27 January 2018 Naki announced through his lawyer that he would not be returning to Turkey due to "massive security concerns" and that his contract with Amed S. K. would be dissolved.

Just three days later, on 30 January, the Disciplinary Board of the Turkish Football Federation ended any possibility of Naki returning to Turkey by banning him for three years and six months (which under Federation rules equates to a lifetime ban) for spreading 'separatist and ideological propaganda'. He was also fined 273,000 Turkish Lira. It seems that Naki's call for people to join a demonstration in Cologne protesting against the Turkish army's offensive in the Kurdish region of Afrin in northern Syria was the reason for the ban.

Naki responded with a personal statement issued via Facebook to Amed S. K. supporters. In it he stated that he couldn't keep quiet whilst people were being killed, he reiterated his desire for peace, "As a man of peace, I could not be insensitive to the war in Afrin because people are dying. I made a call for these deaths to stop and to raise public awareness. I have reacted to the persecution and injustice in the world, and I will show it. This is my human and legal right."

Naki also referred to the ban saying that it showed the political bias of the Turkish Football Federation.

The statement continued with Naki saying, "Surrender is betrayal, resistance leads to victory" referencing the struggles in Kobane and Afrin. He concluded by saying that he hoped to return (to Diyarbakır) one day when there was peace.

Despite being banned from returning to Turkey, and victim of an assassination attempt in Germany, he continued the struggle. On 18 March 2018, Naki announced on his Facebook page that he was travelling to Geneva to begin a hunger strike outside the headquarters of the United Nations to raise awareness of the attacks by the Turkish military on the city of Afrin in northeastern Syria, close to the border with Turkey. Turkish forces and their allies had waged a two-month offensive against the YPG controlled Afrin with civilians, once again, caught up in and displaced by the fighting. On 18 March 2018, the Turkish-backed Free Syrian Army took control of Afrin. Naki's hunger strike began on 19 March and continued until 30 March when Naki and the others taking part in that phase of the protest stood down and were replaced by other activists.

In football terms, Naki has paid a heavy price for his beliefs. It can only be hoped that having survived a shooting and a hunger strike that Naki's sacrifice doesn't become any greater. It is impossible not to have respect for Deniz Naki. One thing is for certain, the young man who symbolically planted the St. Pauli flag in the Hansa Rostock's turf, has moved beyond symbolism into a very real battle between right and wrong. Naki can be considered one of football's most impassioned political activists, a man prepared to risk everything to stand up for what he believes in.

Naki stance hasn't changed, as he stated in *DW*, "I have always been committed to peace and have always been misinterpreted by the Turkish media. I have always been portrayed as someone calling for violence and terror. I have never done that, on the contrary: For me, the ethnic or religious background has never played a role, but always a peaceful coexistence and tolerance."

The charges brought against Deniz Naki by the North Rhine-Westphalia State Police would seem to contradict his statement to be committed to peace. Whether you believe Naki to be guilty of criminal involvement or not, it adds another level of complexity to an already multifarious individual. One thing is certain, Deniz Naki was not your typical professional football player.

Postscript: Hakan Suker

An article about Turkish striker Hakan Suker's enforced exile in the United States published in *The Guardian* on 24 February 2018 has alarming similarities to the case of Deniz Naki. Post-football, Suker had been an MP for Erdoğan's ruling Justice and Development Party (AKP). The President had attended his wedding, but Suker also had links to the cleric Fethullah Gulen, the man Erdoğan blames for the failed coup of 2016. Suker had been indicted for insulting Erdoğan on Twitter, now known as X, and, like many suspected Gulenist supporters, a warrant was issued for his arrest: he was to be charged with being a member of the Fethullah Terror Organisation.

Suker – a hero of Turkish football, leading scorer for the national team and scorer of the fastest goal in World Cup history, escaped to America. Suker's story reads like an astonishing fall from grace, but it highlights the neurosis of the Erdoğan regime. Under the President's rule, democracy hangs by a thread, the regime has imprisoned thousands of journalists, academics, teachers – anyone considered critical of the government or its policies. Deniz Naki might not have the international recognition of Suker, but their fates are similar in that both are now unable to safely set foot on Turkish soil. They are both enemies of the Turkish state.

Chapter 7:
Just 17 or Bigger than Boller? (Match)

Fabian's Höllenhunde (Hounds of Hell) 5 FC St. Pauli 1
15:30, Saturday 11 October 2014, Millerntor Stadion
Testimonial game

You know you are in deep when you are prepared to travel 500 miles to Hamburg for a testimonial game. But nothing was going to keep me away from this one.

I was absolutely gutted I couldn't be at the Millerntor for the final game of the 2013/14 season – a 2:2 draw at home against Erzgebirge Aue – to say farewell to St. Pauli skipper, Fabian Boll. Everyone at the game had said it was an incredible atmosphere and an emotional experience, something that comes through even watching clips on *YouTube*. It was hard not to be moved to tears watching Boller cry as Thees Uhlmann sang *Das hier ist Fußball* in front of a packed Millerntor. Then there was the pyro on the Südkurve and, of course, renditions of *Fabian Boll, Fußball Got!* and *You'll Never Walk Alone*. It was a richly deserved farewell for someone who has taken St. Pauli to his heart. The slogan (invented/ appropriated for Boller) *Für immer mit dir!* or 'Forever with you' – rang true.

Fabian Boll is one of an increasingly rare breed in modern football: a one club man. He began his St. Pauli career back in 2002. Over the next twelve years he racked up 292 appearances for FC St. Pauli scoring 32 goals – taking the club from the third tier to the Bundesliga and making the No.17 shirt his own. Perhaps even more remarkable was that he did all this whilst holding down a part-time job with the Hamburg Police Department. Balancing a professional football career with one in the police would be difficult enough at the best of times – but to do it whilst playing for St. Pauli was even more remarkable.

The club's supporters and residents of the district have a well-known and well-founded dislike of the police. You can't walk more than 100 yards in the neighbourhood without seeing 'ACAB' or '1312' (All Cops Are Bastards) scrawled or spray-painted on any available surface. The dislike and distrust is real. It is borne out of many confrontations and clashes with the police at football or at demonstrations over the previous three decades. The police storming the Jolly Roger pub in an unprovoked attack in July 2009 immediately springs to my mind but – of course – St. Pauli fans and the antifascist left's mistrust of the police runs much, much deeper than that. So, for Fabian Boll to be appreciated and loved the way he is by St. Pauli fans is remarkable. So much so, that you occasionally see graffiti or stickers around the Millerntor proclaiming, 'ACABEB' (All Cops Are Bastards Except Boll). Of course, not everyone fully accepted Boll, but during his time with St. Pauli he has won over the hearts of most St. Pauli fans.

So when 'Bollzen' (Boller's 'testimonial' game) was announced I knew I had to be there. Fabian Boll had scored the winner in my first game at the Millerntor (versus Bayer Leverkusen in 2007) and he's been a constant in my St. Pauli experience ever since. If I was manager, he'd be the first name on my team sheet (not an opinion shared by Roland Vrabec evidently – a decision that you could argue lost him the trust of St. Pauli fans, and ultimately his job). Even coming to the end of his career (and struggling with his hip) Boll was still a steadying force, offering both passion and heart alongside vision and calmness. Sometimes in football, you need players who will dig deep and more importantly inspire those around them to do the same. Fabian Boll is one of those players.

He'd assembled a stellar cast of St. Pauli legends for the game too:

> *Paddy Borger, Bene Pliquett, André Trulsen, Florian Lechner, Moritz Volz, Ian Joy, Christopher Dobirr, Fabio Morena, Björn Brunnemann, Hauke Brückner, Michel Mazingu-Dinzey, Filip Trojan, Marvin Braun, Rouwen Hennings, Florian Bruns, Marius Ebbers, Thomas Meggle, Ralph 'Ralle' Gunesch, Timo Schultz, Sir Charles Takyi, Alexander Ludwig, Felix Luz, Deniz Naki, Carsten Rothenbach, Morike Sako, Olufemi Smith, Robert Palikuca, Fin Bartels, Max Kruse, Andreas Bergmann and Holger 'Stani' Stanislawski.*

Fabian's Höllenhunde (Hounds of Hell) read like an FC St. Pauli dream team from the last decade. Players that we've all pined for when things haven't been going right on the pitch recently. Players that – even individually – we'd love to see in a brown and white shirt just one more time. Seeing them – together – as a collective unit would be something else. Back in 2011 Marcel Eger and Florian Lechner had done something similar with a farewell game held at Altona 93's Adolf-Jäger-Kampfbahn and the atmosphere had looked incredible. St. Pauli fans have a special way of saying farewell to their favourite players and I wanted to share in that.

There was also the opportunity of catching up for a photo and a chat with Ian Joy, left-back turned foreword writer for Pirates, Punks & Politics. He had flown over from the United States for the game. It was a chance not to be missed.

I arrived at the ground unfashionably early, I'd not really processed that this was a (traditional) 15:30 kick-off. I've become so used to dashing from the airport to make it in time for a 13.00 or 13.30 start. It was quiet on the Heiligengeistfeld, no Dom and not many fans milling about. Stranger still, the Fanladen wasn't open. For the first time in seven years of coming to St. Pauli, I wouldn't be collecting my ticket from the Fanladen. Of course, I knew about the ticket situation in advance. Like the Celtic pre-season friendly, the ticketing wasn't being handled directly by the club but by a third-party company, and so the Fanladen didn't have their normal match-day allocation. I'd had to get various people to remind me not to forget my ticket before I left home. In fact, I ended up taping it to my passport, just to be on the safe side.

It felt strange not to see Stefan and the Fanladen crew before kick-off, it was the first of a few key absences over the course of the weekend, that would give the proceedings a slightly different feel. Fortunately, there were plenty of good people around. The Lampedusa gang were setting up outside the Gegengerade and were celebrating the news of a 6:2 league win for FC Lampedusa over the delightfully named 1. FC Turbohorn earlier that morning. FC Lampedusa are now able to play competitive fixtures in the 4th Division of the Hamburg Leisure League. Sadly, although the league has cleared them to play, the league table shows that their results are not allowed to stand. As a result, they sit at the foot of the table with zero points, despite winning most of the games they have played so far this season.

Armed with some posters – provided by FC Lampedusa – to put up in the Südkurve concourse advertising SV Babelsberg 03's 'Refugees Welcome' match in Potsdam the following weekend (gaffer tape stylishly taped around the bottom of my jeans), I made my way into the ground. According to the club, they'd sold around 15,000 tickets for the game, meaning the Nordkurve would be shut. The Haupttribüne was largely empty too, but the Südkurve and the Gegengerade were filling up nicely. Although, again, something was different on the Südkurve: there would be no Ultrà Sankt Pauli for this game.

I appreciate that Ultrà Sankt Pauli aren't to everyone's taste but, for me, their absence today showed just what they contribute to the atmosphere in the stadium. The Südkurve was far from empty, plenty of fans had taken the opportunity to stand directly behind the goal in the space usually occupied by USP. It just wasn't the same. My friend Shaun and I often joke that part of the reason we go to St. Pauli is to *bounce*. Regardless of the score, the importance of the match or the performance on the pitch, there's always the *bouncing*. And the singing. And the choreo. Without USP driving things forward, the Südkurve felt strangely flat. To be honest, it felt as if it were full of tourists, people who had come to sample the atmosphere not to help create it. Now, that might be a little harsh, as I appreciate I could quite easily be classified as a tourist too. It just felt a little different. Part of this, of course, was due to the fact it was a charity game and not a competitive fixture. The silver lining was that it gave the Gegengerade a chance to lead the singing. But for the most part – again, due to the nature of the match – the back-straight was similarly subdued.

But we were here to celebrate, remember and reminisce, so expecting cup-tie atmosphere was a little unrealistic (hopefully we'd be saving that for Dortmund in a few weeks' time). It did flag up to me the opinions voiced by several fans I'd spoken to about the whole event: there was a school of thought that this game was in many ways unnecessary – that Boller had been given a fitting send-off against Aue at the end of the previous season. There was just a hint that this game was milking things a little whilst also promoting a 'cult of the personality' promoting the individual rather than the collective, communal spirit of St. Pauli. I can see their point, although it is not a view I fully subscribe to.

First, the money raised from the game is not going into Boller's back pocket as was the tradition in testimonial games for many years. Instead, money was being distributed to local worthwhile causes (the game raised over €75,000 for charity of which €17,017 went to the St. Pauli-Museum 1910 e.V.). Second, by assembling a cast of former players, Boll was making the event about more than just himself. It was about the collective. The collective of players, managers, and coaching staff that he'd worked with. It was a celebration of everyone, and of their achievements of getting the club back from the financial brink and escaping the wilderness of the Regionalliga. For me, it was the celebration of an era, not an individual.

And, as *Hells Bells* chimed you couldn't fail to be moved by watching the two teams come out. All those players you never thought you'd see again at the Millerntor. It was emotional. So many players, so many memories: Boller, Ralle, Felix Luz, Mo Sako, Flo Lechner, Ian Joy, Florian Bruns... and Deniz Naki.

It left many in the stadium wondering, why isn't Deniz Naki still at the Millerntor? He can't be that old? (He was 25 at the time of this game.) He still has the talent. He is still adored. Surely, here, on our holy field, is where he should be? St. Pauli fans are the ones that will forgive him those frustrating performances when he doesn't quite deliver, but also adore those magical moments when he does things that only Deniz Naki can do. To my mind, he is the perfect game changing 'impact' substitute: 20 minutes to go, trailing by a goal, bring on Deniz. Imagine the lift the crowd would get, the buzz in the stadium? There is no one in the current squad that can change a game like Naki can when he's on form.

This is jumping ahead somewhat. Naki looked like he still had it. So did Florian Lechner (who bombed up and down the right-hand flank like he'd never been away). Another old favourite of mine, Björn Brunnemann, also looked like he could still do a job at this level, even though he is currently plying his trade in the Regionalliga Nordost with Berliner FC Dynamo. Relative youngsters like Rouwen Hennings and Bene in goal, evidently still have the skills to perform at this level (as Hennings illustrated two weeks later when he returned to the Millerntor with Karlsruher SC, scoring one and setting up another in a comfortable 4:0 romp for the away side).

But this game wasn't really about performances, it was about memories and emotions. It was great to see Ralph Gunesch back on the pitch, albeit momentarily. Gunesch was recovering from ACL surgery, so his involvement was limited to booting the ball into touch straight from kick-off, before theatrically being hauled off by Stani on the sidelines. The early substitution – in turn – enabled Fabian Boll to make his own, personal entrance. It was great seeing Charles Takyi enter the fray, and to witness Paddy Borger back between the posts.

You had to feel a bit sorry for the current squad though. They really were on a hiding to nothing. As the game began, it became apparent that they weren't going to get a single decision from Bibiana Steinhaus (refereeing the game for Boller partly because they both share the same employer – *whisper it* – the Police!). It must've been strange for first team squad having to play at half-pace, knowing that the script required a victory for the Höllenhunde. It must've been hard for them too, seeing how much their predecessors are revered and respected. There is a palpable feeling that the current squad just don't connect with the ethos of St. Pauli. Sure, they do the walking tour of the district, they pose for the photographs, but these are young men, professional athletes, pretty much all of whom were born long after the 'Mythos of St. Pauli' first began. They know nothing of *Retter*, of the Regionalliga, of the struggle to kick fascists out of football. Perhaps, today will help them see the importance of that connection between club, fans, and district. The importance of knowing you are not just playing for any old club, you are part of a community – a passionate, political, and principled community. This isn't Hoffenheim or RasenBallsport Leipzig.

It was a rout, of course. Boll got on the score sheet and celebrated with the obligatory knee-slide (it was a day for party-pieces), Mo Sako side-footed calmly into the net (always a delight to see Mo score!) and, of course, Deniz Naki got his goal, scoring with a typically cheeky, 'playground' goal on his hands-and-knees heading the ball over the line. Florian Bruns even conspired to miss a penalty with the last kick of the game. The attendance was announced at a contrived 17,017 and for a while I thought the final score would end up being 1:7. But the match ended in a comprehensive 1:5 win for the Höllenhunde. The other highlight was Ralle, donning a referee's shirt and using the magic spray, pausing as he ran back to the dugout to create an Oz 'smiley' in tribute to the legendary Hamburg graffiti artist who had tragically died the previous month, hit by a train whilst out spraying. It was a heartfelt tribute, and one that felt completely genuine.

Other parts of the day felt more contrived, more pantomime than professional football. As much as we love Deniz Naki, surely there's only so many times he can re-enact the Rostock flag planting? It all seemed a bit too orchestrated. As mentioned, there were no USP, but fortuitously there was one solitary flag on the Südkurve enabling Naki to produce a faithful re-enactment of his famous moment. I hope Deniz does come back, but it must be on the condition of looking forward, creating new memories, not rehashing old ones. In fact, Deniz did his ceremonial flag planting, not once but twice: once at half-time and once at the end. It was fun, but a little laboured.

The final whistle brought a final chance for Boller and his team to take the adulation of the Millerntor. Boll disappeared into the tunnel so he could emerge one more time, this time to an extended guard of honour. Paul Sheridan of The Wakes led the crowd in a rendition of *You'll Never Walk Alone,* the players saluted all four sides of the ground, including the one fan who had got into the Nordkurve.

In many ways, it felt like the end of an era. Will we ever again see a group of players that garner that much respect, that have made that much of a connection with the fans? Only time will tell...

I headed back round to the Fanräume after the game to catch up with a few people including the delegation from Yorkshire.

Then, it was off to meet Sönke, who had managed to get me on the guest list for the post-match party. This was something else entirely. We were armed with copies of *Pirates, Punks & Politics* to get signed by the players (as most of it was written during –

and about – their era). The plan being we could then give these signed copies away in competitions, but really it was just a good opportunity to be a bit star-struck and to see 'behind the curtain' at one of these events. I must admit, I felt more than a little guilty as we pushed passed Fabian Boll himself and the throng of fans at the main entrance to get inside and get our 'access-all-areas' wrist bands. Boll spent a considerable amount of time outside signing anything and everything. We'd also seen Deniz Naki still dressed in full kit, at least an hour after the end of the game, signing things through the fence on the corner of the Gegengerade and the Südkurve. Our group of Museum people headed up the never-ending flight of stairs to the hospitality area at the top of the Südkurve. It was still quiet, but soon the room filled up with players and guests.

To say it was a surreal evening was an understatement. Queuing at the bar next to Fabio Morena, chatting about life at HSVII with him or, even more surreal, starting a conversation with a bemused looking Björn Brunnemann about hair-dye (his shock of punk rock peroxide has been replaced by a more sedate crop in recent years). It was a pleasure to finally meet Ian Joy, who had flown in from Florida (we'd done the foreword to the book via Skype) and it was fabulous to chat to Ralph Gunesch who, to my mind, is one of the most genuine footballers I've ever met.

On a personal level, this was utterly bonkers: just seven years previously I'd watched Fabian Boll score and Brunnemann make his debut in my first ever game at the Millerntor and here I was chatting to the people who made the history that I'd so sketchily documented in the book.

Bizarrely, the more Astra I consumed, the shyer I became. I didn't want to pester these guys too much for photos or autographs. What struck me as I wandered around taking it all in, was that this was *their* night. Yes, we were all gathered here for Boller but, more than that, it was a chance for teammates and friends to get together one more time and relive the memories and the laughs of their time at St. Pauli. This was *their* evening and – although they were all studiously polite to the half-drunk English bloke clutching a book for them to sign – it was important to let them get on with the thing that had made them so great in the first place: being a team, together.

It was this post-match party that made me realise the real importance of the day: it was the chance for the players to be *together* again. Great teams, era-defining teams, have that collective bond. It was a pleasure to sit back and watch them enjoy themselves.

Of course, there was more. Much more. I got to see Thees Uhlmann sing an acoustic version of *Das hier ist Fußball* complete with a verse about Boll and Naki. I got to see Boll and Naki with their arms around each other singing along. I got to watch a 'Greatest Hits' set by The Wakes from the front row. And, of course, I just got to mingle and watch and absorb it all. I spoke to Bibiana Steinhaus about refereeing at the Olympics, I'd seen her at Coventry's Ricoh Arena in 2012. I even got to talk teaching – with German counterparts – sharing its drawbacks and frustrations which seem to know no borders. I can't overstate how lucky I felt to be a part of this. It had been a good day and a great evening.

This was a chance to appreciate a set of fantastic players. Yes, nominally this was Fabian Boll's day but it was actually much more than that. It was a celebration much broader in scope, a celebration of an era. For that, we can strip away the tiny bits of cynicism. It wasn't the celebration of individual success, but a celebration of community. Boll is – and always will be – one of our favourite sons, but we know and he knows that FC St. Pauli is bigger than Boller.

That said – as the current St. Pauli midfield is finding out to its cost – he is going to take some replacing... Thank you Fabian, for everything.

Chapter 8:
Still Lovin' Ewald

With a few notable exceptions, football managers don't tend to stick around long in the modern game. Very few are ever completely embraced by supporters regardless of results on the pitch. Even at FC St. Pauli, no manager had really endeared himself to the Millerntor crowd since Holger 'Stani' Stanislawski, the manager who took the club to the Bundesliga in 2010 and back down to 2. Liga in 2011.

Following Stani came three coaches that many supporters struggled to tell apart: André Schubert, Michael Frontzeck and Roland Vrabec. They all failed to make an impact on the pitch or with the supporters. Following the failures of this trio – which culminated in the sacking of Vrabec in September 2014 – the club changed tack, promoting club legend Thomas Meggle from his position as manager of U23s to first team coach. In hindsight, it was a case of too much too soon. A run of poor results quickly led to Meggle being replaced just three months later in December 2014 by the vastly experienced 60-year-old, Ewald Lienen.

Many readers especially those with only a limited knowledge of German football might have assumed the club had turned to this journeyman manager to steady the ship and to stop FC St. Pauli sliding listlessly into the third division. Those with slightly longer memories or a penchant for watching gory football injury videos on *You Tube* might've recalled the horrific injury Lienen sustained after a tackle by Werder Bremen's Norbert Siegmann in 1981. It's been variously described as 'Football's Grizzliest Tackle' and 'The Foul Unlike Any Other'. The ten-inch-long gash in Lienen's thigh that exposed the bone was so shocking that it requires a strong stomach even when viewing it on the internet some forty years later. Perhaps even more astonishing is Ewald Lienen's reaction to the tackle. Despite his injury he raced across the running track to confront Werder Bremen coach, Otto Rehhagel, whom Lienen believed had instructed his players to foul their opponents. The matter didn't end there. Lienen took legal action against Rehhagel and Siegmann, although the courts ruled that such an injury was part-and-parcel of the game; an acceptable risk in the career of a professional footballer – in the 1970s and '80s at least.

Of course, Lienen was much more well-known in German football circles. His professional playing career spanned eighteen years from 1974 to 1992. He made 551 appearances scoring 95 goals during this time. He began his career with Arminia Bielefeld in 1974, returning for a second stint at the club in 1981. He spent two successful spells at Borussia Mönchengladbach. Lienen won the UEFA Cup with 'Gladbach in 1979, beating Red Star Belgrade 2:1 over two legs, the decisive goal being scored by 1977 European Footballer of the Year, Allan Simonsen (who also holds the honour of being Charlton Athletic's most glamourous signing). Ewald and 'Gladbach made it to the UEFA Cup final a year later in 1980. This time though, they lost out to Eintracht Frankfurt on away goals. German sides had dominated the competition that season, providing all four teams appearing in the semi-finals.

Lienen left Borussia Mönchengladbach in the summer of 1987, dropping to the regional third tier of German football playing for MSV Duisburg. In 1989, he helped Die Zebras win promotion to 2. Liga and in 1991 helped get the club promoted into the Bundesliga. The 1991/92 season would be Lienen's swansong. He retired in May 1992 after Duisburg suffered relegation back to the second tier. During his time in North Rhine-Westphalia, and with one eye on the future, Ewald completed his coaching licence and helped establish the Vereinigung der Vertragsfussballspieler e. V. (VDV), the German professional players union (the equivalent of the PFA in the England).

Following his retirement as a player, Lienen remained at Duisburg, becoming the coach of the club's second string. In March 1993, Ewald took over the reins of the first team, guiding them through the final stages of the season to a second-place finish and promotion to the Bundesliga. It was the beginnings of a managerial odyssey that would last for over twenty years and include managing sides all over Europe. Ewald will continue this part of the story himself.

I was fortunate enough to be able to interview Ewald in person in September 2017. In his two and a half seasons as head coach at the Millerntor, St. Pauli fans had fallen head-over-heels in love with him. What is really interesting to note and also the first point to crop up in our interview was that Ewald was never actually approached for the manager's job at St. Pauli at all.

Back in 2014, FC St. Pauli President, Oke Göttlich, approached Lienen with an entirely different proposition: the recently elected President was looking for someone to fill a new position of Technical Director, a job with a different remit from that of a traditional Sporting Director. It wasn't a post just concerned with the first team, more a role that would help the overall development of players and coaches throughout the club. Göttlich wanted someone with experience and vision; someone who could move the club forward. Ewald Lienen was that person. Outside of my chat with Lienen, I had been told that Ewald's interview for this post had amazed those present – even those who had been in football for a long time – such was the level of detail and insight in his presentation. St. Pauli seemed to have found the perfect candidate at the perfect stage in his career: someone to provide the strategic oversight to take the club to the next level.

As it turned out, it would be three years until Lienen took up the post of Technical Director. Fate, or football intervened. With Thomas Meggle struggling under the weight of expectation and stuck in a run of bad results, the club needed someone at short notice to take over the role of Head Coach. Lienen was already in advanced negotiations for the position of Technical Director, so it seemed logical and sensible to ask him to step in. His last coaching job in Germany had been with Arminia Bielefeld in 2011 (he'd coached AEK Athens and Romanian side Otelul Galati in the meantime) but he readily accepted the challenge of saving St. Pauli from relegation.

You pretty much know what happened next: it was something of a rollercoaster ride but, for reasons we shall uncover, St. Pauli fans enjoyed every minute of it. There was salvation at the Stadion am Böllenfalltor in Darmstadt in May 2015, when Lienen completed his assignment of keeping the club in 2. Liga (despite a final day of the season loss to SV Darmstadt 98 who secured promotion to the Bundesliga). There was the fabulous football and fourth place finish of 2015/16, and the expectation that this would lead to great things, perhaps a return to the Bundesliga at the end of the 2016/17 season – a season that couldn't have turned out more differently. Cut adrift at the bottom of the table with just 11 points at the winter break, Lienen's job was hanging by a thread, only for the most improbable of turnarounds to take place in the second half of the season that saw St. Pauli finish in seventh place. And, let's be honest, after losing at home to 0-1 Stuttgart in the opening game after the mid-season break, who would've thought the season would've ended in anything but relegation and Lienen's sacking? Hell, we didn't think he'd make it to the end of January.

What we didn't know was that during those two and a half seasons, President, Oke Gottlich, was constantly in the background reminding Ewald Lienen about the job he originally applied for. As Lienen said, "He was always thinking: pushing me about the role of Technical Director."

This is the Ewald Lienen I meet at the club offices, just after lunch on the Friday before the home game against 1. FC Heidenhiem. Ewald Lienen, *Technical Director*.

Fairly quickly, we established that he is also Ewald Lienen, *The Man With The Magic Key*. The club offices are busy, and I get the impression that Ewald knows if he tries to conduct this interview anywhere in plain sight, he'll be interrupted hundreds of times. So, with a turn of his key we passed through a number of locked doors and take the elevator to the top floor of the South Stand. We walked to the end of a long corridor housing the Separees (executive boxes, to you and me) and with one final flourish of Ewald's master key, we were inside the box that belonged to Viva Con Agua. It's quiet up here with a fantastic view of the pitch. The only other activity is being conducted by the bloke diligently sweeping the steps of the stand with an elongated dustpan and brush.

Lienen himself looked really well. Slight on his feet, resplendent in a grey Under Armour track top combined with smart work trousers and offset with his trademark glasses, he didn't look anywhere near 63, and seemed to bear none of the usual hallmarks of a man who has spent his life in football. There was certainly no evidence of dodgy knees as he leapt up a couple of times during the interview: once to get a drink from the fridge; and again, to mimic Arsene Wenger's frantic arm actions that he'd witnessed at the recent game between Stoke City and Arsenal.

I'd been granted 90 minutes of Ewald's time and I was keen to make the most of it. My feeling was that – perhaps – my request for an interview had been granted with the tacit proviso that we used some of it to focus on the future, his new role as Technical Director and – maybe – more specifically the club's partnership with Stoke City. But, as a fan and historian, I wanted to delve into the past as well: to try to understand Lienen as a person and get to the bottom of the connection he has with St. Pauli fans.

First, I asked him how his role within the club had changed? And, what exactly does a Technical Director do? It turns out the list is pretty extensive. Primarily, the role is a strategic one, free from the more specific roles of the Financial and Sporting Directors. In theory, Lienen's role is one free from prescribed daily tasks, allowing him to take a more strategic overview of the club. For me, the responsibilities that Ewald listed would have me working around the clock. Here's some extracts from Ewald's list: representing the club in the media and with sponsors; taking a strategic overview of coaching throughout the club *and* taking responsibility for the career development of those coaches; representing the club on matchdays; overseeing international relations and overseas partnerships; representing and promoting the club's social projects (which has included racing round the Millerntor in a go-cart with Nico Rosberg, supporting Viva Con Agua).

At this point, Ewald reached for his iPad, to show me his crazy email list, keen to point out that these are the ones that reach him *after* they have been filtered! He scrolled at high-speed through his inbox, I interrupted to ask him how he copes with it all? He searched for the word in English, "Folders!" He then showed me his highly organised list of folders that helped him sort and prioritise. There was a folder for invitations from sponsors or to speak with fans; there was one for people who email him on a daily basis asking for a job at the club; there were folders for international partnerships, and another for the offers of players he still received, despite no longer being in charge of the first team. It was pretty clear Ewald was a busy man; it's no wonder he had a key that opens pretty much every door in the stadium – he needed it, his role was all-encompassing.

Naively, I asked him how he coped? How different his job must be to that of a coach whose sole focus was on the success of the first team. I had forgotten that he has had a long career in football, becoming a manager in a time before sporting directors, academy coaches and burgeoning teams of support staff. As he pointed out, he was never just a coach. He had worked at plenty of smaller clubs where being manager meant doing a little bit of everything. He explained that during his time at CD Tenerife in Spain, the chief scout had left and it just became another facet of his job, one that enabled him to pretty much travel the world. So, essentially, we shouldn't have worried about Ewald's workload; he was more than used to it and I think he probably quite enjoyed the intensity too.

I asked him if he missed his old job at all? He simply replied that, two or three months into his new post, he didn't. But he also hinted that in his new position, he, "Had the most fun if it was to do with football" – especially if it involved working with the academy. I guess, after a lifetime of day-to-day involvement in the game, you don't get it out of your system that quickly. The other area that was clearly a priority for Lienen was working on the club's social projects. He was quick to mention Viva Con Agua, St. Depri (the excellent project supporting those people suffering from depression, anxiety and mental health issues) and Kiezkick (the established project working with local youngsters). He also spoke of the hundreds of other emails he got about supporting new projects and how hard it was to decide which ones the club should give priority to. He was also well aware that his name and position as a former player and manager could give these projects exposure in the media that they would otherwise never have received. As he said, laughing, "What was going on with Ewald Bienen?" (St. Pauli had recently installed beehives at the stadium and were selling the honey produced under the name Ewald Bienen.) He continued laughing and then, more seriously, suggested that I watch a documentary on *YouTube* called 'More Than Honey'. Leinen had recently spent a week in China (as part of a potential partnership project with a Chinese club) and said he had not seen a single insect during his stay. He laid the blame firmly at the door of farming monoculture explaining that China has almost no bees; instead fields of crops were somehow being pollinated by hand. It showed that beyond the 'Ewaldbienenhonig' word play, there was a serious point to the club's bee-keeping project: even if hosting a colony of bees at the stadium is largely symbolic, it was raising awareness of a truly global environmental crisis.

It is clear that this interest in social projects ran deep with Lienen. And this was something that I was keen to quiz him on.

Even as a young professional at Arminia Bielefeld in the early 1970s, Lienen stood out as someone socially aware and politically active. His political awakening came when faced with the prospect of completing his Bundeswehr (National Service). He had witnessed how serving as a soldier in the Second World War had affected his father and he knew that he wanted nothing to do with war. He explained how he had to sit in front of a commission so that they could, in his words, "Check his consciousness and his desire not to fire a gun." He must've been convincing, because instead Lienen spent his 15-months of National Service doing social work, looking after handicapped children at a residential home.

Ewald Lienen was also actively involved in the Peace Movement (Germany's equivalent of CND in Britain). During the early 1980s, the tension between East and West was at its height and, perhaps, entering its most dangerous phase. Whilst much of Europe was gripped by Cold War paranoia and the real prospect of nuclear annihilation (and those of us who grew up in 1980s Britain are still haunted by *Threads* and *When the Winds Blows* – terrifying television depictions of nuclear Armageddon), Germany, East and West was at its very epicentre. NATO's decision to station hundreds of American Pershing II nuclear missiles on West German soil provoked a huge wave of public protest. In October 1983, nearly half-a-million people protested in Bonn against the deployment of the missiles, whilst a human chain encompassed the United States Army headquarters in Stuttgart. Two years later, in 1985, Ewald Lienen stood as a candidate for the Peace Movement in the election to the parliament of North-Rhine Westpahlia. Lienen explained that it was never his intention to hold elected office; he was simply using his status as a professional football player to generate publicity and broaden awareness of the Peace Movement in West Germany. As a result of his involvement and his position as a professional footballer, he was frequently asked to attend meetings and give speeches at schools and churches.

As Ewald was explaining his involvement in the Peace Movement, I was frantically racking my brains for an equivalent to Lienen in British football in the 1970s and '80s. I drew a blank. British football was deeply conservative (most obviously with a small 'c' but probably with a capital one too). The 1980s were a decade where listening to the 'wrong' sort of music marked you out as a bit different (Pat Nevin). Or, as Graeme Le Saux found out, the simple act of reading *The Guardian* was enough to label you as gay. I asked Ewald if he thought it was unusual for football players to be political? His response was instant, emphatic (and very St. Pauli). He replied, "Everything in football is political!" He just couldn't comprehend it any other way.

I then asked if he had ever felt that his political views had held him back in football? (I wasn't quick enough to link this to Colin Kaepernick's stand against racism and police brutality which saw him frozen out of the NFL.) He didn't; he never felt his political involvement had been used against him or had held him back – as it surely would've done in English football at the time. Instead, he felt – with the benefit of hindsight – that the only person holding him back had been himself.

Lienen had played a couple of B-Internationals for Germany in the 1970s. In 1978, he had the chance to play for the German national team. As he said, he told them to, "Fuck off!" He felt like he had a reasonable chance of making the squad for that year's World Cup in Argentina. However, during his time with the B-team, he had seen how the German Football Federation operated and described it, bluntly, as, "Fucking horrible." He explained that during that time, Amnesty International had written to the

German FA and asked them to formally condemn the actions of the Argentinian Military Junta, but they refused. As a result, Lienen told them, "Don't even think about calling me." Looking back, he thinks he might've made a mistake, not – as you'd expect from a football perspective – but because he believed that he may have had more influence and been able to raise more awareness of the atrocities carried out by the Argentine regime had he travelled to the World Cup.

Lienen recalls Berti Vogts saying, at the World Cup, that he couldn't see any political interference in Argentina. This left Lienen fuming, "But they'd killed them on the field where they were playing." It was clear that, nearly forty years on, Lienen regretted not taking the opportunity to highlight the crimes of the Argentine military dictatorship, lamenting, "As a national team player, I would've had more influence."

During his time at Borussia Mönchengladbach, at the time one of Germany's most renowned teams, Lienen experienced no problems from the club's hierarchy about his politics, instead the club were wholeheartedly supportive. Lienen recalls, "I was club captain and I had a personality – the club accepted that." He then remembered how members from the Christian Democratic Union party had approached the club and said that if Lienen was made captain they would return their season tickets. The club's response was simple: Give them back then. Lienen is our captain.

Whilst no one in football had openly challenged him about his political beliefs, Lienen spoke about another group of politicians from Bavaria who took issue with his opinions. They said, "What does he have to do with politics? He should play football." Ewald recalls replying, "This is your understanding of democracy. It also reveals your character: my task – in your eyes – is to distract the people from politics; to stop them changing or improving society." It's one part of bread and circuses; football performing its role as the opiate of the masses. And Ewald Lienen refused to conspire in it. Unfortunately, he recalls the politicians' standard response at the time when challenged by anyone from the left of the political spectrum. The politicians simply unleashed what was referred to as, 'The argument that kills everything'. In West Germany, during the 1970s and '80s, the default response to anyone questioning the established capitalist orthodoxy was always, 'Go and live the other side of the wall'. Ewald was adamant in his response back then, "No. I don't want to go there, we need to change things here," before reflecting ruefully, "I think we still have politicians like that now."

With such political awareness and a life-long commitment to social change, I ventured the question that I had been wondering for a while: how come it took so long for Ewald Lienen and FC St. Pauli to find each other? Had there been opportunities to join the club earlier in his career? By coincidence, Ewald had met someone just recently who claimed that he had been approached to join FC St. Pauli some twenty years ago, but Lienen himself had no recollection of this. He did recall, at the end of the 1980s, a friend who worked at a Hamburg newspaper suggesting he should visit the Millerntor, but it was not really a career option. The sporting reality was that Lienen and FC St. Pauli were operating at different levels. In short, Lienen was established in the Bundesliga, FC St. Pauli – not so much.

As well as spells in charge of several German clubs, Lienen's managerial career had seen him bounce around Europe. He had two spells in the Canary Isles with CD Tenerife, first as assistant to Jupp Heynckes between 1995-97 then returning as manager in 2002; three spells in Greece and one season in Romania. So the opportunity to work at St. Pauli as a manager never arose either.

One thing he was certain of, when he took the managerial reigns in December 2014, he knew immediately that he was a good fit. As he said, the difference was clear: at the previous clubs he'd worked at he had needed to convince people about his ideas. At St. Pauli he didn't need to convince anyone. Everyone was on board already. He could see it just walking round the empty stadium. To be fair it is hard to be in any doubt reading the giant 'No Football

For Fascists' and 'No One Is Illegal' murals painted on the terraces. But during those first few home matchdays, he marvelled at the banners and wallpapers displayed by fans supporting left-wing political causes.

Lienen clearly connected with the ethos of the club and its supporters, and fairly quickly the fans connected with Lienen. This was established through his – now famous – walkabouts. Pre-match, he would emerge from the tunnel and pump his fists and clap his hands repeatedly over his heart, raising the crowd up another notch in their support. Post-match, regardless of the result, he would applaud the supporters' efforts. It meant so much to us. I asked if it was something he had always done? He recalled that the first time he did it on purpose was at 1. FC Köln in 1999. The club had just been relegated to 2. Liga for the first time in its history. Something, Lienen joked, "that should've happened to Hamburg many years ago!" (and, of course finally did in 2018, when HSV were relegated from the Bundesliga for the first time in the league's 55-year history). It was Ewald Lienen who would lead Köln back to the Bundesliga, and before and after every home game he made a conscious effort to go over and acknowledge the club's most vociferous fans, in the stand behind the goal.

At his first home game at the Millerntor, he did much the same thing with the fans on the Südkurve. The following week, the club's Press Officer was inundated with emails saying, as Lienen colourfully put it, "What the fuck is he doing? What about us?" So, Lienen added the Gegengerade to his walkabout. Then he recalls, "After half a year the Nordkurve was completed. There were more emails. And, so, that stand also became a part of my routine." Lienen was at pains to point out that it was never about him claiming the applause; it was about building a bond between him, the team and the fans.

Once again, there's a complete contrast with British football to be had here. In Britain, players and managers rarely venture out of the centre circle to applaud fans before bolting for the tunnel.

The culture of properly thanking and appreciating the supporters just doesn't exist. Lienen believes that as a coach, not only is it his responsibility to convince the players about his ideas on the pitch, but also that his players should *want* to go and applaud the fans. He recalled his recent trip to Stoke City for the game against Arsenal when not one player went to acknowledge the 5,000 or so visiting supporters.

This provided a convenient segue into the final part of our interview (the part I felt the club probably wanted us to focus on): the strategic partnership with Stoke City that began in 2017. We talked a bit about the contrasting ownership models in British and German football and how the erosion or abolition of the 50+1 model was a real threat to the game in Germany. Ewald talked about the inflationary bubble in football, the product of television money and funds from obscenely wealthy owners. He pointed out that bubbles tended to burst. But how did all this relate to St. Pauli's partnership with Stoke City, an arrangement that was greeted with quite some consternation by most British based St. Pauli fans? What was a club, like FC St. Pauli, a club with such a clearly defined identity and established set of values doing getting into bed with Stoke City? Arguments swirled around Twitter in the days that followed the announcement. Stoke's Labour supporting chairman was cited, as too was Stoke being dubbed the Brexit capital of Britain. There were concerns about some Stoke fans' links to the far-right. There was sympathy for the group of twenty-or-so Port Vale fans that had been regularly journeying to the Millerntor for years. The discussion wasn't particularly pretty. And that was before Stoke visited the Millerntor for a friendly and sung their reworking of the Tom Jones song *Delilah*, the version that celebrates sexual assault.

It was pretty clear that Ewald was unaware of this controversy. Maybe, it was something that had consumed us – as British-based St. Pauli supporters – far more than anyone else. For what it is worth, I think St. Pauli could've partnered with any British club and there would've been rumblings of dissatisfaction. After all, part of the reason we were all drawn to St. Pauli was because we'd had enough of British football – especially, the sexist, misogynist 'lad' culture that prevails too often in too many stadiums in Britain.

What was clear was that Lienen regarded this first and foremost as a sporting partnership. As he began to explain the constraints that St. Pauli operates under it began to make more sense. As he stated, "St. Pauli can't sell its soul." It is not like other clubs. It won't rename the stadium or revoke or bend the 50+1 rule. So the club needs to find other ways to compete. The partnership with Stoke provides that opportunity. St. Pauli has to find a way of getting better without spending money. There was a chance that through this arrangement with Stoke City, the club might have be able to field players in the first team that they couldn't possibly afford otherwise. These were players that Stoke may have bought with an eye firmly on them playing in their first team in two years' time, but for those two years, these players could be playing for St. Pauli. It benefitted Stoke too: they could give their young prospects – who weren't quite ready for the Premier League – competitive football in 2. Liga, rather than limiting them to the slightly sterile environs of U23 action in England. Lienen believed this competitive match experience would be the defining factor in a footballer's progress in the future. He believed that, increasingly, due to improved training and coaching, players were coming through that had similar technical and physical attributes. He believed that the key factor in a player's development was going to be their 'game intelligence' – something that could only be properly honed through experience in competitive match situations. He felt that the partnership with Stoke could provide this.

Lienen had already spent a few days in Stoke, looking at their coaching set up and taking in a number of matches – from youth level through to the aforementioned first team game against Arsenal. He was due to return to the Potteries the following week. He saw the relationship as an attempt to gain a sporting advantage, saying, "We have to live this and see if it works out. We will learn from them and hope to get to the Bundesliga. Once we achieve promotion, then everything is about staying there. After two or three seasons you begin to be established."

Sometimes, as international, ideological St. Pauli fans we can be too focussed on the club's ethos and almost forget about the football. And whilst, as we have seen, Lienen is clearly political, he is also a man who has spent his life in football. And being in football means wanting to be the best you can possibly be, to compete at the highest possible level. With this in mind, the tie-up with Stoke made more sense. It is FC St. Pauli trying to compete in a football environment without selling its soul. The partnership with Stoke City is best viewed as an attempt to do just that – compete on the football field. It might not be the perfect alliance, but it is better than the alternatives.

About halfway through our hour-and-a-half long discussion, Ewald Lienen said something that made me fall a little bit more in love with him, something that I have been saving for the end of this piece, because it captured everything I've ever felt about this club in one statement: "This (the fans' political values) gave me a special feeling. I knew I was not just a coach winning the next game, but a coach defending our ideas and values." This is precisely why we are Still Lovin' Ewald.

We wrapped up our interview with talk of a Manchester based get-together of Ewald and British-based St. Pauli fans – as he's flying in-and-out of Manchester when visiting Stoke. We gathered up our stuff and shook hands, Lienen last out of the door as he needed to lock up, using his 'Key to Rule All Keys.' He'd kindly given me 90 minutes of his time and it had been absolutely fascinating. I came away from the meeting feeling relieved: Ewald Lienen might not be out there on the pitch on matchdays, pumping his fist to his chest, but from everything I'd just heard it was clear that his heart still beats for St. Pauli.

As an aside, the partnership with Stoke City that Lienen was speaking so optimistically about in 2017 was dissolved just two years later. The union yielded two pre-season friendlies and a couple of unsuccessful loan deals between the sides. Both clubs issued a joint statement to a largely uninterested football media (at least outside of Hamburg and Stoke-on-Trent), it read: "The partnership has brought the clubs closer together and led to a number of benefits, including two pre-season fixtures, coaches and officials from both clubs sharing knowledge and many intangibles. However, after two years – and as a result of other priorities and a change in personnel at both clubs – we have mutually decided to discontinue the formal partnership whilst remaining on good terms." The English side's relegation from the Premier League in 2018 after ten seasons would have also played a part.

In June 2022, Lienen's association with FC St. Pauli would come to an end too but not before his role had evolved again, finishing his seven-and-a-half-year spell at the Millerntor as the club's 'Value and Brand Ambassador'. His enthusiasm and personality will be missed around the place by both fans and colleagues alike. It took a long time for St. Pauli and Ewald Lienen to find each other, but it was a union worth waiting for. Club President Oke Göttlich summed the time up by saying: "We have experienced a lot together – and I can only say: I am an Ewald fan." You and 30,000 others, Oke.

Chapter 9:
Sleepwalking (Match)

FC St. Pauli 1 Arminia Bielefeld 0
15:30, Sunday 6 May 2018, Millerntor Stadion
2. Bundesliga

Looking back with the benefit of hindsight, the 2017/18 season was a bit of a roller-coaster – albeit one with more lows than highs. Dismal back-to-back 4:0 and 5:0 defeats did for manager, Olaf Janßen two games before the winter break. New boss, Markus Kauczinski, started reasonably strongly with four points from the two home games before Christmas (a 2:2 draw with Duisburg and 2:1 win over Bochum).

And, after the first game back in 2018, things looked almost positive as we opened with a 1:3 away victory in Dresden. A dramatic last-minute Christopher Avevor headed goal gave us a memorable 3:2 win at home against pantomime villain, Marvin Ducksch's Holstein Kiel, but after that there was a run of eight games that we either drew or lost. The 2. Bundesliga table was ridiculously tight (again): the top 4 teams were in a race for the two automatic promotion places and the play-off spot, whilst pretty much everyone else – from fifth to eighteenth – was running the gauntlet of relegation.

Unlike the 2015/16 season, when Ewald Lienen led a spirited second half of the season revival, this season felt like it was listlessly slipping through our fingers. For all of March and most of April, it felt like the players, the team and the fans were sleepwalking towards relegation. There just didn't seem any spirit left to fight it off. As the weeks slipped by, the odds-on relegation started to change from unlikely to inevitable. Some even talked of it being necessary – a chance to reset the clock – if you don't mind borrowing an analogy from somewhere else in Hamburg... There was no feeling of togetherness. No #KLASSENHALTEN painted in giant letters on the Nordkurve (as there had been in April 2016). No sustained anger or prolonged frustration, just a sort of nothingness, a collective shrug of the shoulders, an acceptance of our fate. There were even players signing new contracts that were only valid if we stayed in the second division. If we didn't, it was hard to see how relegation would impact them, as they would jump ship to somewhere else. It was all very strange.

Fortunately, things changed with a convincing 3:0 home win over an equally lackluster Greuther Fürth (spoiler alert: even after this dismal result, Fürth somehow also managed to avoid relegation). It meant we went into the final home game, and penultimate game of the season with a chance that a win might be enough to keep us up. At the very least, a win would keep us in the mix until the final game away in Duisburg the following week. Anyhow, Shaun and I were reunited in Hamburg for this one and Shaun was bringing along his daughter (and my Goddaughter), Laura, for her first trip to the Millerntor (and for a post-exam blowout). It was a bit weird travelling separately, my flight from Heathrow arrived first, meaning I was able to watch The Big Man disembark his Manchester flight, walk down the steps, kiss the ground then shake his fist and shout something inaudible at the sky from my position on the viewing balcony at Hamburg Airport.

We met the other side of the customs gate. Shaun was looking spritely as was Laura who had got in from a party at 02:45 before having to get up again to go to the airport at 03:30. Oh, to be young and able to survive on 45-minutes' sleep. I feel tired just thinking about it.

On our way to the stadium, we spotted some graffiti sprayed on the wall, it read, 'We will win!' Could it be an omen? Even if the graffiti was referencing anarchism's ultimate victory over capitalism rather than St. Pauli beating Arminia Bielefeld (as if there's a difference). We made it to the ground super early, picking up our tickets and dropping off a small present for Stefan who was – sadly – departing the Fanladen for a new job heading up the fan liaison between HSV and St. Pauli. Thanks for everything you've done for us over the years, Stefan – it's really appreciated.

Shaun and Laura managed to bag a sneaky afternoon powernap (thanks to the more traditional 15:30 kick-off) whilst I had a meeting with Christian from the club about the forthcoming trip to Detroit. I had been asked to moderate a discussion panel featuring representatives from both FC St. Pauli and Detroit City FC. It was good to chat with Christian, and to try and get plans in place for the USA trip. However, my pessimism was so overwhelming that I can't say I was 100% concentrating. I was convinced we'd be occupying the relegation play-off spot that would – in turn – see the US tour cancelled.

At the end of the meeting Christian took me out of his office to watch the team arrive from our position above the Südkurve. He said he would be able to tell whether we'd win today's game by watching how the squad got off the bus. The players were greeted by young fans chanting and clapping. The team seemed in a good mood, high fiving the youngsters. Christian seemed happy. I wasn't so easily convinced.

Then I quickly headed back to the hotel to collect Shaun and Laura and avail myself of my 'lucky' brown, white and red ribbons. For some reason, I decided that my hair tied back with ribbons could be just the impetus the team needed to secure victory. In truth, I was just desperately trying to convince myself. I'm also not entirely sure how much the ribbons were for FC St. Pauli collectively avoiding relegation or more selfishly for me getting the opportunity to visit Detroit (even though both things were intrinsically linked).

The atmosphere inside the stadium was pretty good. We were on the Südkurve, joined by the lovely FC Lampedusa guys. Laura and Shaun were on the pre-match beer, I was too nervous. From the first few minutes, it was clear that Arminia Bielefeld weren't going to be a pushover like Fürth. In fact, if there was any pushing over to be done, it was going to be done exclusively by Bielefeld, who had the look of a particularly physical 1980s rugby league side about them. One player had his shorts hitched up so high around his massive thighs that he looked like he'd mistakenly turned up at the Millerntor instead of Craven Park or Odsal. The game wasn't pretty, and it just felt like however well we performed Bielefeld still had the capacity to score from a well-drilled corner or set piece.

However, it was St. Pauli that took the lead, shortly before half-time. From where we were standing, low down in the Südkurve, it was impossible to tell anything other than the fact that we had scored. Yiyoung Park broke into the penalty area down the left, and somehow the ball was in the net. Ever the pessimist, I couldn't even celebrate – it was obvious, we'd scored too bloody early. There was no way we were going to stop this Bielefeld side from bundling the ball into the net through sheer brute force, and probably with the very last kick of the game. But as the second half wore on, a St. Pauli win became more of a possibility. For all their physicality and aggression, Bielefeld didn't offer very much in the way of creating chances. Shaun – always more objective and astute in his analysis of football than me – pointed out Bielefeld's lack of both a Plan B and, indeed, anyone with the ability to beat a player. They were completely one-dimensional. As the clock ran down, Bielefeld's menace faded. As the effort expended in their overly physical approach saw them visibly wilt in the May sunshine.

The final whistle brought a 1:0 victory and three valuable points. The celebrations intensified as other scores filtered through. Uwe Stöver led the charge onto the pitch as the news came in that we'd secured our 2. Bundesliga status with a game to spare. I'm guessing the club had two squad planning scenarios dependent upon the division they'd be playing in next season. I'd wager Uwe's job will be infinitely more pleasurable planning for life in 2. Liga rather than 3. Liga. There was a palpable sense of relief all round the stadium. I whispered a 'thank you' to my 'lucky' ribbons, now 'officially' lucky. We were safe from relegation, and I was going to be heading to Motor City, USA. The post-match celebrations with the players were particularly enjoyable – they received a rapturous reception from the Gegengerade. Then, after more celebrations, the whole squad walked along the front of the Südkurve shaking hands with fans at the fence. We'd done it: we'd woken from our slumber just in time to secure another season in the second tier of German football. Perhaps, we should be aspiring to more, but right then it felt good just to be safe.

Post-match the place was heaving. We couldn't get near the wine bar to start with, so made do with bottles of Jever from the beer sellers around the ground. Whilst we were drinking, we ran into our old friend Thomas who had brought a copy of the *Übersteiger* fanzine for me and a wonderful, bespoke braun-weiss pig for Laura knitted by his niece.

We finally made it back to the wine bar and, with Laura's hangover from the previous night seemingly remedied by beer, we decided to do the sensible thing and proceed straight to the pink prosecco. There was still quite a queue at the bar, so it made perfect sense to order two bottles. From there, the evening was the usual wonderful mix of prosecco, friends and warm Hamburg sunshine. At some point, we made our way from the wine bar to the Jolly and switched from prosecco back to Jever, occasionally spiced up with a rogue Mexicana. We chatted for ages to everyone, including Marco from Calgary, who'd used his entire year's annual leave (and sick days) on a trip to Hamburg to watch St. Pauli (his annual leave began in April, it was only 6 May!) There was the obligatory stag party from the Britain, who hadn't got tickets for the game (hurrah!). They were not so subtly taking the piss out of me and Shaun behind our backs for our stupid hair (amongst other things) – not that we gave a toss. As ever, I was on the early flight back to London, whilst Shaun and Laura had a leisurely mid-morning departure. I needed to be on the 04:35 train back to the airport. You could tell it was Sunday night/Monday morning because the Reeperbahn was eerily quiet as I sleepwalked to the station.

So, all's well that ends well. We avoided relegation. The hashtag *#FCSPGoesUSA* can actually 'Go USA'. And I'd got a whirlwind trip to Detroit to look forward to. As it turned out, it was the other Hamburg club that were the ones sleepwalking to relegation. The clock finally stopped for HSV. However, rather than gloating at the demise of our suburban rivals, we should learn a lesson from it: there are only so many times you can dodge the relegation bullet, it will get you in the end. We needed to look back on 2017/18 as a warning shot across the bows. It was time for our beloved pirate ship to plot a course to a higher league, and not keep getting sucked into the relegation whirlpool. Well, we live in hope.

Chapter 10:
G20: Welcome to Hell

*"Capitalism is a social relationship of domination and violence that is leaving a trail of devastation behind it: ecologically, economically, and socially. A swath of devastation that is depriving people of their livelihood everywhere... The proclaimed triumph of capitalism is nothing less than hell on earth for many people. When we called our alliance "Welcome to Hell", that's exactly what we meant: to make the rulers' G20 meeting in Hamburg – a bit of a hell for which they are responsible and for which they stand." – **G20: Welcome to Hell, autonomous & anticapitalist alliance against the G20-summit in Hamburg**

If Angela Merkel personally chose the Hamburg Messe convention centre as the venue for the 12th G20 summit she must've spent three sleepless nights between 6-8 July 2017 wondering what she had done. Merkel – born in Hamburg – was probably in a hotel far enough from the conference site not to be kept awake by the constant hum and swooping searchlights of the police helicopters that patrolled the sky. However, many of the city's other residents would've looked out the windows of their flats and apartments and wondered what the hell the German Chancellor had unleashed.

There was another school of thought: that the location was chosen as a deliberate provocation of leftist, anti-capitalist and anarchist groups. That the authorities knew the trouble locating the G20 in the middle of St. Pauli and surrounding districts would create. That it would provide an opportunity to demonstrate the full power of the state when it came to repression of the inevitable protests. That repression wouldn't just manifest itself in the violent police operation that was well documented in videos, reports, and blogs over the course of the summit. It would extend far beyond that. The protests would legitimise a fresh wave of oppression against leftist groups, justify the enabling of stricter laws against future demonstrations and protests and, most damagingly, prompt the long and drawn-out incarceration and trial of activists from across Europe who were arrested by police snatch-squads on the streets of Hamburg. There were even theories that the hosting of the G20 in Hamburg was an attempt to use the power of the German state to 'clean-up' the districts of Sternschanze and St. Pauli by creating a conflict that would turn popular opinion against the existing residents of the district, thus accelerating the gentrification of the area.

In the run up to the G20, the residents of St. Pauli probably had more pressing concerns than the ongoing battle against the gentrification of the Kiez. The arrival of the world's leaders would have a very real and tangible impact on their daily lives. A 'Red-Zone' was to be created around Hamburg Messe that restricted access to those with the correct accreditation. The massive police presence, random ID checks and roadblocks would make daily life more arduous for residents.

Of course, there had been significant disturbances at previous G20 summits. London had seen protests in 2009, and a year later, in Toronto over 1,000 protestors were detained in custody making it the largest mass arrest in Canadian history. In 2011, the G20 gathering was held in Cannes with the French police able to seal off the resort and limit protestors to the nearby city of Nice. The G20 already had an established history of protest.

St. Pauli and the surrounding districts also had an equally established history of protest. In the autumn of 1986, police had raided the squatted flats on the Hafenstraße to evict residents. There were frequent violent clashes between police and protestors that culminated with 12,000 people marching through the streets in support of the Hafenstraße residents and demanding an end to police discrimination. The action was ultimately successful – with the council drawing up an agreement that provided the residents a degree of security from eviction and harassment. In December 2013, there were further clashes between protestors and police over the attempted eviction of squatters from the popular Rote Flora autonomous community space (housed in an old theatre in the heart of the Sternschanze district). Over 8,000 protestors assembled to defend Rote Flora despite the authorities declaring the area of the city as a 'Danger-Zone' which gave them even more repressive powers to break up demonstrations. The police were quick to use tear-gas and water cannons to break up the demo – which came not long after similar police violence during the city's 2013 May Day protests. Much like the victory for the residents of the Hafenstraße squats in the later 1980s, the demonstrations helped secure the future of Rote Flora as a social space when – in January 2014 – the council announced that they had ceased with plans to demolish the building.

So, inviting an assortment of over thirty presidents and prime ministers alongside the leaders of the World Bank, World Trade Organisation and the United Nations to meet at a city centre venue located just a stone's throw from the districts of Sternschanze, Schanzenviertel and St. Pauli with their long tradition of activism and anarchism was not a wise move. The fact that deeply divisive and right-wing leaders in the shape of Theresa May, Recep Tayyip Erdoğan and Vladimir Putin were in the ascendency only poured fuel on a fire that had continued to burn after almost a decade of austerity and the associated fall in living standards that had become more pronounced following the global financial crash of 2008. Then, there was Donald Trump. President Trump had been inaugurated into office in January 2017. He'd spent the first few weeks firing-off executive orders (24 in his first 100 days in office) that introduced a raft of regressive policies. There were travel bans from Muslim-majority countries, the infamous proposed wall along the border with Mexico and an increased drive for deportations via an empowered Immigration and Customs Enforcement (ICE) agency. All this led to the United States feeling like an increasingly hostile environment for numerous immigrant communities. There was the repeal of his predecessor's Affordable Care Act (Obamacare) which had given access to affordable healthcare to tens of thousands more US citizens. On top of all this policy was the almost daily volley of vitriol that gushed forth from the President's mouth via the medium of Twitter. The G20 in Hamburg would also be Trump's first as Commander-in-Chief of one of the world's most powerful nations. In short, an unstable former reality-TV star had his finger on the button of one of the largest nuclear arsenals on the planet.

Supporters of FC St. Pauli (along with numerous other anti-capitalist groups from across the continent) had been planning their opposition to the G20 months in advance of the summit.

On 28 April, Ultrà Sankt Pauli, Zeckensalon, Supportblock Gegengerade and Nordsupport coordinated a stadium-wide day of action that coincided with the home game against Heidenheim. Banners and placards were held aloft around the stadium. The tifo on the Südkurve was a subtle play on words proclaiming: 'G20 to Hell' and supported with the message, 'No War But The Class War'. After the match, around 3,500 demonstrators marched from the stadium in the direction of the Hamburg Messe exhibition centre. However, in a foretaste of things to come, the Hamburg Senate refused to allow the protest to culminate at the main entrance of the venue. They claimed this was because the demonstration exceeded

1,000 people but it probably owed as much to groups like USP being seen as 'problematic' by the German authorities. The protest was low-key and passed off peacefully, albeit coming to an end some 800 metres short of its intended destination.

In the weeks preceding the summit, the German state increased security and checks at the borders with Belgium and Denmark in an attempt to stem the flow of foreign-based anti-capitalist activists reaching Hamburg. The police established a mass detention centre in an industrial unit located to the south of the river Elbe. The site had previously been used as a refugee detention centre but was repurposed for the duration of the G20. Temporary courts were also established in a series of shipping containers on the same site. Judges were empowered to remand those accused of an offence (or those suspected of planning one) for an initial period of 10 days. These temporary courts were a clear signal of intent. The authorities were planning for mass arrests and incarceration.

Much of the talk in the mainstream media would focus on the violence that erupted around the G20 summit. However, the protests would be much more varied, creative and joyful than depicted on the news reports. For example, the '1,000 Gestalten' (1,000 Figures) protest was a collective art performance. 1,000 artist-activists covered from head-to-toe in grey clay walked zombie-like through the streets of Hamburg before coming together to shed their grey exteriors revealing brightly coloured t-shirts and celebrating their 'awakening' by dancing and shouting. The grey clay-encrusted figures represented individuals who had lost their collective purpose and had become trapped in a world of personal progress; the shedding of their grey shells symbolised the joy of breaking free from an increasingly individualised society and rediscovering a sense of community and collective solidarity. The organisers successfully carried out the most visually arresting performance of the weekend, one in which people from all over Europe participated and that was notable for the fact that it was many of the participants' first ever experience of a collective art performance. After the event, a spokesman for '1,000 Gestalten' summarised the action: "We want to put back in memory how compassion and public spirit conveys identity for a society. Our campaign is a further symbol for the fact that many people do not want to put up with the destructive impact of capitalism any longer. What will save us in the end is not our account balance but someone who will offer their holding hand."

In the days before the summit, the police carried out a number of raids on camps set up by protestors – demolishing tents and pepper-spraying occupants. The most notable of these raids happened at Entenwerder Park on the banks of the Elbe, where police waited until nightfall to break up the camp, despite the highest court in Germany granting protestors clearance to stay there. It was a pattern that was to continue in the days that followed wherever protestors tried to set up base.

As the week progressed, nightfall would often bring localised skirmishes between activists and police – who were intent on disrupting any attempt by protestors to pitch tents and rest.

It was at this point, on the morning of Thursday 6 July, that FC St. Pauli intervened to help with the situation. In coordination with the organisers of the (legally approved) camp at Entenwerder, the club made 200 sleeping spaces available to activists in the Haupttribüne (somewhat ironically using the one stand in the ground that is dominated by corporate seating and hospitality boxes).

The club had already agreed to host the 'FC/MC' 'alternative' media centre over the duration of the G20 summit. At daily press briefings – held at 09:30 each morning – activists were given a platform to talk about the summit itself and the associated protests in a space that welcomed critical thinking and went beyond the mainstream media's summary of events. Despite being hosted in FC St. Pauli's South Stand, the media centre was not run by the club or any singular political entity. Instead, it was a non-hierarchical collaboration of activists designed to engage in discussion about the events unfolding around them. You might be forgiven for thinking the 'FC' part of the name was a reference to hosts 'Football Club' St. Pauli? Instead, it was more ambiguous than that. The assumed name for the collective was 'Federation of Competences' but as the organisers noted themselves, the acronym could equally have stood for: 'Forget Capitalism', 'Fruitful Collaborations', 'Future Culture' or more. The media centre live-stream was able to disseminate information and video almost as it happened. There were also social spaces for journalists and activists to be able to compile their reports in safety. Throughout the duration of the G20, discussion panels were also broadcast including one on Friday 7 July that featured FC St. Pauli's Ewald Lienen and Sven Brux who discussed the aftermath of the previous evening's' Welcome to Hell' demonstration. The mood in the temporary studio was sombre. There were calls for both the police and protestors to stand down, insisting that they 'avoided a second Genoa' – referring to the death of two activists at the 2001 G8 Summit in the Italian city. At this stage of proceedings there was a very real fear that the violence unleashed by the police at the 'Welcome to Hell demo the previous day would escalate and that there would be fatalities on the streets of Hamburg.

Other parts of the stadium also offered activists sanctuary from the invasive police presence elsewhere in the district. The Fanladen together with the amateur football department ran a tournament – 'Football vs. G20' – on the FeldArena pitches behind the North Stand. A community kitchen was set up in the Fanräume along with live music and the all-important mobile phone charging facilities whilst the Museum/Weinbar handed out soft drinks, drinking water and allowed people to shower off the pepper spray used by police. FC St. Pauli had – once again – found itself at the heart of a protest movement, the Millerntor providing a relative oasis of calm in the maelstrom of protests and police brutality that had engulfed the rest of the district.

Although, most evenings leading up to the G20 summit had seen confrontation between police and activists, the first major (and approved by the Hamburg Senate) demonstration was the 'Welcome to Hell' rally and march scheduled for the late afternoon and evening of Thursday 6 July. The politicians were in town; it was time to make the people's opposition known. Crowds began to assemble by the Fischmarket and along the Hafenstraße adjacent to the banks of the Elbe ahead of the march which was scheduled to leave at 19:00. The march was meant to follow the extensive permitter to the 'Red-Zone' heading out first through Altona, then via Sternschanze avoiding the heavily fortified Hamburg Messe exhibition halls. The rally had passed peacefully with people enjoying speeches and music from sound systems. As 19:00 approached the crowds started to coalesce – with most participants at the front of the march donning black clothing and masks – as a 'Black-Bloc' of anonymous and autonomous protestors.

Ahead of the Black-Bloc, blocking the road in front of them stood hundreds of police in riot gear. The sheer number of officers blocking the route seemed incompatible with the idea of the march being allowed to proceed. It has been reported that the police were refusing to let the march begin unless members of the Black-Bloc removed face-coverings that were concealing their identity. The police knew that this was a demand that was never going to be met. However, they also cynically let the march move forward a few hundred yards along St. Pauli Fischmarkt into a section of the road that forms a natural gulley with a high brick wall on one side and a multi-storey carpark on the other. Suddenly, the front section of marchers found themselves hemmed in on all four sides. There was no way out on either flank; ahead, the way was blocked by riot police and behind them was the main body of around 10,000 protestors stretching back into the distance. It felt like a trap.

After a prolonged stand-off in which the tension continued to build, the police made their move. They attacked the Black-Bloc from the front and the back. Video footage collaborates the events. Police bombarded the now separated front section of the march with tear gas whilst snatch squads of officers in riot gear went after protestors. The front few rows of the Black-Bloc resolutely held their ground in the face of this onslaught. This allowed others – with the help of bystanders on the walkway above – to haul themselves up the brick embankment and out of the line of fire. Police watercannons then moved in to disperse those protestors and onlookers on the footpath above as the last of the Black-Bloc protestors were either snatched by the police or scrambled up the brick wall. The confrontation continued on the raised walkway, with the water cannons continuing to push protestors back, this time forcing many to leap down an eight-foot drop onto the concrete beside the Elbe River.

With the Black-Bloc broken up by the riot police and either arrested or scattered around the district, the rest of the 'Welcome to Hell' march remained penned in by the police, their water cannons and armoured vehicles. At around 20:00 – three hours after the march was supposed to begin – the main body of protestors was finally allowed to proceed in the direction of the Reeperbahn.

By 23:00 the march had headed north, reaching Sternschanze where their progress was blocked by more police. From here, a pattern emerged that would last most of the night. Activists would set up barricades in the street only for water cannons and riot vans to regularly try and break up the protests.

At first light on the Friday morning, plumes of thick black smoke could be seen rising across the St. Pauli district and that of Sternschanze – Hamburg had become a battlefield. The police had struggled all night to regain control. Much of the smoke stemmed from burnt out luxury cars that had been set on fire by protestors or from multinational retail shops and banks that had been attacked. This was not the G20 that Angela Merkel had been expecting – or was it?

One of the first tasks of the FC/MC media centre on Friday 7 July was to send out a tweet explaining that from 06:00 that morning a ban on demonstrations had been put in place by the authorities covering most of the city. However, this didn't mean an end to protests. Instead, there was a change in strategy. The second day of the summit was all about small scale protests designed to disrupt and slow down the mechanics of the gathering. Rolling blockades were set up – activists staged sit-ins on roads leading to Hamburg Messe causing delegates to be held up and the start of that morning's proceedings to be delayed.

Meanwhile, another group of protestors successfully managed to blockade the port of Hamburg, disrupting the flow of goods for a couple of hours, before they too were moved on by police. These anti-capitalist protestors were taking a slightly different approach by directly targeting a hub of global commerce. Interviewed by a reporter from *Vice*, a spokesperson for Ums Ganze (an association of anti-capitalist autonomous groups) stated: "Our goal is to show that capitalism is not only the authoritarian regime of the G20 but also the normality of capitalism which happens every day. People dying at the borders of Europe. We live in a world where people die on national borders while the goods we consume every day can cross the globe freely."

On the Friday afternoon, activists once again gathered outside of the Millerntor Stadion. It was the starting point for the 'Colour the Red-Zone' demonstration that planned to block delegates from listening to a performance of Beethoven's 9th Symphony at the Elbphilharmonie concert hall in the HafenCity. There were also further clashes between protestors and police on the Hafenstraße with protestors being kettled by police. At this point, the feeling on the ground in Hamburg was that the police were becoming more indiscriminate and violent – frequently targeting people who were not actively involved in the protests.

By nightfall, the police – increasingly frustrated and tired from two long days facing-off against protestors – were losing their control over several streets in Sternschanze. Fires once again burned, and shops were looted – for a few blissful hours the streets belonged to the protestors with the police forced to withdraw to the periphery. But reinforcements were on their way in the shape of

GSG-9 special forces units. Finally, in the early hours of Saturday morning, the police re-established control of the Schanze.

Saturday 8 July was the final day of the G20 Summit. After two nights of intense skirmishes between protestors and police, the final day of demonstrations had a very different feel. Over 50,000 people took to the streets – a coalition of many different pressure groups and activists. The final day felt more like a carnival, with families with children in pushchairs walking alongside riot police who seemed to have dialled down their violent rhetoric. There were still confrontations – usually caused by police snatch squads breaking into the march at different points but the dynamic of the protest and the policing felt markedly different. The mood was more celebratory than angry.

In the end, the protestors fell short of their stated desire to stop the G20 summit from taking place in Hamburg although this was never an achievable objective. However, they did much to disrupt proceedings, and even more to shine a light on the differing world views held by those in power and those on the streets. The three days of demonstrations and protests had taken months (if not years) of planning, they had brought together activists from across the continent. They had also highlighted how far the authorities were prepared to go to supress and undermine popular protest.

The world's mainstream media were forced to cover the protests although – of course – most of them spun their coverage to focus on the rioters and the activities of mysterious Black-Bloc with their covered faces. The number of police casualties was massively inflated by the media – all in an attempt to paint the police and the authorities as the 'good guys'. People on the ground in Hamburg knew that the reality was very different. FC St. Pauli's decision to host the FC/MC media centre at the Millerntor allowed for the dissemination of an alternative narrative – one much closer to the experience of those on the streets.

It would've been easy for the club to shut up shop and literally board up its exterior for the duration of the summit and to have trotted out the famous trope that 'sport and politics don't mix'. However, as we know, at FC St. Pauli sport and politics are so deeply entwined that it was impossible for the club to sit on its hands and do nothing whilst outside the stadium the district burned.

Hosting the G20 summit hundreds of yards from the stadium of the most political football club in the world could be viewed as a mistake or as a provocation. It certainly gathered together all the different strands of capitalism and the global shift of power to the authoritarian right and dumped it right on the football club's doorstep. There was no way that the club and its active fans were going to shrug their shoulders and walk away. FC St. Pauli was part of the fightback. The club itself played its part offering sanctuary to protestors. The supporters of St. Pauli were there on the streets alongside anti-capitalist and anti-fascist protestors from around the world. It was how you would expect it to be. From the riots on the Hafenstaße in 1986; the coming together of supporters and residents marching against the proposed Sport-Dome three years later; right up to the defence of the Rote Flora in 2013, the fans and inhabitants of St. Pauli have always taken to the streets to stand up to oppression. At the 2017 G20 summit the whole world was watching and, hopefully, a new generation of activists was inspired.

The world's leaders had experienced the wrath of the people at close quarters. Donald Trump had been dispatched back to the United States with his tail between his legs, it was even rumoured that protestors caused his wife, Melania, to 'miss an appointment' because she was trapped in her hotel. However, having welcomed Trump & Co. to hell in July 2017, I don't think anybody had expected that, under a year later, FC St. Pauli would be taking the fight to Trump's home turf: to Washington DC, Detroit and beyond.

Chapter 11:
Detroit's Soul/Welcome to New York
(Matches)

Detroit City 2 FC St. Pauli 6
International Friendly
18:00, Saturday 19 May 2018, Keyworth Stadium

Let's deal with the criticism first: there was a lot of cynicism surrounding the motives behind St. Pauli's United States tour – a viewpoint I can completely understand.

On the surface the tour looked like a marketing venture: it included visits to commercial partners including, (controversial) kit manufactures, Under Armour, as well as Levi's, whilst frequent references to 'growing the brand', gave the trip the feel of a commercial land-grab. On top of all of that, this was *Trump's America* – what on earth were a club like FC St. Pauli doing visiting a country whose president specialises in building literal and metaphorical walls; who issues travel bans to nations he deems undesirable; who repeals government legislation providing healthcare to American society's most vulnerable, who puts babies and small children in cages and whose misogyny and prejudice are laid bare for all to see – *daily*

– via his Twitter account? This felt like a very different trip to St. Pauli's winter training camp in Cuba back in 2005, a trip which inspired player, Benny Adrion, to found Viva con Agua – a charity that has since provided clean drinking water to thousands of people in developing nations.

Closer to home, there were even whispers that the US tour was an unnecessary distraction that contributed to St. Pauli's slump in form during March and April, leading them to flirt with relegation (ironically, putting the tour itself in jeopardy). The murmurings were that the club should concentrate on securing its league position rather than – in pop music parlance – 'trying to break America'.

In the end, a 1:0 victory against Arminia Bielefeld in the penultimate game of the season at the Millerntor secured our 2. Liga status; lifted the spirits of players and fans alike and – of course – meant that the tour could proceed.

So, to the actual tour... Yes, there was a visit to Under Armour headquarters for the usual photo opportunities and 2018/19 kit reveal. Yes, the players were kitted out in Levi's gear and did some promotional appearances in stores during the first part of the tour. But let's not forget that Levi's sponsor the St. Pauli Music School at the Millerntor run by Dave Doughman, who works with local kids and community groups. But perhaps the first indication that this tour wasn't just about 'growing the brand' and selling shirts, came when the squad posed for pictures in front of The White House with a rainbow flag to celebrate the previous day's International Day Against Homophobia. Uber-cynics could argue this action was still in line with the positioning of St. Pauli as a 'rebellious' brand, but those of us who support the club, who understand the motivations of those in charge, know that it was more than that – it was genuine. Standing against, fascism, racism, sexism, and homophobia isn't a marketing gimmick, it's literally what the club stands for – it's part of our DNA.

From Washington it was on to Detroit for the first game of the tour against Detroit City FC. I'll hold my hand up at this point and admit I didn't know anything about Detroit City. I understood the reasoning behind the tour's other match in Portland, but my knowledge of the club ethos and the fan scene in Detroit was non-existent.

This is where I should've trusted the club and those in charge of organizing the tour. It didn't take much of a look on the internet to ascertain that Detroit City are not your typical American sports franchise. Playing in the National Premier Soccer League (NPSL), the fourth tier of the very much in flux US soccer pyramid, Detroit City FC were founded in 2012 as a community club. The fan base is fiercely loyal and fiercely political. The club and its fans have self-financed the renovation of their Keyworth Stadium. Detroit City FC aren't doing all this with the long-term ambition of becoming another Major League Soccer franchise. As I would become increasingly aware over the course of my trip, these fans bloody hate the MLS.

For all the cynicism and misconceptions about St. Pauli's trip to the United States, there was one precise moment when I knew it was all going to be okay. I'd only been in Detroit for a couple of hours, I'd got the $2 airport shuttlebus downtown and made the 10-minute walk to the hotel (once again, I'm convinced the US adheres to a different scale for mapping, as it only looked like a couple of blocks away). I found myself sat in a hotel room with Shawn and Sam from the *Fell In Love With A Girl* podcast, when my mobile phone rang, an unknown German number calling. Assuming it was something to do with the tour, I answered it.

"Hello, Nick? It's Ewald..."

I managed to hold it together reasonably well for the duration of the call, but as soon as I hung up, I couldn't contain my excitement. Ewald Lienen had phoned me! Not only that, but he was sending the team bus back to the hotel to collect us and take us to the distillery where the players and officials were holding a meet and greet with fans and their counterparts from Detroit City. It just seemed so typically Ewald. He'd been told I should've been on the bus to the venue, and when I wasn't he took it upon himself to call me and sort it.

What he didn't know was that just before he phoned, we'd been listening back to and repeating a voice memo sent by Svenja from NYC's East River Pirates that told me how to correctly pronounce both "Oke Göttlich" and "Ewald Lienen!" I wasn't particularly nervous about hosting the Q&A session the next day, in fact I was very much looking forward to it, but I was petrified that I'd say both Oke's and Ewald's names wrong when introducing them.

It was pure *Beetlejuice*. I'd literally just said Ewald Lienen's name three times and he'd called. From then on, I instinctively knew everything was going to work out just fine.

We gathered up our stuff and headed down to the lobby of the ridiculously enormous MotorCity Hotel & Casino to begin living the dream. It's fair to say I've never really grown up. I remember going on school trips when I was about 11 or 12 pretending that whenever I got on or off the coach, I was on the team bus heading to the Cup Final. Or when I was going on a package holiday to Spain and stepping off the plane into the warm Mediterranean night with the buzz of cicadas in the background, imagining I was about to play in a particularly tricky European Cup tie... And here we were, in Detroit, waiting for the team bus to come back and collect us. Finally, at the age of 46, I was on my first 'End of Season Tour' albeit as a hanger-on, eeking out my minor part moderating a panel discussion for all it was worth.

Things just got better from there on in. We arrived at the distillery which was packed with players, officials and fans. I'm not sure Shawn and Sam could believe it any more than I could. Here we were, stood next to players we'd watched, and they'd podcasted about. Everyone was so relaxed. Eventually we plucked up courage to engage them in conversation. Ewald was as charming as always, the players too. Shawn is a massive fan of Philipp Heerwagen, and

I wondered if he was having one of those 'never meet your heroes' moments? If he was, he needn't have worried as Heerwagen was so lovely and so generous with his time. In the absence of Jan-Philipp Kalla from the tour (who'd stayed behind in Germany to take his coaching badges) it felt like Heerwagen had stepped up to fill the void by being the embodiment of everything it means to be a St. Pauli player. Whatever topics we discussed, he just instinctively 'got it'. He clearly understands the ethos of St. Pauli as much as anyone. Heerwagen's off-season travels, that included a trip into North Korea, are about as far from the standard footballer's trip to Dubai as you can get.

It's fair to say I'd not really connected with this group of players, not in the same way as I had with those from the Boller-era, where it seemed like most of the squad including: Fabian Boll, Ralph Gunesch, Deniz Naki and Bene Pliquett had close links to the fan base, the culture and the district. But whilst chatting to Heerwagen, he was keen to point out that it wasn't just the likes of him and Kalla who understood what the club represented, he insisted that all of the players were aware that St. Pauli was special and that things were different at the Millerntor than at other clubs. This was reassuring to hear, especially coming off the back of a season where it seemed that players and fans alike had spent much of the season sleepwalking towards relegation. It certainly helped dispel some of the doubts I had about this current group of players from as far back as Fabian Boll's testimonial game in 2014.

Certainly, the way the players and staff interacted with fans on this trip went a long way to eliminating the feel of a 'disconnect' between the team and supporters that I had been building up in my mind. By the time we left the event at the distillery, I already had the feeling that this tour was about more than just commercial gain: it also served as a bonding experience, not just between the players but between the team and supporters. I think the fact that so many St. Pauli fans came to Detroit helped to reinforce the point that Heerwagen had made earlier: playing for St. Pauli is different. It is special – yes – first and foremost, these young men are professional athletes, with a short and precarious career in the professional game, but they do realise the St. Pauli experience is something unique.

Of course, it was fun too. Everyone was enjoying a drink which relaxed the mood. Oke and Sean Mann, one of the co-founders of Detroit City, stood on the bar and made speeches. Diminutive midfielder, Richy Neudecker couldn't believe that someone had written a book about FC St. Pauli in English and was insistent that I put my number in his phone so he could call me the next day to get a copy. It was one of those evenings (spoiler: he never phoned).

From the distillery, it was back aboard the team bus to head over to St. Andrew's Hall to watch Chicago punk band, Rise Against.

The security check to get into the gig was an eye-opener: we were casually advised that we wouldn't be able to take any firearms or knives into the event – and there was me worried about getting my mobile phone charger in.

It was here that I began to realize the sheer number of US fans who had made the trip to Detroit for the game. But first, we were joined by the final member of our group: Shawn from New York (henceforth referred to as 'New York Shawn', as opposed to 'Canadian Shawn' – confused?) Her flight had been slightly delayed, but she still made it in time for the concert. It was great putting names and faces to the Twitter accounts of fans from across North America – it gave the first real inkling of a 'coming together' of the 'Nordamerikurve'.

By this stage, I'd been awake nearly 26 hours and was flagging badly. I'll also admit that I'm not a massive fan of shouty punk bands. The team coach was also doing a shuttle run back to the hotel, to get the players home at a respectable hour (they did have an important international friendly match to play the next day!). So, I ducked out of Rise Against, and headed back to my room to fall asleep to the gentle melodies of Belle and Sebastian, something much more befitting of a man of my advancing years.

I remember Canadian Shawn getting back to the room a couple of hours later. He was clutching a Levi's jacket given to him by Philipp Heerwagen. In our slightly delirious state, we weren't sure if the evening had been a dream. So, we resolved that if the jacket was still hanging on the back of the chair in the morning, it would've been real and us not imagining some surreal childhood fantasy where we got to go on the team bus and hang out with the players. Fortunately, for our sanity, the jacket was still there when we woke up.

We woke up late though, which meant a bit of a scramble to source breakfast before the discussion panel at 11:00. After being unable to locate any food outlets the previous evening, I was surprised to find that there was a whole plaza – the size of a small shopping centre – in the hotel dedicated to serving food 24 hours a day. Oops.

From a hurried breakfast it was up to the 13th floor to the hotel's ballroom where I was hosting a discussion panel entitled: *Detroit City FC and FC St. Pauli – A different kind of football?*.

The view from the top of the hotel was spectacular, you could see the skyscrapers of downtown Detroit, the Ambassador Bridge that connects the city to Canada (to the South!) and the iconic, derelict behemoth, Michigan Central Station. The assembled panel was equally impressive: Sean Mann (co-owner of DCFC) was joined by FCSP President, Oke Göttlich; Ewald Lienen added to the St. Pauli contingent; academic and author, Dr Stefan Szymanski; Jackie Carline, the head capo from Detroit City's Northern Guard supporters group; and Christian Weiss from Levi's Europe.

There were between 50-75 people in attendance, and they were able to hear the panelists speak about how the match between Detroit City and FCSP came about, the similarities between the two clubs and the differing sporting models at work in Europe and the United States. What became apparent was that the similarities between both clubs in both outlook and fan culture clearly outweighed the differences. The highlight, for me, was Ewald

Lienen floating his (hypothetical?) idea for a global left-wing Super League, involving clubs like St. Pauli, Detroit, Livorno, FC United, Clapton CFC, etc. I think I just about pronounced everyone's name correctly too.

Next, it was game time. We got a cab out to The Fowling Warehouse in Hamtramck for the pre-match gathering. As we arrived, the heavens opened, unleashing a torrential downpour. We took shelter with the Northern Guard under their beer and BBQ gazebos. It was a good opportunity to chat to both the Detroit fans and the international brigade of FC St. Pauli supporters that continued to arrive from all over North America. I found myself having a beer with Soren and some of the Cosmos guys who'd recently arrived after making the 12-hour trip, overnight in a minibus from New York. There was a moment of worry that the heavy rain might cause a delay to kick-off, with the water having to be swept off the artificial surface, but fortunately the deluge abated.

As the rain eased off and the skies cleared, I made a dash for The Fowling Warehouse – a bar-cum-bowling venue. Inside, it was packed with fans of both teams, many playing a curious mash-up of ten-pin bowling and American football. It looked like fun, but with my experience of American Football exclusively limited to binge-watching *Friday Night Lights*, I decided to forgo my Matty Saracen moment as QB and save myself the embarrassment of failing to fell a single skittle with a badly executed Hail Mary.

Soon it was time for the march to the stadium. We assembled in the parking lot outside The Fowling Warehouse. The Northern Guard were in full voice, drums beating and an array of flags fluttering in the wind. Despite their fearless reputation and disdain for anyone who isn't 'Detroit' the Northern Guard welcomed us with open arms. St. Pauli Totenkopf and rainbow flags mixed in with those flying Detroit's distinctive gold and rouge. Later, someone commented on social media that there had been a Union Jack in amongst the Detroit fans, this wasn't the case: the flag was Basque – red, green and white, definitely not red, white and blue. A similar accusation was made later, as the FC St. Pauli fans produced a rainbow smoke choreo at kick-off – it was mistakenly thought that the smoke was red, white and blue in homage to the United States: it wasn't; it was rainbow coloured (although the orange smoke miss-fired).

The march was another highlight of the trip, from witnessing the FC St. Pauli President scramble down a grassy bank to the moment we emerged from underneath a railway bridge and I fully appreciated the sheer number of fans involved. The drums were relentless, and the smoke kept popping. We assembled behind a banner that read: *From St. Pauli to Detroit Gegen Rechts! Goodnight Alt-Right.* It was in this moment that the purpose of the tour, the reason Detroit City were our hosts became clear: this wasn't about marketing or merchandise, this was about solidarity – pure and simple.

Right here, in the middle of a closed-off highway, surrounded by good people, was the counterpoint to Trump's fascist America. And football, soccer, whatever you wanted to call it, was the conduit for the resistance. In this moment, as countries retreat into themselves; as the menace of nationalism and patriotism rear their ugly heads, football – the world's game – makes these artifices irrelevant. Standing amid the Northern Guard and the assembled collective of St. Pauli fans it felt like they could build no wall high enough to contain us. Football knows no borders.

The feeling intensified the closer we got to the stadium. The march took us through a series of streets and houses occupied by many people from new immigrant communities. Detroit City's Keyworth Stadium is located in the Hamtramck district of Wayne County, Detroit – an area that has welcomed both refugees, asylum seekers and other migrating peoples from conflicts in Afghanistan, Syria and Iraq. This might have seemed surprising to those of us who had been focusing on the plight of refugees within Europe. Compounded with Donald Trump's signing of Executive Order 13769 in January 2017 – that suspended all refugee admissions for four months and banned Syrian refuges indefinitely – the casual observer might've been surprised to know that over 30,000 refugees from 52 different nations had been resettled in Michigan over the previous ten years. It was certainly heartening to hear that Trump's racist and Islamophobic policy decisions didn't represent the country. Here in Hamtramck, as elsewhere in the United States, there are good people on the ground helping those in need. These are ordinary people engaged in projects giving support and solidarity to those forced to flee their homes and countries. Indeed, in 2020, just a couple of streets away from Keyworth Stadium, a development of six new houses under the name 'Freedom Village' was completed to provide quality housing to refugee families.

It struck me, how in most contexts, in most places, a mob of football fans marching through the streets towards the stadium in a part of town that housed a majority immigrant population would've struck fear into the hearts of those residents. I'd seen it enough times growing up, going to football in the 1980s: pissed-up football fans shouting racist insults at people going about their business in the vicinity of the stadium – shopkeepers abused, families intimidated. Back then, doors remained firmly shut and people hid behind closed curtains, fearful of being victimized by thugs. But not here. Here the mood was entirely different: residents and fans exchanged smiles and took photographs with each other. The mood was relaxed, jovial, curious – despite the smoke and drums and noise, this wasn't a threating experience – it was celebratory. It was only afterwards that I learned of the ticketing scheme that allows Detroit City supporters to pay extra on their tickets to support local kids getting in free to matches.

If you are looking for similarities between St. Pauli and Detroit City, then the symbiosis with the local community is a major one. Back in Hamburg, St. Pauli 'the club' has long been synonymous with St. Pauli 'the district'. The same was true here in Hamtramck. Detroit City FC might be a new club, but their raison d'être was to put down roots in the local community; to develop meaningful and lasting relationships with local people. This is how you build a football club from the ground up; it is the exact opposite of the dominant US franchise model. It's why FC St. Pauli were playing this friendly and not a game against, say, New York City FC or LA Galaxy.

As the march to the ground reached its conclusion at the gates of the Keyworth Stadium, the St. Pauli contingent gathered together and Ewald Lienen – standing on the porch of the house nearest the stadium – led the singing. We then passed through a cursory security check and into the ground. Open seating runs the length of the pitch on both sides. The far side belonging to the Northern Guard was already three-quarters full, with flags waving in the wind. Keyworth has the feel of a high-school, or small college American Football stadium (again, my experience is limited to *Friday Night Lights* and the Netflix documentary *Last Chance U*). The gridiron markings were still visible on the artificial turf, a playing surface that, perhaps, gives away the fact that this is the fourth tier of US Soccer. The pitch was uneven, recalling the rumpled green baize of a Subbuteo pitch hastily set out on a lounge carpet on Christmas morning.

We made our way to the guest-bloc and found a spot on the bleachers near the front. I hung my *Yorkshire St. Pauli - Our Friends in the North* banner in prime position above the St. Pauli bench and leaned over to get goalkeeper, Robin Himmelmann to take a picture of it from the pitch. The banner was in good company, alongside those of fan groups from Buffalo, Detroit, New York and Toronto.

The St. Pauli section started to fill up steadily, a mixture of hardcore fans from across the continent – including those that had travelled from Mexico – supplemented by more casual fans intrigued by the spectacle of a German second division side playing against the local team.

With the teams lined-up in the centre-circle, there was an acapella rendition of *The Star-Spangled Banner* – I'm not a fan of

American sports' obsession with either the anthem or the military but, sung unaccompanied, it was strangely moving. As kick-off approached, the Northern Guard hoisted an impressive tifo spanning much of their side of the ground. The Detroit and St. Pauli club crests bookended the words: *Forged from the same bones,* and central to the display was a Totenkopf (Detroit fans adopted the skull-and-crossbones after their beleaguered city was repeatedly described as being dead). It was mighty impressive and backed by a display of smoke and pyro. Not to be outdone, the St. Pauli section unleashed the aforementioned rainbow smoke display. It is worth noting that travelling St. Pauli fans had to organise their efforts exclusively over social media and that many fans were flying in, which complicated matters somewhat. So huge respect must go to Ernie from the Buffalo supporters' group who managed to get 26 smoke canisters into the stadium simply by putting them at the bottom of a large bag. I'm not so worried about how he got them past the stadium security (I'm pretty sure they'd been given the nod that smoke canisters were okay). I was more impressed with how he managed to lug them round with him all day, they weighed a ton! Ernie's canisters were supplemented by more smoke from the guys from New York Cosmos and the results were impressive – I'm not sure those watching on local cable TV would've been able to see much of the match for the first few minutes after kick-off such was the density of the pyro; the St. Pauli bench, sited directly in front of us, was certainly lost in the fog for the early part of the match.

The Northern Guard were loud right from the start, especially impressive when you consider the stadium has no roof and you'd normally expect the noise to drift away like the smoke into the early evening sky. The St. Pauli section took a little longer to get going, despite the best efforts of President Oke Göttlich who stood singing with the fans throughout (no corporate hospitality for him). As we found out later via social media, substitute goalkeeper, Philipp Heerwagen went one step further and watched the second half in the middle of the Northern Guard support section on the opposite side of the pitch.

For all the criticism Ultrà Sankt Pauli get for dictating the singing on the Südkurve, we were clearly missing them at the front with a megaphone directing the chanting. Things improved after the break as we got a bit more coordinated, but I'm not sure we did St. Pauli's usual away support justice in terms of noise – although Detroit City fans reassured us that evening that we were the loudest visiting fans ever to have graced Keyworth.

The match – as always – largely passed me by. Detroit took the lead after just eight minutes, following up after Heerwagen spilled the initial shot, but I had the strange sensation watching St. Pauli that the result was never in doubt. The difference between a full-time professional team and Detroit's semi-professionals was evident in the little things: the strength on the ball and the St. Pauli players' speed of thought and decision-making. In fact, and this is in no way meant to be disrespectful to the home side, but the biggest stumbling block felt like the pitch, the uneven surface and unpredictable bounce catching the St. Pauli players out on several occasions. Sami Allagui equalised after 21 minutes and from then on St. Pauli exerted their control, going in at half-time 3:1 up. Despite wholesale changes from both sides at the break, St. Pauli remained in control with the game finishing 6:2 to the visitors.

But this really wasn't about the result or about the football *per se*. This was about the unifying power of football, political football, uniting people with similar values and ideals. This was about building meaningful connections between two clubs and two sets of fans, a show of international solidarity.

FC St. Pauli gets a lot of criticism from cynics, glib comments about supporters being football hipsters or fashionistas from other fans who find it easier to mock the club's international popularity than to try and understand it. However, I don't think it is any coincidence that St. Pauli are touring the United States right now. I don't think it is any coincidence that in the last 18 months countless numbers of US fan groups have been established and risen to prominence on social media. It's a clear and direct response to Trump's America. FC St. Pauli and the values it represents has become a focal point for football fans around which to coalesce opposition to his repugnant regime. Sure, the subversive skull-and-crossbones branding, and punk band connections play a part but, dig a little deeper and this popular symbolism is backed up by something more. FC St. Pauli fans have been fighting a similar fight for decades: they have been at the fulcrum of sport and political activism since the mid-1980s. Let's not forget one of the main reasons the loose collection of punks, squatters and anarchists first gathered together on the Gegengerade all those years ago was due to the growing threat of Nazi groups organising brazenly on the terraces at German football clubs at the time. St. Pauli fans served as a counterpoint to the real threat of fascism. As it was then, so it is now.

I appreciate these are all generalisations, but there are concrete examples too: earlier this year, the FC St. Pauli Buffalo fan club held a screening of the Audience Network's *Religion of Sports* documentary about FC Lampedusa entitled *Here to Stay*. Back in May 2017, the American documentary makers had spent time in Hamburg interviewing those involved in St. Pauli's official refugee team. The screening of the documentary in Buffalo inspired volunteers from Journey's End Refugee Services to set up a refugee football team. In New York, the East River Pirates have forged close links with New York Cosmos' Antifa fan group Brigada71, they also regularly hold fundraising events supporting refugee charities. Whilst in The Fowling Shed prior to today's match, fans from FC St. Pauli Toronto held a silent auction of signed St. Pauli and Detroit City memorabilia to raise money for 'Cash n' Cleats' making football accessible to refugees by providing football boots and financially supporting Freedom House – a project established over 35 years ago for asylum seekers – in Detroit.

These newly formed North American fan groups are among the most active and passionate supporters' clubs to emerge in recent years. Part of that must be put down to establishing a direct counterpoint to the hostile political climate being pushed by Trump, Breitbart, and other prominent right-wing voices.

Being a FC St. Pauli fan is to be part of the resistance. Sport is a vital medium in the fight back against the establishment's divisive right-wing narrative. You don't have to look much beyond Colin Kaepernick protests to see how powerful that message can be – it's no surprise Kaepernick has been frozen out of the NFL. The owners, the establishment are scared. The lengths they are going to outlaw 'taking a knee' and other examples of solidarity shows just how worried they are.

Setting up a fan group or wearing a St. Pauli hoodie, isn't going to single-handedly alter the course of US politics, but it plays an important role connecting like-minded individuals. Groups working locally are making a real difference to the lives of refugee families, but we also shouldn't dismiss the importance of the symbolism. Sometimes, just seeing someone else in your city or town wearing a skull-and-crossbones hoodie can be enough – just knowing that there are other people out there who believe the same thing, who want to push back against America (and the world's) drift to the right. Of course, I'm not completely ruling out the possibility that the person wearing that t-shirt or hoodie isn't some wannabe-hipster who just thinks the skull on the front is a bit edgy, but I'm pretty sure most people are better informed than that. And this tour can only help in that regard.

Just prior to the end of the match I was approached by Michael Wehner who was clutching a hubcap with a Detroit St. Pauli sticker dead centre and *Meister der Motorstadt* written underneath in permanent marker. He said he got the idea from listening to me describing how the players were presented with a similar hubcap when they finished runners-up in 2. Bundesliga in 2009/10 (and thereby missing out on the trophy for winning the league which

– of course – looks an awful lot like a hubcap!) He wanted a few of us to go on the pitch and present the team with this, the most appropriate of trophies, for a victory in Motor City, Detroit.

Once again, I was living the dream. All my football supporting life I'd wanted to go on the pitch at the end of a game and celebrate with the team. Sometimes I have to pinch myself and think, "How the hell did – I – a middle-aged bloke from a provincial town in England, end up here, on the pitch with the team?" It was incredible; a real honour to be part of it. New York Shawn gave a short speech and handed the trophy to Richy Neudecker – and there we were in the middle of it all! I was then able to get some great photos and videos from the pitch looking back at the St. Pauli fans in the stands as the players went to greet them.

As I was standing there soaking it all in, I was reminded of a conversation I'd often had with my friend, Shaun. We would often lament players in English football disappearing down the tunnel as soon as the final whistle sounded without so much as a backwards glance. We said that if it was us out there, we'd walk round the entire stadium shaking as many hands as possible. And then here I was – on the pitch – with that exact opportunity (albeit I wasn't actually one of the players!) So, I decided to wander over to the Northern Guard on the far side of the pitch and acknowledge their fantastic support. I shook hands with both Northern Guard capos and said a "Thank You" to as many people as possible. I'm sure most fans were – quite rightly – thinking, 'Who the hell's this random bloke with rainbow ribbons in his hair and why's he shaking my hand?' But it felt like the right thing to do. What Detroit City fans have done at the Keyworth Stadium is incredible, perhaps unparalleled in US Soccer. They have created an inclusive, progressive and welcoming environment for everyone in Detroit with an interest in football. And they've done it themselves. It was also the Northern Guard who created the atmosphere inside the ground today; us St. Pauli fans were just playing the role of enthusiastic guests. This was their house. And they rocked it.

The Northern Guard then got some proper recognition when the entire St. Pauli team came over and joined in the singing and scarf-twirling. Considering Detroit City fans' reputation as fiercely pro-Detroit and against everyone else, it was another wonderful moment of international comradeship and solidarity. Once again, you got the impression that FC St. Pauli's players understood.

The teams slowly made their way back to the dressing rooms (which were proper old school, no modern luxury here: they reminded me of the detritus-strewn Sunday League changing rooms of my youth – I just hope there was more hot water!)

We returned to the stands, still a little in awe at what had just happened. Fans milled around chatting before finally leaving the stadium and heading to the after-match party at The Magic Stick Club. This provided another opportunity for St. Pauli and Detroit City fans to drink and chat late into the evening. It was one of the most relaxed parts of the trip as finally there was a decent amount of time to catch up with people, although I think most of us still left at the end of the evening feeling like we'd not had a chance to talk long enough to everyone. These occasions are almost as important as the game, as it gives a real chance to talk politics and share experiences plus – of course – drink!

Both sets of players were present and – again – were happy to chat and pose for selfies with a never-ending stream of fans. Like the previous evening at the distillery, the players seemed warm and genuine, and their responses to questions were far removed from the sterile responses we've come to expect from professional footballers.

The team bus back to the hotel left around 12:30, the players and those travelling on to Portland had to be up and in the hotel lobby again at 06:30. As we got off at the hotel, Ewald Lienen mentioned going for a 05:00 run around Detroit. I like running, but a 05:00 start on four hours sleep with a hangover, meant not even I could contemplate that. Ewald on the other hand is made of sterner stuff (although I did subsequently find out, he didn't make the run either!)

And that was Detroit... For Shawn, Shawn and Sam the adventure would continue in Portland, I had to be back in school on the Tuesday morning, so extending my trip was an impossibility. But just for Detroit alone it had been worth it.

I'm sure part of the rationale was to sell more shirts. FC St. Pauli is a club that still needs to compete on the pitch in Bundesliga 2 and that requires money, but St. Pauli is also a club that won't sell its soul or its stadium name to the devil to generate income. We are not like other clubs, which means we must approach things differently. So, whilst North America is a potential market for merch sales, I don't believe that it was the primary driver for this tour.

The tour was about making connections; building relationships between clubs and supporters' groups that share the St. Pauli ethos. Put simply, in a language even Donald Trump could understand, it's about building bridges and smashing down walls. It's about comradeship and solidarity with people through football. It's about inspiring and supporting each other through shared ideals. It's about supporting LGBTQ+ rights and establishing refugee football teams. It's about reaching out and being inclusive at a time when the dominant political and media narrative is to divide and exclude. It's about being part of the fight back.

I already knew that this sort of scene existed in Portland (the next stop on the club's US tour). What made the trip to Detroit so special for me was seeing this resistance there too. We can all sometimes be guilty of painting pictures in broad brushstrokes; quick to demonise America and Americans for falling under Trump's spell – but we must remember that there are many, many more people that oppose him and his ideology. Football fans in Detroit, in Portland, across the continent are loud and visible in their opposition to this right-wing bullshit.

Like FC St. Pauli, Detroit City FC aren't perfect. Like FC St. Pauli in Germany, they are often held up as the standard bearers of anti-fascist, supporter-driven football in the United States. From a distance it is easy to view both organisations existing in a perfect, idealist bubble. But we all know, reality isn't like that. Detroit City and the Northern Guard lead the way in inclusivity in US soccer. But there is always room for improvement. The work Detroit City do to make watching football accessible and affordable to those in the local community is admirable. There is always one criticism that is levelled at the club and its supporters – one that might well be unfair and due to lots of different factors – and that's that those supporters inside the stadium are predominantly white. 79% of Detroit's population is African American and as such there is a considerable under-representation of black supporters on the bleachers at Keyworth Stadium. Not for one moment do I think this is due to racism or discrimination from the club's supporters. Quite the opposite. But there is work still to be done to make the club's support truly representative of the city.

But look at me – visited Detroit once and think I'm qualified to comment on socio-political issues in the city! I'm not. If this trip taught me anything, it is that I knew shamefully little about Detroit before my visit. All I really knew was the cliches. The poverty and insecurity that followed the decline of the motor industry that resulted in a dramatic decline in its population, that in turn contributed to the city itself filing for federal bankruptcy in 2015. Of Tamla-Motown and the city's importance in the history of soul (only on my return did I make the links between Motown and the songs and artists on my Dad's home-made compilation cassettes from the 1970s). And – more recently – of Eminem and the semi-autobiographical film *8 Mile*. Like I said, I was dealing exclusively in stereotypes and cliches. On my return, I discovered and devoured Stuart Cosgrove's *Detroit 67: The Year That Changed Soul*. It made me wish I could have my time in Detroit all over again. I learnt so much about the 1967 riots and the murder of three young black men at the Algiers Motel for which no members of the Detroit Police Department were ever convicted. I was also left in awe of the sheer number of hit songs that came out of Detroit in that era. Again, if I could have my time in Detroit again, I would've been sure to visit the Motown Museum, 'Hitsville USA' on West Grand Boulevard just three miles south and east of the Keyworth Stadium. It was a pilgrimage FC St. Pauli president, Oke Göttlich (himself a founder of a music label, Nonplace Records) made time to include in his Detroit schedule.

New York Cosmos 2 FC St. Pauli 1
International Friendly
19:30, Thursday 23 May 2019, Rocco B. Commisso Stadium

I'm not sure that too many of the Nordamerikurve fans thought that the Boys in Brown would be back on their side of the pond so soon after 2018's visit to Detroit and Portland. But here we were – a year on – standing on Brooklyn Bridge with the team, coaching staff, President Oke Göttlich, Ewald Lienen and a swarm of media people from various organisations who were meticulously documenting the tour on tape and on film. As per last year, a few of us fans (hangers-on, I'd guess you'd call us) had managed to tag along for the ride.

From some quarters, the same criticisms that were levelled at the club last year for touring the United States surfaced again this season: wasn't this just a corporate junket bankrolled by Levi's and other sponsors to increase our merch sales in the Land of the Free? There was also the added complication of the tour only going ahead if we *didn't* finish in third and qualify for the play-off spot for promotion to the Bundesliga (which, for the most cynical, could've been viewed as an incentive *not* to pursue promotion).

After last year's experience, I knew this wasn't the case. Sure, commercial activities and marketing played a part, but there was also the opportunity to renew the connection with American St.

Pauli supporters who – as we discovered on the trip to Detroit and Portland – are both as passionate about St. Pauli in a sporting context as they are politically active and motivated in their opposition to all things right-wing, fascist and Trumpian. In short, these fans connect with the team but more importantly they identify with the club's core values. This is why the tour was important.

The day before I had arrived the squad began with a sight-seeing tour of New York. Yes, it included Levi's flagship store on Times Square being illuminated with the St. Pauli Totenkopf but it also included a visit to Trump Tower, where the team stood together as one behind a series of rainbow flags (flags that the Trump administration has banned from being flown at US embassies around the world). It was a small act of resistance but an important one – I can't think of many other professional sports teams who would've acted as one in this context.

This year's tour opponents, New York Cosmos and FC Buffalo, are members of the newly formed National Premier Soccer League, both have a left-wing, antifascist fan scene – with Cosmos' Brigada 71 being particularly active countering the rise of the far right both on the streets of New York and, perhaps even more worryingly, in the stands at MLS club, New York City FC. Both matches on the tour were less about the action on the pitch and more about the connections between fan groups in the stands.

On the Wednesday (the day before the Cosmos match), in amongst all the sightseeing and photo-ops, the squad joined a kids' training session on an AstroTurf pitch in the middle of China Town – all under the watchful eye of new boss, Josh Luhukay. Then, in the evening, they mingled happily with fans at the Knitting Factory over the bridge in Brooklyn at a gig by punk bands, Desperate Acts, Face to Face and Kitschkrieg. The squad of players was a mix of experienced professionals like Kalla, Himmelmann, Allagui and Knoll with a supporting cast made up from members of the U23 and U19 teams which – with the US' strict 21 drinking-age policy meant some of the travelling party weren't able to partake in the liquid refreshments flowing both at the gig and afterwards at the East River Bar. I ducked out of the after-party, knowing I'd be back there after the game the following evening, but also because I needed to be hangover-free to host this year's panel discussion entitled, *The Rise of Independent Football* the following morning.

The panel was a mix of club owners/presidents and active fans and we managed to cover a good range of topics as we tried to nail down exactly what was meant by 'independent football'. Oke Göttlich and Detroit City FC's CEO, Sean Mann were veterans of last year's panel; they were joined by Tim Kelly, President of Chattanooga FC and Joe Barone, Vice President of the Cosmos. From the discussion, it became apparent that FC St. Pauli are held up as an example of how to do things differently in an increasingly homogenised, bland and corporate football world. Fan representation came from Shawn Roggenkamp from the East River Pirates and Anthoney 'Prez' Stephens, an active Cosmos supporter (familiar to many through his stint as a presenter for Copa 90). They were able to contribute significantly to the discussion, especially on the topics of fan activism, and antifascism.

The match, that evening, against New York Cosmos was taking place at the Rocco B. Commisso Stadium at the very tip of Manhattan Island and involved a bit of a slog on the metro out to 215 Street. When I arrived, there were only a few people milling about, amongst them Joe Barone, New York Cosmos Vice President. We continued our chat about the challenges facing US soccer outside the closed shop of the billionaire franchisee world of Major League Soccer.

Not long after, the heavily branded St. Pauli team coach arrived at the stadium, optimistically offering the promise of 'Rock 'n' Roll Football' which I thought had been trademarked by Jurgen Klopp and certainly wasn't a label that could've been applied to St. Pauli's performances in the later stages of the 2018/19 season. And, of course, Klopp's gegenpress actually went by the name 'Heavy Metal Football'.

Unlike Detroit's Keyworth Stadium, there was only a set of bleachers on one side which meant that St. Pauli's Nordamerikurve congregated down one end of the pitch length stand whilst Cosmos' impressive '5 Points' supporters positioned themselves nearer the other goal. It is fair to say that, even on a Thursday night in New York a friendly between a second division Bundesliga side and the Cosmos wasn't a massive draw. The reported attendance of 1,500 seemed a bit optimistic and, in numbers, the crowd fell well short of the 7,000 sell out in Detroit the year before.

However, Cosmos' active fans fall firmly in the same category as Detroit City's Northern Guard (don't ask me to pick sides, I love *all* fan groups with a solid left-wing, antifascist ideology). I'd first come across 5 Points out at Cosmos game at Hofstra University deep in the suburban sprawl of Long Island in 2014. It was the day I chased Pelé around on a golf cart (he was in the cart, not me, he got to it first). But my main memory was of the intensity of the Cosmos support. They were loud, constant and political. I hadn't expected it. My view of the New York Cosmos had been firmly rooted in the glitz and glamour of the NASL at its 1970s peak: kits with massive collars; really bad AstroTurf pitches; ageing global superstars like Beckenbauer, Chinaglia, Carlos Alberto and Dennis Tueart cashing-in on one, final payday whilst living the high-life in the city that never sleeps. If you want to wallow in that stereotype, watch *Once In A Lifetime (The Extraordinary Story of The New York Cosmos)*. I'd also followed the various reboots that the club had been through in the intervening years, including one re-launch that was backed by British businessman (and David Beckham's former personal manager), Terry Bryne, former Liverpool CEO, Ricky Parry and Eric Cantona and also included the release of some fantastic Umbro retro-styled apparel.

But at Hofstra, it was the fans that stood out. And, despite not even having a first team to support last season (only Cosmos B took the field in 2017/18), the supporter culture has remained undimmed ever since.

It was these fans that brought the Rocco B. Commisso stadium to life. The teams emerged to a blaze of green and white smoke that was shared with the St. Pauli fans making up the Nordamerikurve. The pyro was impressive and atmospheric but what really stole the show was the banner that ran along almost the entire length of the stand. The quote read, *Love is free, it can dwell in no other atmosphere* and was from anarchist writer and activist, Emma Goldman who first came to New York from St. Petersburg in 1885, fleeing a rise of Antisemitism in Russia.

Recession, strike action and events in the United States drew Goldman deeper and deeper into anarchism. In 1886, she and Alexander Berkman planned to assassinate industrialist Henry Clay Frick who was a staunch anti-unionist and had opposed the Homestead Strike near Pittsburg. Frick was wounded in the unsuccessful attempt to kill him and whilst Goldman escaped prosecution, Berkman was sentenced to 22 years in jail. Goldman was also charged with 'incitement to riot' in 1893 after speaking to a crowd of over 3,000 people in Union Square, New York. She was also implicated in the assassination of US President William McKinley by Leon Czolgosz in 1901, something that both Goldman and Czolgosz repeatedly denied, although it was an action that Goldman refused to condemn, leading to her being referred to as 'the high priestess of anarchy'. Goldman spent more than a decade touring the US speaking about women's suffrage, equality, and contraception. In response to the United States involvement in World War One, she organised the No Conscription League in New York. She was imprisoned and then deported by J. Edgar Hoover who considered her and Berkman 'as two of the most dangerous anarchists in the country'. She continued her writing, speeches and activism after being deported back to Russia. She also travelled throughout Europe, was involved with the CNT in Barcelona during the Spanish Civil War before living out her final years in Canada. She died, aged 70, in Toronto in 1940.

For me, this was the first of two standout moments that I took from the tour. I love history, especially socio-political history, so it is always great to discover something new. As a result of the tifo, discussions with those responsible and a bit of a read around on the internet I have learnt a lot about one of America's leading anarchist-feminist figures of the early 20th Century.

In the current political climate in the United States, referencing such a powerful feminist figure was incredibly prescient. Of course, Trump's ongoing war on migration and multiculturalism continues unabated – with walls, fences, detention centres, children locked in cages. But his misogyny and sexism has also emboldened the right in its attack on women – in both attitude and policy. Just prior to St. Pauli arriving in the United States, the state of Alabama passed legislation making abortion illegal. A direct result of Trump's election, we now have a situation in America where women no longer have the right to determine what is happening to their own bodies. On May 15, Alabama's governor signed the most restrictive anti-abortion law in modern American history. If enabled, the law would allow abortions only if the mother's life is at risk or if the foetus cannot survive, but not in cases of rape or incest. The pro-life, anti-abortion lobby has become worryingly mainstream (Friday 24 June 2022 was a dark day in American history, with the Supreme Court overturning the 1973 Roe v Wade case that had legalized abortion in the United States). By choosing Emma Goldman as their tifo, Cosmos fans were declaring their hand as part of the resistance to this alarming cultural and political lurch to the right.

The match itself drifted by in the background; Cosmos went ahead early on before Sami Allugai equalised from the spot. Back in the bleachers the pyro and the smoke continued unabated. In the second-half the St. Pauli fans conga'd down to join their Cosmos counterparts, unleashing even more smoke and trading songs. In amongst this feel-good atmosphere Cosmos scored a late winner but nobody really cared. By this time, FC St. Pauli had two keepers on the pitch: Korbinian Muller had taken over from

Robin Himmelmann in goal at half-time, but for the last 15 or so minutes Sven Bordersen put in an industrious shift as an old-school centre-forward. This was very much a St. Pauli side in holiday-mode, but credit to Cosmos for putting in a focused, professional performance and coming away with the win. During the match, Brigada 71 also displayed banners supporting fellow fans who have been deported by the United States Immigration and Customs Enforcement agency. The banner read, 'FCK ICE' and included painted pictures of absent fans, Danny and Julio. There was also another good political banner which belonged to the 'MuJu Antifa: Muslim-Jewish Antifascist Front' – a street-level network of Muslim and Jewish activists and agitators dedicated to fighting against Islamphobia, Antisemitism and the rise of far-right white supremacists, like the Proud Boys. Once again, it is organisations like MuJu Antifa that are on the streets confronting the violent right-wing extremists who have been legitimized and encouraged by the policies and tweets coming from Trump's Oval Office.

Both sides remained on the pitch enjoying the post-match celebrations, engaging with the fans and posing for a joint team photo under a banner, #ProRelForUSA calling for promotion and relegation in US soccer. The closed-shop nature of the MLS, where potential owners need to demonstrate and provide assurances for their considerable wealth before being granted a franchise and then have their investment ring-fenced because clubs can't be relegated remains one of the most contentious flashpoints in US soccer.

Post-match, it was back across the Williamsburg Bridge to the East River Bar and an acoustic set from Thees Ulhmann that culminated with a sing-a-long rendition of *Das Hier Ist Fußball*. Myself, Sam and Shawn from *Fell In Love With A Girl* podcast only made it back for the end of the gig as we had been stuck on the world's slowest train back from the stadium. Players and officials hung around chatting with supporters before boarding the team bus back to the hotel. Fans of Cosmos and St. Pauli carried on drinking late into the night.

With the New York leg of the tour put to bed, it was time to head upstate to Buffalo.

FC Buffalo 0 FC St. Pauli 2
International Friendly
15:00, Saturday 25 May 2019, Robert Rich Sr. All High Stadium

The next morning, myself and 'New York' Shawn had managed to blag our seats on the team bus for the 8-hour coach journey north to Buffalo. We met up with the team just off Times Square and took our places on the bus with the squad. At 47, I think my days of genuinely believing I could've been a professional footballer are finally behind me, but it didn't stop me living the fantasy in my head as the coach made its way through the streets of New York – thanks to the tinted windows who wasn't to know that I wasn't the club's first summer signing?

Unfortunately, I had to earn my keep and was put to work by Sönke helping to tidy up the English subtitles for the 1910.eV. Museum's recent exhibition videos. It turns out travelling on a first team bus isn't too dissimilar to a school trip. The only difference being the players are much better behaved than the kids, nobody was sick, and I wasn't asked every two minutes, "Are we nearly there yet?"

What was evident was the maturity of these young players. There were no Wimbledon-esque hijinks. I was comfortable enough to have a nap without the fear of waking up to find my eyebrows had been shaved off or someone had drawn on a comedy moustache on my face with a Sharpie. It was also interesting to watch professional athletes getting excited about the opportunity to go and watch other professional athletes. The club had secured five tickets for the Toronto Raptor's NBA basketball play-off against Milwaukee Bucks the following evening. The players had to write down their reasons for wanting to attend and then the names were drawn out of a hat and their explanations read out. I think it was Marvin Knoll who went with the persuasive line of argument that he was the best at NBA 2K19 on the PlayStation. The five chosen players were genuinely ecstatic to be going to the game.

There were a couple of breaks along the way. The first at a service station-cum-truck stop, where the players were able to marvel at the range of calorific, peanut-based snacks available for purchase.

Then there was a late lunch in the town of Owego at the newly restored Belva Lockwood Inn. Following the Emma Goldman quote at the Cosmos game, the Belva Lockwood connection/coincidence was the second prescient moment of the tour. Belva Lockwood had purchased the building in 1863 and had run it as a girls' school called The Owego Female Seminary. Lockwood went on to become the first female Presidential candidate in the United States when she stood for office, representing the progressive National Equal Rights Party, in 1884 and 1888 (or the second woman, depending on the historical interpretation/validity of Victoria Woodhull's candidacy). She stood for election at a time before women even had the right to vote. She was also one of the first female lawyers in the country and she successfully petitioned congress to become the first woman to practice before the United States Supreme Court. Her political work and writings focused on women's suffrage, and she remained a vocal activist for female equality until her death in 1917. She was also an advocate for world peace, editing a journal called *The Peacemaker* and even attending the International Peace Congress in London in 1890. I'm not sure if the stop in the town where she first taught and at the restaurant bearing her name was a fortuitous or deliberate part of the tour itinerary, but – once again – it seemed an appropriate riposte to the current misogynist bullshit that is taking hold in the United States. The proprietors, Ike and Julie Lovelass, were certainly keen to point out the correlation between Lockwood and FC St. Pauli's core-values.

The lunch was delicious and the history fascinating, as was the juxtaposition of the beautifully restored Victorian-era home with the boldly branded Rock 'n' Roll team bus parked in the driveway.

We were back on the bus for the final two-hour leg of our journey to Buffalo, and by this point most of the occupants were opting to sleep off their late lunch. However –somehow – just like kids on a school trip, the players had a sixth sense that we were reaching the journey's end and the chat and energy levels increased sharply as we rolled through the outskirts of Buffalo. I think the players were looking forward to the opportunity to stretch their legs and the prospect of a night on their own, free from official 'meet and greet' duties.

There was no such down time for the fans: we were off to a Nordamerikurve meet up organised and hosted by Ernie and FC Buffalo St. Pauli. More beer was consumed and international friendships formed.

The next day was game day. FC Buffalo's home stadium is on the campus of the Robert Rich Senior All High School, an imposing brick building that wouldn't look out of place in the opening credits of *High School Musical*, or even *The Breakfast Club*. The pitch shared markings and goalposts with the school's American Football team, which was a little confusing and gave rise to the possibility of a freak goal being scored by hitting one of the gridiron uprights (or additional crossbar) and rebounding to a forward to slot home. I seemed to be the only person in the ground even remotely excited by this possibility, which was especially embarrassing as I tried to explain my idea to Richy Neudecker as he stood in the tunnel waiting to go out on pitch.

Before the game, Nordamerikurve had congregated in a nearby carpark for the complete US sports tailgating experience. More American St. Pauli fans joined the meet, drank beer and exchanged origin stories before heading to the stadium together in a small but vocal fan march. Again, the crowd was hovering around the 1,500 mark. The pyro wasn't quite as prolific as in New York, although some of the St. Pauli travelling contingent were able to get in a couple of smoke bombs. The atmosphere in the away section was good, with less regular fans able to join in the singing thanks to the *Pirates, Punks & Psalters* song sheets handed out to newcomers. There was vocal support to from President Oke Göttlich and members of the supervisory board who joined the fans for the game.

A banner made by Atlanta and Buffalo St. Pauli supporters' groups ran along the front of the guest-bloc and read, 'FCSP Means Radical Antifascism!' It was supplemented at kick-off by another wallpaper that stated, 'Let's Fight Nazis! Wanna Joyn?' it was a dig at former St. Pauli left-back, Ian Joy, who now works in sports broadcasting and has links to New York City FC. It is the feeling of Atlanta and Buffalo St. Pauli that Joy was not doing enough to publicly denounce the NYCFC fans that have been expressing right-wing sentiments in the stands. It is only right to point out that we don't know what Joy has been doing behind-the-scenes to oppose this outbreak of fascist support at NYCFC, sometimes not all battles can be fought most effectively in public. I'll leave you to make up your mind on that one.

Nobody completed the American football crossbar challenge, but St. Pauli did record a relatively comfortable 2:0 victory courtesy of a goal in each half, first from Sami Allagui and then Kevin Lankford. And this time it was goalkeeper Korbi Muller's chance to have a run out up front in the second half.

Kevin Lankford's aunt and uncle had travelled up from Virginia to watch him play. They arrived dressed in Heidenheim tops bearing his name but left wearing St. Pauli t-shirts. There was a lovely 20 minutes after the game when Lankford sat in the stands chatting and catching up with his family.

The rest of the players came over and thanked the St. Pauli support. It is also worth mentioning the excellent fans from FC Buffalo who contributed to the atmosphere and showed their support for progressive causes through banners, flags and songs. As mentioned previously, the Buffalo St. Pauli fan group – along with active fans from FC Buffalo – and inspired by the work of FC Lampedusa in Hamburg are also closely aligned with Journey's End Refugee Services based in Buffalo. They have supported them in the establishment of a refugee football team with the aim of bringing people together through the medium of football. They have arranged donations of boots and kit, as well as going down and supporting games. It is another example of how St. Pauli (and others in football) have helped inspire people to become involved in supporting refugees in their local communities.

Again, football fans are helping provide a counterpoint to the government narrative. Trump's administration houses refugees and asylum seekers in former World War Two internment camps; the football community reaches out and tries to support and integrate refugees through the universal language of football. The contrast couldn't be stark.

The evening after the match was the last of the official fan/team events. Held at the grand sounding Buffalo Town Ballroom, it was a chance for more beers and more discussion as well as some punk rock karaoke with a live band. Myself and Shawn were ever so slightly gutted to be denied the opportunity to bash out a version of Nirvana's *Smells Like Teen Spirit* because St. Pauli president, Oke and Justus from the Fanladen stole our song. To be fair, it probably saved the whole of Buffalo from a traumatic vocal performance from me, but I did feel I was deprived of the moment I had been waiting for my entire life...

The players didn't partake in the karaoke (well, not the St. Pauli ones, there were a few contributions from their counterparts from FC Buffalo). Instead, the squad were mostly glued to the TV watching the Toronto Raptors record an historic play-off victory (cheered on by Himmelmann, Knoll and co., watching in the arena).

The night at the bar was another opportunity to chew the cud with the St. Pauli great and good. I am always astounded at Ewald Lienen's depth of knowledge in all aspects of football, it was also interesting (and a little scary) to find out the very real financial cost of conceding that last gasp goal in Fürth on the final day of the season. It cost the club a significant sum in terms of playing budget for next season. I didn't realise the calculations were made on a complicated average of points over previous seasons, not just the past campaign. It is one advantage of a tour like this, that you can have these discussions and broaden your knowledge of St. Pauli and the machinations of German football.

The next day, I was heading home to London via New York. The team were flying out of Toronto and had the opportunity to stop off at Niagara Falls. Some of the board also went to watch the MLS match between Toronto and San Jose Earthquakes before heading down to Jack Daniel's headquarters in Lynchurg, Tennessee, as the two parties renewed their sponsor relationship.

It is true that we all take different things away from our tour experience. And the reality is the tour had a combination of motives and objectives. But I still believe, at the heart of it was the desire to show solidarity with St. Pauli supporter groups and like-minded clubs and fans in the United States during these increasingly hostile political times. As was the case last year with Detroit and Portland, the choice of opponents on this tour was deliberate and a statement of intent. New York Cosmos and FC Buffalo fans are firmly committed to taking an active stance against racism, fascism, sexism and homophobia – all of which are receiving increasing legitimacy under the Trump administration.

For me, the tour was a chance to catch up with old friends (and make new ones); it was the chance to pretend I was a professional footballer and travel on the team coach to an away game; but – most importantly – it gave me the opportunity to learn about such political visionaries as Emma Goldman and Belva Lockwood. Their contribution to the tour may have been incidental to some, but for me they were potent reminders that the struggle for gender equality and the battle against misogyny is steeped in history but always ongoing.

The USA isn't Trump or Alabama; it is Emma Goldman, Belva Lockwood and everyone carrying on the fight for equality in their wake. It is about a long and proud history of resistance to the regressive elements in society. It is about smashing the patriarchy. And football, FC St. Pauli, all of us – can play a part.

Footnote: The fervent supporters of New York Cosmos have continued to be frustrated and aggrieved by the club's ownership issues and problems in securing a permanent home stadium and an unstable US soccer pyramid constructed on constantly shifting sands. After the friendly match against FC St. Pauli in May 2019, the Cosmos played in the inaugural National Independent Soccer Association's (NISA) Fall Season that commenced in August 2020. They finished bottom of their group in the NISA Fall Playoffs – a tournament hosted in its entirety at Detroit City's Keyworth Stadium. By the start of the NISA 2021 Spring Season, the New York Cosmos went on a hiatus citing the ongoing logistical and financial difficulties of the Covid-19 pandemic as their reason for not competing. At the time of writing they remain in hiatus. There has been disquiet amongst the Cosmos fan scene, many who feel that the current owner Rocco B. Commisso (yes, the stadium where St. Pauli played Cosmos was named in his honour) has put all his energy into his newly acquired Serie A team, Fiorentina who he purchased in 2019. It is a sad situation for the Cosmos and their supporters, not least because 2021 should've seen them celebrating their 50th anniversary on the pitch. Instead, fans were left only to reminisce their incredible legacy and lament their current position.

Chapter 12:
Global Brand Versus Local Activism and Sustainability – Welcome to the Contradiction of St. Pauli

As we know, FC St. Pauli is not a typical football club. It is certainly not a typical global brand. Despite this, FC St. Pauli, through its 'skull and crossbones', 'Jolly Roger' or 'Totenkopf' symbol has become one on the most iconic brands in world football. The transformation of the Jolly Roger from a symbol of rebellion into a trademarked brand is contentious enough to be worthy of a book all to itself. However, the Totenkopf remains at the heart of the St. Pauli story, its journey symbolic of the wider dilemma faced by FC St. Pauli supporters over the last 30 years, as they attempt to swim against the sporting, political and economic mainstream tide.

At the heart of the 'Contradiction of St. Pauli' is the fact that the club *is* different. It is not a club built on sporting glory: there are no league titles, no trophy cabinet packed with the polished silverware of yesteryear. Instead, the club has gained notoriety for the values it represents rather than its sporting achievements.

David Goldblatt wrote in *The Ball is Round: A Global History of Football* – in the context of the modern game being consumed by globalisation and an influx of investment – that, "The bottom line for those who follow football is not calculated in money or power, but in victories and pleasures."

However, for most FC St. Pauli fans whilst the bottom line certainly isn't money or power, it isn't about victory either. Instead, pleasure (and considerable pride) is derived from adhering to a broad *for-and-against* value system. Being a St. Pauli fan is about standing *against* fascism, racism, sexism, homophobia and commercialism and standing *for* equality, fairness and social justice. True, on-the-field success isn't completely irrelevant to supporters but, unusually, it is not the primary focus. Indeed, recent flirtations with promotion to the German top division sparked lengthy debates, pitching the merits of promotion against the dilution of the club's identity.

Fast forward to the third decade of the 21st century and technology, particularly the internet and social media, has made the world a much smaller place. David Goldblatt also noted that, "In an epoch characterized by unprecedented global interconnectedness, the most universal cultural phenomenon in the world is football."

This interconnectedness has changed the way we watch, support, and consume every aspect of football. The geographical ties of localism have loosened, with a generation of fans as likely to watch Real Madrid or Paris St. Germain every week on the internet as they are to support their home-town team. Of course, globalism and localism are not mutually exclusive, plenty of football fans do both: support their local football club and a team on a faraway continent.

Historian Eric Hobsbawm recognised the rapid transformation of football into a global business and the impact this has had on existing local and national identities. Hobsbawm stated: "Essentially, the global football business is dominated by the imperialism of a few capitalist enterprises with global brand names

– a small number of super-clubs based in a few European countries."

Hobsbawm expanded on this theme at *The Times Cheltenham Literature Festival* in 2007, "Since globalisation it's been possible for a consortium of wealthy clubs in a particular set of Western European countries to build themselves up as global brands which have relatively little contact with their original local roots and hire people from all over the world. They make money by selling goods, such as t-shirts, by television and to a diminishing extent by people watching [live] football."

Of course, in many ways, Hobsbawm's analysis is correct. Top European clubs are powerful brands, commanding global support and earning huge sums of money through sponsorship and television rights. It was a standing joke in English football during the 1990s that Manchester United fans were more likely to come from London than Manchester. These days the 'Cockney Reds' phenomenon is dwarfed by a truly global fanbase – with Manchester United fans almost as likely to come from Beijing, Darfur or Los Angeles as Manchester.

Often, globalization focuses on the negative, but there are positives too. Twenty years ago, it would have been impossible for a global audience to have watched the mesmerizing skills of Lionel Messi or the ruthless finishing of Erling Haaland in real-time, but now their every move is screened live on television or streamed on the internet for the world to enjoy.

The globalization and availability of information has also made it possible for football fans to make informed choices. Allegiance to a particular football team no longer has to be made on locality or handed down through the generations. Sure, plenty of people use it as an excuse to 'support' the biggest and best teams in the world, but not everyone. This availability of up-to-date information has enabled fans to research, identify and support teams for a whole host of different reasons. This partly explains the level of support for FC St. Pauli on a global scale.

As word of St. Pauli's unique mix of football, social activism and politics began to spread – via articles in magazines, websites and online discussion forums – more and more people with a left-wing outlook began to take an interest in the club. Once again, the Totenkopf had a crucial role to play. For years, the skull and crossbones symbol with the words 'St. Pauli' printed underneath has been sold on t-shirts and hoodies. The simple iconography appealed to people who identified with the alternative, punk ethos of St. Pauli.

The story of Doc Mabuse – the singer in the band Punkenstein introducing the skull and crossbones to the Millerntor Stadion is one of legend. In 1986, he nailed his Totenkopf flag – which he had either bought or 'appropriated' depending on the version of events told – to a broomstick and took it onto the Gegengerade. It was the beginning of a phenomenon, but it is only part of the story.

There is another man integral to the legend of the Totenkopf – his name is Steph Braun. Steph worked in a screen-printing workshop on Clemens-Schulz-Straße. He had already developed several t-shirt designs featuring a skull but wanted something that uniquely represented the district of St. Pauli. Braun explained, "I wanted to make a t-shirt that linked to the district of St. Pauli. I was interested in real skulls. I went to a Leonardo da Vinci exhibition of his anatomical drawings. I thought it was great, I wanted the skull to be anatomical, in black and white but not the same as the two-dimensional 'Jolly Roger' pirate flags that have been around for hundreds of years."

The bones were drawn by local artist Mats Mainka, they had originally been intended to be part of an 'Anti-Batman' t-shirt (Batman, starring Michael Keaton, was released in 1989 to an enormous fanfare and high-profile marketing campaign). The connection to the district was made by the text 'St. Pauli' written in block capitals underneath the skull and crossbones. The t-shirt was sold in local record stores but, crucially, the St. Pauli Fanladen also started selling the shirts. They were a success, helped in part by

St. Pauli's three-season stint in the Bundesliga between 1988 and 1991.

Steph Braun recalls how the Totenkopf was so successful that everyone was screen-printing their own versions. Whilst Braun didn't have a problem with this, once the club started selling t-shirts at the Millerntor the sales of his t-shirt declined dramatically. This forced him to trademark the version of the Totenkopf that he had created. Towards the end of the 1990s, the club started producing more and more merchandise featuring Braun's Totenkopf design. The Fanladen was forced to stop selling his shirts as suddenly they were classed as counterfeit merchandise. Braun then went to the club threatening an injunction and eventually an agreement was reached which transferred his trademarked design to FC St. Pauli.

Hendik Lüttmer, now Head of Marketing for Merchandising at FC St. Pauli was working in the Fanladen during that period. He remembers the time when the Totenkopf was more closely connected with the district and the radical section of the St. Pauli fan scene than the club itself. He explained, "There was actually a lot of resistance against it from the club – so the Totenkopf was actually an anti-symbol for the club at the time. FC St. Pauli then was really still quite old and bourgeois; the skull and crossbones did not represent the club. But, of course, as FC St. Pauli became more professional in its approach to marketing itself, they became more interested in the Totenkopf as they could see its commercial potential. There was real tension between the club and the Fanladen at this time. Then, there was the attempt by the club to bring out its own version of the skull and crossbones, which led to a trademark dispute that was finally resolved sometime around 1998 with the rights transferring to the club."

The fact that – even when the club gained the trademark – they chose not to add the 'FC' part of their name on the t-shirts meant that the Totenkopf remained synonymous with both club and district.

In the early days, there was no organised marketing campaign or conscious effort to promote the brand. St. Pauli via the skull and crossbones became 'cool' through exposure in the right places via the right people, rather than through a coordinated campaign of marketing. So much so that the St. Pauli hoodie has become football's equivalent of the Ramones t-shirt. Just as many people who wear the iconic Ramones t-shirt design are unaware that it even belongs to a band, many people wearing the St. Pauli hoodie are completely unaware of its connection to a football club in northern Germany.

Of course, St. Pauli being St. Pauli (and not, say, Manchester United) managed to contrive a way in which *not* to benefit financially from such a successful brand. In 2000, with the club in financial crisis, President Heinz Weisener sold 50 per cent of the club's merchandising and marketing rights (which he himself owned) to a company called Upsolut. It was a decision that would have long-lasting ramifications for the club. The deal that meant St. Pauli hardly profited at all from the merchandising of its Totenkopf. Indeed, it wasn't until November 2015 that the club finally agreed a deal to buy out Upsolut, paying nearly €1.3 million to re-acquire the merchandising rights and therefore the ability to generate income from the sale of skull and crossbones branded merchandise.

Perhaps the fact that the club hadn't quite mastered the finer aspects of Hobsbawm's global capitalist model is also part of St. Pauli's appeal, although there are those in German football that would argue that the St. Pauli brand is marketed to the nth degree – something that it is hard to disagree with when the skull and crossbones has endorsed everything from toasters to Sky TV boxes. As Hendrik Lütttmer said, "Over the last 15 years I have actually printed this symbol on every kind of shit there is and – yet – I think it is still the strongest symbol in football worldwide." Whether this opinion is true, is open to debate. However, there are certainly no other symbols or crests within football that can claim such counter-cultural resonance.

A prolonged period of time lurching from financial crisis to financial crisis and yo-yoing between the divisions has only added to St. Pauli's status as fashionable under-achieving outsiders. The club's popularity continued to grow. It is often said that FC St. Pauli are many German supporters' second favourite team, especially among those with a fondness for the underdog or the perennial loser. Andreas Rettig, former CEO of FC St. Pauli, cited a survey commissioned by sports marketing agency, *Sportfive* that showed 19 million people in Germany alone are 'sympathetic' towards FC St. Pauli. Of course, the club's fan base is not just confined to Germany. There are numerous registered supporters' clubs across the globe. The number of officially registered fan clubs surpassed 500 in 2011, the growth of social media platforms like Twitter, now called X, has also contributed to the proliferation of international fan groups.

Support from musicians across various genres has also broadened St. Pauli's global appeal, particularly in the world of punk, where Norwegian band Turbonegro, Slime and the Italian band Talco all having strong links to the club. Alex Rosamillia from rock band, The Gaslight Anthem frequently takes to the stage in a St. Pauli hoodie or cap. Scottish group, The Wakes even recorded a song called, Pirates of the League about the club whilst Calgary-based punks The Pagans of Northumberland recorded a song simply entitled St. Pauli. Such a close association with punk, in particular, and music in general has helped sustain the club's counter-cultural appeal.

Of course, one consequence of having such a broad fan base is the risk of alienating those supporters at the core. It is one of many tightropes that the club itself must walk, balancing commercial expansion, on-the-field success and the ethos of the club. It is an impossible task to keep everyone happy. This conflict of interests is brought more sharply into focus during the rare periods of footballing success.

In 2009/10 the club celebrated its centenary by winning promotion back to the Bundesliga. The club being back in the top-flight of German football for its 100th year had a certain fairytale quality to it. Unfortunately, one of the main things promotion to the Bundesliga achieved was to bring to a head long-running differences of opinion between those that ran the club and those that supported it. *It was a clash of two cultures: on the one hand, the corporate money-making opportunity that promotion to the Bundesliga offered; on the other, the wishes of the core local fan base who felt that their ideals were being betrayed in pursuit of commercial greed that amounted to a significant erosion of St. Pauli's unique fan culture.*

The Sozialromantiker 'Jolly Rouge' movement was the manifestation of this clash of cultures. This was covered in more detail in *Pirates, Punks & Politics*. But – in short – dissatisfaction with a number of decisions especially the leasing of one of the executive boxes in the new Haupttribüne to a local strip joint, Susi's Showbar, riled fans.

The supporters behind Sozialromantiker Sankt Pauli were already concerned with the direction the club itself was heading and also the unity of the fan scene. Fissures and disagreements between different groups were starting to call into question the very nature of supporting FC St. Pauli. Yet, within a matter of weeks, these same fans were to come together in a show of incredible unity and solidarity.

In December 2010, a petition by Sozialromantiker Sankt Pauli to the club (with an accompanying set of demands) had attracted more than 3,000 signatures. Moreover, the protest had really caught the imagination of FC St. Pauli fans. The protest had also developed its own iconography. In a clever subversion of the club's official Totenkopf symbol, fans started producing a homemade appropriation, the 'Jolly Rouge'. The black skull and crossbones on red background had its own history: it was the flag pirates chose to fly when they intended to take 'no quarter' or no prisoners. It was a perfect iconography, a twist on the original Jolly Roger brought to the Millerntor by Doc Mabuse and popularised by Steph Braun's t-shirts, all those years before. The same Jolly Roger that had itself been appropriated and trademarked in complicated licensing agreements for corporate gain – an image that had been repackaged and sold back to the fans as a symbol of 'rebellion' and 'counterculture'.

It felt like something had been taken back, and soon homemade 'Jolly Rouge' flags, posters, stickers and flyers were being produced by fans all over the district. It was as if someone had awoken the DIY ethos of punk, a simple act of symbolic subversion, enthusing the entire fan scene with a desire for change.

On 4 January 2011, Sozialromantiker Sankt Pauli called for a day of action at the home game against Freiburg. Under the banner of the Jolly Rouge and the slogan, 'Bring Back Sankt Pauli', they urged fans to turn the Millerntor into a sea of red in protest at the club's continued refusal to meet the demands of the fans. In the build-up to the game, the internet was alive with photos and blogs detailing the flags and banners that were being created.

After the game somewhere between 500-1000 fans defied the wintery rain to march in solidarity with the district of St. Pauli through the streets. The movement had expanded beyond football. Under the banner of 'Bring Back Sankt Pauli – Reclaim Your District', fans and residents gathered to protest against the creeping gentrification and urban regeneration that was not only depriving residents of social spaces but that continued to push rents in an upward spiral, thus forcing out those people at the very heart of the St. Pauli community. In one way it was a familiar tale, one that harked back to the demonstrations on the Hafenstraße and the protests against the Sport-Dome. Nearly twenty-years had elapsed but still fans and residents alike were coming together to preserve the St. Pauli way of life as it came under threat from outside sources.

As a direct result of the protests, the club announced that it was going to set up a working group of club officials to review all new advertising campaigns, to ensure new companies adhered to the existing criteria. In the short term, many of the other issues, including the continued renting of an executive box to Susi's Show Bar, remained unresolved. Pole dancing during the match was banned but dancing was still allowed both before and after the match. However, the real success of the Sozialromantiker's campaign was threefold: to bring unity to a fragmented fan scene; to strengthen the bonds between fans and residents of the district; and to re-open meaningful dialogue between the fan base and the club. For club officials, it was a timely reminder that any commercial activity must be carried out with the broad consent of the fans. It also exemplified the contradiction of being a global brand – albeit an alternative, counter-cultural one – and remaining true to the ideals that shaped the club's image in the first instance: local activism.

In the years that have elapsed since the Jolly Rouge protests of January 2011, the club – relegated back to the Bundesliga 2 at the end of the 2010/11 season – experienced a period of relative stability on the pitch, consolidating its position as a second division club. But what were the longer-term ramifications of the Sozialromantiker protest? One of the strengths of the St. Pauli fan scene is its self-reflection and capacity of critical thinking and, as such, there will never be a complete consensus between fans and club. However, it is broadly agreed that following the Jolly Rouge protest, the club has listened and adapted its commercial strategy. Interviewed in January 2016, a member of Sozialromantiker St. Pauli reflected on the impact of the campaign: "The most lasting impact might be the proof that it is still possible to initiate a large-scale campaign at FC St. Pauli. It has also raised the awareness for the consequences of marketing – not just on the feelings of supporters, but also regarding the long-term value of the 'brand'. At this level it is difficult to determine what degree of influence this Jolly Rouge protest had, but it is quite likely it has at least some impact on decisions taken in that area even today."

Key personnel at the club have changed too in the years since 2011. In November 2014 a new President and Supervisory Board was elected. Many members of the new board have long associations with the active fan scene, and this has gone some way to restoring trust between the club and its supporters. President Oke Göttlich was a fan and activist before his appointment, he too also held the flag of the Jolly Rouge. Sozialromantiker Sankt Pauli shared this optimism over Göttlich's appointment.

Of course, due to the very nature of St. Pauli, there will always be controversy and criticism of the club's commercial activities. St. Pauli's fan base is reflective and critical, but criticism of the club is frequently voiced from the outside too – from those who think the club isn't worthy of its 'kult' status and is in fact just another heavily marketed football club. In February 2016, *SportBild* ran an article with the headline, 'St. Pauli is always unlikeable' – journalist, Jochen Coenen criticising the club for its forthcoming kit sponsorship deal with US manufacturer, Under Armour. The kit deal had already been extensively debated by St. Pauli fans; the 'Under Armour will equip us' discussion thread on *stpauli-forum.de* ran to over 100 pages. In addition, there had already been discussions between fan representatives and the club. Sozialromantiker Sankt Pauli acknowledged this improved communication between the Supervisory Board and supporters, "There are already some examples for that, the most prominent being the contract with Under Armour. Different groups were invited before the publication of the deal to explain its character and get feedback. One of the results was the formation of work groups on different topics, such as the social work the new outfitter intends to support. Representatives of these work groups travelled to the US so that both sides could get to know each other and the way they are working. Most likely that is the first time anything like has taken place at any major sports club worldwide."

The Under Armour deal is a good example of the additional scrutiny and constraints FC St. Pauli is subject to. For most professional sports teams, having to consider a kit supplier's links to the United States military or the production of clothes linked to hunting would not be such a visible issue. Among St. Pauli fans such considerations are paramount. The improved communication and understanding that there is no perfect solution is emphasized by Sozialromantiker, "The kit deal is a good example for the complexities and constraints that come with being a club in professional football. Does Under Armour tick all the boxes we would like to see, e.g. the location of production, minimum ecologic impact, price for the jersey? Probably not. But this ideal company does not exist, especially not at a size that is relevant to satisfy the needs of a team in Bundesliga 2; can handle the logistics and is willing to pay the money FC St. Pauli is asking for. There are some positive factors as well, e.g. support for employees joining unions and well-funded charity work that is integrated into the organization of the company."

So, perhaps, a middle-ground is being sought by both fans and club. After nearly 30 years developing a unique fan culture and seeing it grow into something people all around the world can identify with, a fragile balance is being achieved. Those in charge of the club are acutely aware of this unique situation: Andreas Rettig stated in an article for *Die Welt* newspaper: "We need to hammer out a balance between our social responsibility, our sporting ambitions and the economic situation. We want the greatest sporting success taking into account our values, ideals and guidelines."

The buy-back of merchandising rights from Upsolut, was acknowledged by Andreas Rettig as a 'cornerstone' of the club's strategy. Rettig respected the history and symbolism of the skull and crossbones brand, "From our experience, the Totenkopf is a synonym for buccaneers/pirates, a rebellion against the establishment and a stance against the mainstream. In our view, these are positive aspects, as we see them as part of our culture as a club."

Yet the risk of over-exposure of the St. Pauli brand remains, but as Sozialromantiker point out there are positives to be drawn from such a global reach, "Yes, over-exposure and marginalising the meaning of the symbol might water down the brand and result in the Totenkopf showing up in unintended contexts. On the other hand, there are reasons for the success. Can't we be proud of the reach? Isn't it a possibility to communicate our ideals and ideas, no matter how small that is reflected in every single sale?"

Being a globally recognized brand remains a double-edged sword, as highlighted by club historian, Christoph Nagel: "FC St. Pauli is a source of pride and enjoyment for many people living in the district, but of course as a brand it also is part of driving rents and property prices up. A couple of days ago (this interview with the author took place in February 2016) I found someone commenting on Facebook that he had never heard of a district named St. Pauli but only of the club... That is certainly an extreme, but in quite a few ways recognition for the club may today actually be bigger than for the district."

It would be unusual for the most radical solution to this problem to emanate from the President of FC St. Pauli, but the issue of branding is something Oke Göttlich has thought long and hard about. Göttlich made the comparison between FC St. Pauli and the Berghain techno-nightclub in Berlin, saying (albeit jokingly) – in a 2016 interview with the author – that St. Pauli is the Berghain of football. Göttlich was interested in the way Berghain don't do any branding or take any sponsorship. There is no commercialism at all, with people just attracted by music and reputation. Göttlich, at least theoretically, considered applying this strategy to FC St. Pauli, "I even made the calculation in my head. How much money would it cost to not brand St. Pauli at all? It is about €15-20 million per annum. Without sponsorship and branding, how would we refinance this, if we wanted to stay as independent as possible? Let's discuss paying €300 for a season ticket with no branding at all."

It was an interesting and – *it is important to stress* – purely hypothetical discussion. But it shows how even at the Presidential level, the club is prepared to think differently. The reality, of course, is that the success of the St. Pauli brand (especially now that the club controls the merchandising rights) gives the club more freedom to act independently and exercise a choice over the commercial partnerships they enter into.

Perhaps, Oke Göttlich's parallel between the music industry and football is quite apt. Of course, it is familiar territory for Göttlich; he has spent much of his career in the independent music sector and was the CEO of *Verband unabhängiger Musikunternehmen* (Association of Independent Music Companies) – a lobby group representing the interests of independent music companies in the face of the big multi-national players in the music industry. The parallels with FC St. Pauli and the independent music sector are there to be seen. It is the classic 'Indies versus the majors' – be they football clubs or record labels. FC St. Pauli needs to compete in the same sphere as much bigger, more financially powerful football clubs, but central to its existence is retaining both its independence and the core beliefs initially defined by the punks and anarchists of the Hafenstraße and refined over the following 30 years by a generation of fans and activists.

There will always be claims that the club has 'sold out' and has become just like any other football club but they are claims that are difficult to completely substantiate given the amount of activism that is embedded in both St. Pauli as a club and in its fan base. St. Pauli isn't a club that plays lip service to its supporters. The 50+1 rule means that members will always have a controlling say in major decisions. Sozialromantiker Sankt Pauli are optimistic that the club and its supporters remain as active and radical as in the 1980s and '90s, "With larger numbers and more involvement in actually running the club, the politics and actions became more diverse. Supporters who started to follow the club as children or students became well-established in jobs and started families. Existing organizational structures make work more efficient, but also offer less flexibility. But you will still find large numbers of supporters out on the streets to try to stop right wing demonstrations, support charity work, and fighting for the rights of football fans."

Despite the numbers of fans attending home matches increasing by about 10,000 in 2022 compared to 2006, the number of active fans has remained fairly constant. Christoph Nagel puts the number of socially active fans at a couple of hundred at best (but this highlights the difficulty of precisely defining 'socially active'). He believes that the influence of fans (on the decision-making process within the club) is much bigger than it was in the 1990s or 2000s. What is interesting – as was the case with the Jolly Rouge – is that it remains possible to mobilise a lot of popular support from a relatively small active fan base.

Whilst most research on FC St. Pauli's unique fan culture focuses on its beginnings in the 1980s, the challenges the club and its fans face today are just as interesting. The battle against racism, sexism and homophobia are ongoing as is the fight to stop the erosion of fan culture by creeping commercialism. As we shall see in a subsequent chapter, even the St. Pauli fan scene isn't completely immune from accusations of sexism.

As we move through the third decade of the 21st Century, another dynamic has risen to prominence when trying to maintain the difficult balance between commercialism/global brand expansion and local, supporter driven, activism. That dynamic is environmental sustainability.

The football industry like every other aspect of contemporary capitalism has been forced to consider its environmental impact and carbon footprint. It is now not enough just to generate significant sums of money through merchandising and lucrative commercial sponsorships. Increasingly, society is demanding environmental accountability and increased sustainability.

FC St. Pauli have been switched on to this changing dynamic. There have been actions that are perhaps a little performative or tokenistic such as the *Ewald-Bienen-Honig* (Ewald-Bee-nen-Honey) initiative that saw colonies of bees installed at the Millerntor to boost Hamburg's urban bee population and produce local honey named after St. Pauli icon, Ewald Lienen. But there have been other decisions that should have much more of a lasting impact.

The most notable of these was the decision not to extend the club's contract with Under Armour at the end of the 2020/21 season. Undoubtedly, the backlash from supporters and lacklustre sales figures had an impact on the decision not renew but not many within the fan scene would've predicted the club's next move. Instead of signing with another kit manufacturer, FC St. Pauli took the bold step of moving the production of all kit and training gear in-house. This was a decision that had its roots in a motion passed at the AGM of 2016 to commit to the sustainable and fair production of all of the club's merchandise. The club founded a sustainability working group in 2019 and had been working towards hitting environmental, fair trade and sustainability targets for general merchandise ever since.

The working group established a strict 'Social Code of Conduct' that all suppliers must adhere to. The Code of Conduct places emphasis on dignified working conditions and fair pay for all those working in the St. Pauli merchandise supply chain.

FC St. Pauli are the first (and so far, the only) football club to be a member of the Fair Ware Foundation – a non-profit organization improving working conditions in the textile industry. As such, the club is subject to an annual audit. As for the garments themselves the club's merchandise is Fairtrade accredited. It also adheres to the Global Organic Textile Standard that monitors the production and processing of all organically produced natural fibres. The Global Recycled Standard also ensures that there is traceability and accountability in the process of using recycled materials in merchandise production at St. Pauli.

Former Commercial Director, Bernd von Geldern, acknowledged that it had been a long process but, "We wanted to be sure we'd be launching the most sustainable teamsport collection in the world." Of course, other kit manufacturers have been producing kits with improved environmental credentials for a number of seasons. Adidas have been working with Parley for the Oceans since 2015, with their football shirts and other products being made from recycled ocean plastics. But, to the best of Bernd von Geldern's knowledge, no other kit supplier has provided a complete range of teamwear that is made from recycled materials. In short, these accreditations mean that the Totenkopf is only ever printed either on recycled or organic materials.

All the sustainably produced FC St. Pauli merchandise carries a 'Sustainable Product' logo which includes the strapline, 'Not perfect but better'. This is an acknowledgement that the club's environmental impact can always be reduced and that the journey towards sustainability is always ongoing. In an interview with Bernd von Geldern, conducted by the author in May 2022, the club's then Commercial Director hypothesised of a time when supporters could exchange old jerseys for new ones in an expanded recycling scheme that perhaps would offer a discount on a new shirt if an old one was returned. It is clear that – once again – people in high places at St. Pauli are prepared to think outside of the box to look at solutions that go against the existing merchandising orthodoxy.

The launch of FC St. Pauli's own *Di!Y* kit label in the summer of 2020 was the result of thousands of hours of hard work by both the club's Sustainability Working Group and merchandise team. All items that were released as part of the teamwear collection were ethically produced and as sustainable as possible: 'Not perfect but better'.

Of course, the DIY ethos at St. Pauli has a long history. It is symbolised by the production of the famous Totenkopf t-shirts in a St. Pauli basement by Steph Braun (and others) that stretches back to the late 1980s. So, it represents some clever marketing to brand the club's in-house production as *Di!Y*. Martin Drust, the club's Head of Marketing explained, "The core of FC St. Pauli is DIY - do it yourself - and that's actually the core idea behind this brand. Instead of constantly moaning that a kit supplier isn't good enough or can't equip us sustainably enough, it's about saying we'll do it ourselves... Unfortunately, you can't trademark DIY, so we came up with the idea of simply adding an "I". In the long version, it actually means "Do it, improve yourself", but we won't use that. Instead, we're assuming that *Di!Y* will enter into everyday language, so people understand we have the courage to take this matter into our own hands."

Bernd von Geldern was keen to get the message across that this isn't just about the team jerseys, "It'll be the most sustainable teamsport collection, with all 55 products. We'll make everything ourselves, from the socks to the rain jackets."

Of course, this move to in-house production represented quite a financial gamble. The previous deal with Under Armour had been good financially for the club. By launching *Di!Y* the club was taking a financial risk, something that was only exacerbated by the Covid-19 pandemic. However, it was a risk that paid off. The club sold 30,000 jerseys during the 2020/21 campaign – meaning all stock was sold-out. This was considerably more than the number of Under Armour shirts sold during the previous 2019/20 season. It is difficult to say whether this was due to the quality of the *Di!Y* jersey designs and fabrics or because a large number of St. Pauli fans had voted with their feet and had committed to not buying shirts produced by Under Armour. The reality is probably a mixture of the two: strong, classic shirt designs and a willingness amongst supporters to back the club's decision to pioneer an ethical and sustainable in-house brand.

The club had also dodged a bullet that many other kit suppliers and clubs faced during the pandemic. With *Di!Y* products predominantly being produced in Turkey and Portugal they were not impacted by the disruption to supply chains that companies who had based their manufacturing in the Far East fell victim of. Of course, St. Pauli fans were quick to point out that the Erdoğan regime in Turkey is considered extreme and has victimized its own citizens as well as those of Kurdish extraction. Many St. Pauli fans and activists on the left would disagree with housing garment production in Turkey, but again – and this may be a considerable ethical stretch – the motto, 'Not perfect but better' can be applied.

The looming environmental crisis isn't going away, it also isn't going to be solved by the merchandising decisions of a second-tier

German football club. But, once again, St. Pauli is trying to find another way even at a difficult juncture in history.

Sustainability is another element to add to the mix and the contradictions of St. Pauli. Of course, in an ideal anti-capitalist world the club wouldn't need to generate revenue by selling vast amounts of skull and crossbones merchandise. Yet, without those original and iconic Totenkopf t-shirts spreading the word you could question whether a small football club with an anti-fascist fan base from the docks of Hamburg would've risen to be a standard-bearer for a different type of football? Perhaps. Andreas Rettig, former FC St. Pauli CEO, provided the most succinct response to the contradiction of being a global brand and yet adhering to the principles of the local fan scene, "FC St. Pauli has become the club it is because of its fan scene. The values for which the club stands were forged by local supporters but are valid globally."

To return to Eric Hobsbawm for a moment: his fears were that, in an era of globalization, local identification with a football club and 'popular sentiment' were incompatible with business, politics and economics. For the majority of football clubs, he appears to be correct. FC St. Pauli might just be the exception. The club will continue to juggle the seemingly contractionary responsibilities of being a sustainable, global brand that remains rooted in local activism. It won't be easy, but then nothing at St. Pauli ever is.

Chapter 13:
St. Depri – Wir Sind Immer Für Uns Da

FC St. Pauli and its supporters are renowned all over the world for their outward fight against racism, sexism and homophobia. However, in recent years, a group of St. Pauli fans have joined together to fight a much less visible but no less malign adversary: depression.

These are changing times – often for the worse – but one area of discourse that bucks this trend is the increased awareness and understanding of mental health. This includes more open discussion, increased support, and a move towards a parity between mental and physical health. Once again, football has a role to play, and the fans of FC St. Pauli have been proactive in this regard.

St. Depri is an initiative set up by fans of FC St. Pauli, established to support people struggling with depression themselves or the friends, colleagues or family members supporting individuals struggling with their mental health.

St. Depri was established by a group of supporters in response to losing one of their friends, Michel, who died by suicide on 28 August 2014. A day later, in the Jolly Roger, in amongst the maelstrom of emotions – sadness, anger, grief, disbelief – those mourning their friend, decided to do something positive and establish a group that enables people to come together, talk, listen and support each other. The St. Depri website sums it up succinctly: "We want to use this terrible event to help others who are also affected. We do not want to hide any more depression in the St. Pauli fan scene; we want to make it visible; we want to talk and to clarify." It is a brave and noble statement, because so many instances of depression remain hidden, often because those people suffering from depression are so good at hiding it. Even if they aren't good at concealing their illness, they can be extremely reluctant to engage in support that could help them. Men are particularly reluctant to recognise, acknowledge, or seek help for their depression – and often the very last thing they want to do is talk about it. Friends of Michel noted how he had become withdrawn in the weeks before his death. His roommate at the time assumed that this was due to stress at work. But the withdrawal ran much deeper than that. It is not always possible to counter that withdrawal from the world with the offer of support and conversation, as the individual suffering from depression must be open to it – but talking can help. It can be an important first step. There is no miracle cure: medication may work for some, counselling for others. Equally, none of these things may make a blind bit of difference but talking is often the first step along the road to seeking help.

Football's high media profile means that the suicide of a professional footballer generates a lot of media coverage. German football was rocked by the death of former national team goalkeeper, Robert Enke in November 2009. Enke's tragic story was retold by Roland Reng in *A Life Too Short: The Tragedy of Robert Enke*, possibly one of the most haunting football books ever written.

FC St. Pauli lost a former player to depression in July 2014, when 33-year-old Andreas Biermann died by suicide after a long and public battle with depression. Five years earlier, the death of Robert Enke had prompted Biermann to go public about his own illness. On 21 November 2009, Andreas Bierman released a statement via his club FC St. Pauli. The words were stark: "I, Andreas Biermann, 29 years old, married and father of two children, am a professional soccer player at FC St. Pauli and have been suffering from depression for several years. I attempted suicide on October 20, 2009."

Biermann's football career had been hampered by niggling injuries and it was during his time on the side-lines that he developed an obsession with playing poker online that further compounded his illness. With the full support of the club – and just two days after Robert Enke's death – he was admitted to the depression ward at the Klinikum Nord clinic in Hamburg-Ochsenzoll where he spent 58 difficult days and nights.

Biermann also wrote a book documenting his fight against his illness, titled, *Depression: Red Card* published in Germany in 2011 (although, as far as I am aware, there is no English version). He started diarising his experiences of depression during his stay at the clinic in Hamburg-Ochsenzoll. He wanted to be open about his illness and document his experiences. On his first day at the clinic, he wrote: *"Hiding and disguising no longer helps, but has also partly contributed to the fact that I am here now. I want to tell everything, even if it's embarrassing for me. That is precisely the aim of this matter, to get everything on the table in such a way that it is no longer so burdensome." In common with many sufferers, Biermann had become a master at disguising his illness to the outside world. He wanted his time in therapy to be the start of a new beginning for him and his family.*

For those struggling with depression, recovery isn't a linear process. The same was true for Andreas Biermann. The left-sided defender had spent over a decade in professional football, playing for a variety of club's including Hertha Berlin, Chemnitzer, Union Berlin and Tennis Borussia Berlin before joining FC St. Pauli in 2008. Injury limited him to just ten appearances in a two-year spell at the Millerntor. Yet, despite a debilitating knee injury, Biermann continued to play football with FSV Spandauer Kickers in his home city of Berlin.

It was in Berlin, on 19 July 2014, that Andreas Biermann died by suicide. It came as a shock to the whole German football community, including those who had known and played alongside Andreas at FC St. Pauli.

Similarly, in Britain, the death of Gary Speed in 2011 shocked everyone, and took the world of football completely by surprise. The common consensus was that Speed was such an outwardly cheerful character. However, he too had developed that outward persona to successfully mask his illness.

Perhaps the only positive to emerge from such tragedies was that it opened a discourse on the topic of depression in football and – as an extension of that – in life. That's why I felt such a swell of hope and pride that fans of my club, FC St. Pauli, had taken things one step further and set up a support group for people suffering from the illness.

St. Depri offers real, ongoing support. Not just for those suffering directly with depression or anxiety but also for their friends and families. The group meets on the third Thursday of every month in the Fanladen. They are supported by psychologists and psychotherapists along with others who have experienced or are experiencing depression. The sessions begin with a talk on a particular topic before expanding into more informal open discussion. People can suggest topics for discussion in advance. Prior to the roundtable discussion, people can come to the Fanladen to receive practical support with letter opening. For anyone who has suffered from depression or anxiety the sheer act of their opening post (especially when linked to bills and finance) can be almost impossible. This leads to the inevitable build-up of unopened letters, and it can become difficult to break the cycle. The St. Depri letter opening allows people to be supported in opening letters and reading the enclosed documents, it also offers them advice on how to proceed with issues that arise.

St. Depri also offers a pioneering 'godparent' project. The service acknowledges that during a particularly bad bout of depression it may become impossible for the person suffering to even contemplate leaving the house. The godparent project pairs up those people struggling with their mental health with other St. Pauli fans. The idea is that they will come and knock at their door and give them the support and motivation they need to leave the house. This commonly occurs around St. Pauli home games when the godparent will travel to the stadium with them. But it is not limited to attending matches, the service is also a way to help people to continue to engage and attend the St. Depri monthly discussions, it has even been utilised to get people out of the house and to the shops. The central tenet to this service is that both parties – those suffering with depression and the godparents – are united by their support of St. Pauli. It is hoped that this common ground provides a connection and generates conversation. The St. Depri website even has short biographies of some of the godparents, so that those interested in support can request a godparent based on common interests, age, gender or location. It is all about making connections and developing a support network fostered by a common love of St. Pauli.

There are other activities too: yoga, an active sports group and even courses at the Levi's Music School based inside the South Stand at the Millerntor. The Covid-19 pandemic made the work of St. Depri much harder (and simultaneously more vital). Where in-person group meetings were not allowed due to Covid restrictions, the meetings took place online. Indeed, the March 2022 topic for discussion was, 'Depression during and as a result of the pandemic'.

Nothing beats face-to-face interaction, and St. Depri were delighted to be able to return to its regular monthly meetings at the Fanladen as the pandemic began to subside. The supporters that established and run St. Depri remain committed to helping anyone suffering from depression. It is something that fits with the song, *You'll Never Walk Alone* that is often sung on the terraces of the Millerntor. The idea is that nobody should suffer alone – that everyone should have the opportunity to talk openly about their depression. The project is a fitting memory to Michel and other members of the St. Pauli fan scene who are no longer with us.

No matter how we are feeling, St. Depri are always there for us.

Chapter 14:
We Need to Talk About Bochum (Match)

VfL Bochum 1 FC St. Pauli 1
Bundesliga 2.
18:30, Friday 30 October 2015, Ruhrstadion

I've worried about this chapter a lot. It has been the most difficult to write. I am also conscious that it contains the least St. Pauli or football content of any chapter in this book. That said, it was partly due to the establishment of St. Depri in 2014 that gave me the courage to share my experience. I would say skip over this chapter, but the subject matter is important. Even if you can't personally relate to it, the withdrawal and the shutdown documented below might remind you of a family member or a friend.

Writing about mental health, especially in a football context, simply wouldn't have happened even a decade ago. Fortunately, things have moved on. This is essentially a chapter about depression, and how football – as a constant in my life – has been used as a coping mechanism, sometimes successfully, sometimes not.

Normally these 'Match' chapters are loosely based around a game I attended, but as the title of this chapter suggests, we need to talk about Bochum. I didn't make it to FC St. Pauli's away game against VfL Bochum at the Ruhrstadion back in October 2015 (a 1:1 draw for those who are interested, featuring a rare Jan-Philipp Kalla goal).

At the time I told everyone that I missed the plane because I was stuck in a traffic jam. It was about 04:00 when I left for the airport. It was pitch black and pouring with rain but there was absolutely no traffic to get stuck in – even my excuse was rubbish.

I missed my flight because, at that moment, depression had me in a stranglehold and anxiety had paralysed me. All the way down the motorway to Heathrow, I was going/not going/going/ not going. It was a battle that ate up the miles. In the end anxiety won. I came off the M40, parked up in the services, crawled into the back seat and went to sleep for a couple of hours.

I woke up as it got light (I'd slept quite well, it's reasonably roomy in the back of a Citroen Berlingo). You'd imagine I'd be feeling guilty, right? Guilty for wasting money I could ill afford on a flight I never took. Guilty of letting the people at the Fanladen down over tickets. (Don't worry, I texted them in plenty of time and my ticket went to a good home.) Guilty for being such a mess?

But I didn't feel any guilt at all – only relief. Real, palpable relief that I could feel coursing through my veins.

You see, when the twin forces of depression and anxiety combine, they do so with devasting effect – and all I want to do is withdraw from the world. And when they hit hard, I'll even want to avoid the things I love most – including football.

Bochum wasn't the first St. Pauli game I missed because of an anxiety attack either. In the early days of going to St. Pauli games it used to happen a lot. I would lose my nerve the night before, crippled with anxiety and make up excuses as to why I wasn't going. But it hadn't happened for quite a few years, so it was a bit of a shock when it hit me. I thought I'd overcome it, because watching St. Pauli has become one of the few things I do where I feel completely at ease.

When I analyse it, missing the Bochum game was part of a longer-term shutdown policy. I guess the best analogy I can come up with for my shutting down is that I have compartmentalised my life into sections, a bit like a fuse box. For the last seven years, teaching has drained so much of my life force that to survive I have had to shut-off so many other areas of my life. To continue the analogy, it is like an electrician switching off all the different circuits to try and identify where the fault is. Only, the problem wasn't with any of the individual circuits that I shut off; the problem was that I had completely overloaded the system – overloaded my ability to cope.

First to go, almost unnoticed, were things like watching TV and reading books. This crept up on me, as I was so busy in the evenings preparing stuff for the next day that I didn't even notice that I no longer tried to stop work and have some downtime at the end of the day. Hell, most evenings meals were expertly eaten one handed as I typed away on my laptop with the other. I guess when I started teaching, I just accepted the loss of evenings as collateral damage for starting a new career relatively late in life. I was used to working hard, so I could cope – at least that's what I thought. I imagined that after a year or two I'd have things sorted and I'd be able to have my evenings back again.

I was also completely blindsided by the virulence of the workplace bullying. The conduct of senior management in school was disgraceful and quite unlike anything I had experienced in my years working in other sectors. It was subtle yet relentless, gradually eating away at your confidence and self-worth. A deliberate and calculated drip feed of leadership gaslighting that undermined all staff and left us powerless to confront the management.

Gradually – as the depression and anxiety took hold – it became impossible to have any kind of social life, maintain friendships or relationships *and* hold down my job, so they were the next things to get switched off. Again, it happened slowly at first. Some people (quite rightly) gave up on me, either because they got bored of my moaning about work or fed up with the last-minute cancellations and excuses. Others, I just shut out of my life.

The trouble is with all this is, it's self-perpetuating. It reached the point where I went out so little, that the sheer thought of socialising filled me with dread. So, I made excuses. I stayed in, even though it meant that I was often letting real friends down.

This next bit sounds even more dreadful typed out: my dad had another round of cancer in the time I was suffering with depression, and I probably only saw him a couple of times. There are other reasons for that too (like he moved to the actual end of Wales) but the real reason is nothing to do with geography and everything to do with the fact I didn't have the emotional capacity to juggle his physical illness, my mental state and hold down my job. The illness finally took my dad in 2020 but – thank God – by that point I had recovered enough to patch up our differences.

With friends and family pretty much shutdown, football and my own kids were about all that was left. So I shut down football.

Football has been a constant in my life for as long as I can remember. Aside from the enjoyment and obsession, I realise now that football has helped me manage my mental health. The collective nature of the crowd helped me cope and manage various feelings of anxiety, uncertainty, or depression. As the pure euphoria of being a kid and loving everything about football was replaced by teenage angst, I used to take comfort in sharing of emotions with the crowd. I loved those shared feelings. If we won, we were all happy. If we were denied a blatant penalty, we were all angry. If we lost, we were all, err, depressed? It was that simple.

Those collective feelings always used to embrace me on the slow shuffle out of the ground at the end of the game. There, in a confined space exiting the stadium, it didn't matter who you were – or what was going on in your life outside of football – in those few minutes before you spilled out onto the street and dispersed in different directions, you all felt the same. As a shy teenager, without many friends, I took enormous comfort in that. It was a reassurance that would often last all weekend. There was comfort in knowing, even after a particularly gutting last-minute defeat, that there were 17,000 other people that had all had their Saturday night ruined. It worked the other way too, of course. Knowing that all those other people on the terraces would still be buzzing about a win just like you, long after the final whistle had blown and they had returned to everyday life.

I took a lot of strength from those collective emotions. In many ways, it was (and still is) easier than dealing with individual ones. Sociologists have made careers out of writing about our need for a collective identity. It's not exclusive to football. Religion used to do a pretty good job fulfilling that need – only in recent times has its grip on the populace lessened.

But sometimes it is unhelpful too. You can hide behind your support for a football club or, if you are that way inclined, your faith. It is sometimes much easier and safer to invest all our emotions in something abstract like football than, say, another human being. Despite this, I have found that being able to have football to identify with has been – on balance – a good thing.

The way I get my fix of watching football now is very different to my youth. Gone are my fortnightly trips to Vicarage Road with my dad. Gone is my Watford season ticket and those shared collective emotions of victory or defeat. Truth is, I fell out of love with going. I fell out of love with the commercialization and gentrification of English football. But if you've read *Pirates, Punks & Politics* you will know that already. You know that, instead, I found something far more fulfilling. I found FC St. Pauli.

I only get to three or four St. Pauli games a season, but the experience is so much more rewarding that I wouldn't swap it for the world. I guess I found a real collective experience, one that goes beyond the superficial (and temporary) feelings brought about by winning or losing. I found a football club and a fan scene that shares my political ideals and values in a way I never thought possible. Even though I live hundreds of miles away in a different country, even though I can't speak the language, I feel a sense of belonging that I have never felt anywhere else.

For a variety of reasons, I never felt like I completely fitted in with mainstream football in Britain, yet the Millerntor feels like home. Through talking to people, realizing we share similar views and have similar aspirations for football and for life, we feel like we really belong to a tangible community. It is a community that exists in and around the Millerntor and the district of St. Pauli, but it is also a community that extends beyond Hamburg – with a little help from the internet and social media – to London, Brighton, Yorkshire, New York, Brazil and beyond.

And that's when I think, what would I do without this club? Coincidentally, the years of falling in love with St. Pauli and the sense of belonging that it has fostered have loosely coincided with my toughest years of wrestling with depression and anxiety. Make no mistake, the depressive feelings and thoughts have always been there, in the background, I recognise that now. The feelings I used to put down to my pessimistic nature or my inbuilt cynicism, went beyond that. Fortunately, the periods of anxiety and depression are by no means constant, they come and go. And I've been lucky, there's been times when I've gone years without them, but during the last four or five years the attacks have become more frequent and vicious.

Simultaneously, I have been really lucky. *Pirates, Punks & Politics* opened lots of doors for me and it made me do stuff outside of work. This wasn't always easy but, somewhere in my head, I made the decision that talking about the book, doing presentations and attending seminars was something I had to do. It was almost evangelical. I was on a mission. And I'm glad I did. It kept me going, gave me some focus outside of work and I really enjoyed it – and I have met some amazing people along the way.

In other areas though, I continued to shut down. And eventually that shutdown seeped into football too. Which is why I bailed out of Bochum.

Why the Bochum game though? When I analyse it, the fact that it was an away game played a part in my decision. I've worked out that when I'm suffering, there are familiar safe places where I feel comfortable and – conversely – places that fill me with dread. When I'm feeling anxious, routine and familiarity play a big part in keeping me calm. I have safe spaces where I feel at ease. The gym is one – I can stick my headphones in and know that nobody will approach me. Going for a long run works in the same way. It might seem strange, but the Millerntor is one of those safe places too. This is partly because I know how it all works – the familiarity of a matchday routine. Partly because of the comforting anonymity of being part of a crowd. But also, it feels like home.

It's comforting because it reminds me of being a kid. Of going to football with my dad, getting lost in the crowd and forgetting that the rest of the world exists.

Also, I've done the Heathrow-to-Hamburg trip so often that it has a clockwork familiarity (another reason why making up a story about missing my flight was so ridiculous, I know exactly how long I need to get to the airport and always build in a sizeable contingency!). My trip to Bochum didn't have that same familiarity. It would've required me to step outside my comfort zone. Travelling to a new airport, making my way to a new ground in a strange city on my own. With my anxiety going through the roof, I wasn't ready for that.

I guess that 'familiarity' theory holds true, as a few weeks later I made it across to Hamburg without the slightest hint of panic. I've got my next trip booked and I know I'll make that too. I need to because football remains a sanctuary. And despite what I think when I'm depressed, I really need football. It's part of the fabric of who I am. And when you're lost in a bout of depression, you need to cling on to anything that reminds you of who you are.

However, not going to Bochum wasn't my lowest point (although it was the last time that I missed a game due to feeling so bad). But, before you worry about reading through another eight pages of self-pity, bear with it a little longer, my story does have a happy ending.

On 3 January 2020, I sat down and reflected on my mental health journey of the previous ten years in a blog post somewhat dramatically entitled *The Lost Decade*. I've included some of it below:

–

"You lost, get over it!" seemed to be the riposte of the decade.

It applied to so many things: the general elections of 2010, 2015, 2017 and 2019; Scottish Independence referendum; Brexit; Trump; FC St. Pauli in pretty much any DFB Pokal game in last ten years.

But it is not just football and politics where I've felt I I lost this past decade. I've also been adept at losing friendships, confidence, the ability to cope in social situations, contact with close family. If I'm honest, I pretty much lost a whole decade to depression and anxiety. It took me a long time to write about missing a St. Pauli game because I was paralysed by depression and anxiety. It felt cathartic when I did, but I wasn't out of the woods yet.

In February 2017, I hit rock bottom. I locked myself in the disabled toilet at work and decided I didn't want to carry on. I wanted to die. This wasn't the first time I had felt like this, but it was the most acute. The pressure of work; of getting students through their exams (or rather making sure they did well enough for the school to avoid the scrutiny of Ofsted and others); the pressure of trying to please everyone, every single day had beaten me. It was an impossible task, it had worn me down over the years, but my own anxiety and inability to think rationally had broken me. I hadn't figured out, or at least come to terms with the fact that in my job (and most jobs under late capitalism) you can never work hard enough. In education particularly, results are never good enough; lessons can always be improved; marking can always be more detailed; and management, government and parents will always demand more of you even – or especially – when you've nothing left to give. I'm aware this isn't just a teaching phenomenon. The fact that employers always demand more is prevalent across all professions. It's something that has been brought more sharply into focus following a decade of austerity and the impact of the Covid-19 pandemic. What I am saying is, I know it is not just me. The mental health of hundreds of thousands of people in this country and across the world has suffered over the last decade.

Back to February 2017. The following day, I got an emergency appointment at the doctor. I remember going into the room and not knowing what I was going to say. I thought back to my previous visit a couple of years earlier, when the (male) doctor was dismissive. He told me to 'man-up' and to switch jobs (not so easy when your whole self-worth has been eroded by your current profession). But, this time, the doctor couldn't have been nicer. All I had to say was that I was a teacher, and I was really struggling with stress and depression, and I felt like she instantly understood.

She put me on some tablets and suggested a website for CBT. I told her how stubborn I was and that taking tablets felt like a sign of weakness, defeat or giving in. She reassured me it wasn't. I explained how the last time I'd tried antidepressants, I'd been too paralysed by the depression to book another appointment when my tablets ran out after a month, so she gave me a six-month prescription. It was probably only a 10-minute appointment, but I felt like – at last – someone understood.

I started the tablets; I didn't notice much difference at first. Then one afternoon in the gym, I felt that familiar feeling. The one where everything starts sinking and you feel more crushed and broken by the second. Interestingly, I'd long used exercise as a way of coping with the depression, literally trying to 'run off' the stress – something to do with endorphins, I think.

But, as my depression took root, I noticed that the exercise was less and less effective. In fact, the only way I could really feel anything other than numbness was to push myself so hard on the treadmill that it hurt, really hurt. That was pretty much the only way to stop the feelings of despair: to push myself so hard physically that I was in pain. The relief was only ever temporary. As soon as I stopped the intense exercise and went to finish off my routine with a cool-down, I could feel the depression kick in. It was horrible. I'd often leave the gym feeling worse than when I went in.

Anyhow, there I was cooling down at the end of a workout and I could feel myself start to slide, I could feel the despondency begin to take a grip on me. But – then – it stopped. Well, it didn't stop, but it levelled out. I didn't metaphorically crash through the floor into the depths of despair like usual. It was the drugs. The only way of describing it was that they formed a very real, tangible safety-net that stopped me from falling, stopped me from being dragged under. After a couple of minutes, I felt okay. Not brilliant, but okay. Good enough to go and get on with the rest of the day. It was incredible. I thought it might be a one-off, but at the same time I knew. I knew it was the medication kicking in. It was a revelation.

It continued like that. I kept noticing that at the point when I would normally spiral the safety net caught me. Family noticed it, people at work noticed it. I became adept at thinking to myself: "You were going to go then, but the bloody drugs saved you!" It was such a liberating feeling.

When my six-months was up I went back to the doctor (a different one again). I explained all of the above but felt confident enough to ask if they would increase my dosage. This is something I would never have done before. When I was at my lowest, I would've been convinced that they would stop my medication altogether, that I shouldn't be allowed access to it, that I didn't deserve to be helped. But here I was asking about the possibility of bumping it up slightly. So that rather than scraping by, fighting the depression, I could go one step further and feel vaguely happy about things. Six-months previously, I simply wouldn't have believed such a status was possible. Destroyed, broken, defeated were the only states I knew.

I've been on the higher dosage for three years now. It has transformed me. I wouldn't say that I'm a de-facto 'happy person'. I'm not, far from it. I'm still as cynical and as world weary about things as ever – after all, 'a pessimist can never be disappointed' and I still support St. Pauli, the most under-achieving football team of all time! But for the first time in at least a decade, I am more at peace with myself. I'm looking forward to things. I can do stuff again. Occasionally, I can even interact socially with people. I still have the down moments, but I acknowledge them, and I recognise that most of the time the safety net will catch me and stop me spiralling.

So, what has all this got to do with football?

Well, the anti-depressants have given me enough confidence, enough perspective to realise that having some time off at the weekend isn't a betrayal of your job, it's healthy. As a result, I've been going to lots more football. And writing lots more about football.

FC St. Pauli have been for so long my safe space, my refuge from the monotony of everyday life. Make no mistake, those trips (when I was well enough to go on them) gave me hope. They saved me. Being able to go to the Millerntor, to be around beautiful people who shared my politics, my passion, my outlook on life kept me going. Trips to Hamburg are akin to recharging your soul, your life-force. They make me believe that another world is possible. I owe so much to so many people over there.

Then, back in the summer of 2018, Clapton CFC – formed as a breakaway from Clapton FC – started up. I'd been to the old Clapton a few times and loved it. But this new club was something else. I felt like I belonged right from the start. Before I knew it, I was going to all the home games I possibly could. It was like I'd found a little bit of St. Pauli at the bottom of the M11. As the season progressed, I got more and more involved. Bess and I made a 30ft banner that went across the top of the stand that read, 'We are the Clapton. Always Antifascist'. I somehow stumbled into being one of the club's unofficial photographers. I joined some committees. I felt like I was part of something. I can't be in Hamburg for every game, so finding something like St. Pauli in London has been a godsend.

I might've lost a decade in a battle with depression and anxiety, but without a shadow of a doubt it has been football – via St. Pauli and Clapton along with some prescription meds – that stopped me going under.

> **Note:** I know that depression can't always be solved by tablets or therapy. I know many people are suffering from much more severe symptoms. I got lucky. But I don't for one moment think this is over. I worry constantly that, one day, medication will stop working for me, or that I'll have to come off it. I also worry that all I am doing is masking the problem, papering over the cracks of my reality. But, for now, I am accepting that there is a chemical imbalance in my brain and the medication is helping to rectify that. And – compared to how I used to feel – I'll take that.

Writing about depression is strange. On one hand, it is cathartic to be able to try and make sense of how you feel. But then, nagging away at you is the feeling that you are just being massively, self-indulgently attention seeking. It's not that though – I'm not writing about it for sympathy, attention or even hugs. I don't want this to be our topic of conversation when we next meet. In fact, I'd prefer it wasn't mentioned at all, I hate talking about it. But writing feels good, it is my way of explaining myself. Also, there's the chance that writing about my struggles might help other people who are experiencing something similar.

It doesn't stop there though. There's a big part of me that knows my depression is a massive first world luxury. I watch the news, see the people fleeing war and disaster, travelling across Europe with nothing, risking their lives crossing the sea, then living in inhumane conditions in refugee camps and think, what right do I have to feel miserable? I know the answer – none.

Also, I've been lucky enough to be able to afford to travel and watch the team I love at the Millerntor. I've been lucky enough to write a book about it and represent the club (in some small way) at conferences and on tour. You would be justified in arguing, "How could he do all this and be depressed?" I don't really have an answer. My experiences with St. Pauli were the high points of the last decade, but even they couldn't completely mask the bad times.

Like all of us I carry the guilt. I have friends who have battled through far more trauma in their lives than I could ever comprehend. That, of course, makes my depression feel selfish, but it doesn't change how I felt inside. I understand now that doing nothing, taking no action, and pretending everything was okay was probably more selfish. My inability to address my depression certainly had a negative impact on those closest to me.

This is the important aspect of my depression that I now need to take ownership of. It's probably also the hardest one: owning all the holidays, family days out, evenings and weekends that I ruined when my depression was at its worst. Over the course of a decade those events stack up. It is easy to feel sorry for yourself, but it needs recognising that family members and close friends suffer the effects of your depression too. Trying to come to terms with my illness and do something about it took a long time, but it was worth it, I only wish I had got there sooner.

That was my story. I know it was self-indulgent, but it is why I think that St. Depri is one of the most important aspects of St. Pauli fan culture. It is imperative for people to know they are not alone. The common bond of supporting a football team brings people together and can – if fostered in the right way – provide enough of an emotional support network for people to begin to seek help.

Chapter 15:
Working Class Wine Bar

To people of a certain age, the concept of a wine bar is everything that was wrong with the 1980s distilled into one pretentious social space. It's yuppies; it's shoulder-pads; it's posh blokes dealing shares on their over-sized mobile phones; it's the gentrification of former working class districts; and it's that sleazy Wilmot-Brown bloke running The Dagmar in *Eastenders*.

But then, in 2015, came the 1910-Weinbar.

St. Pauli *is* different, so it makes sense that the very concept of a wine bar in St. Pauli would be different too. Even so, it would be entirely reasonable to conclude that the very existence of a wine bar at the world's most famous punk club would add more fuel to the fire for those that think that St. Pauli has sold out and is just a pastiche of the alternative culture it claims to represent. Also, isn't the existence of a wine bar in St. Pauli further contributing to the gentrification of the district that fans and residents have been battling against for years?

Perhaps it is wise to rewind to the beginning of the story. There is no better person to put the record straight than Sönke Goldbeck, member of FC St. Pauli's Supervisory Board and – more importantly in this instance – one of the key figures behind the 1910 - Museum für den FC St. Pauli e.V. project.

Sönke is perfectly placed to put the Museum's 1910-Weinbar into the correct – St. Pauli – context. The first wine bar with direct FC St. Pauli connections was set up by Heiko (who had worked for many years in the Fanladen) and Raphael. Located to the north of the Millerntor on Neuer Kamp it was christened 'Weinbar Sankt Pauli'. Its initial goal, alongside serving a range of great wines, was to finally dispel the myth that is prevalent in northern Germany (as well as 1980s Britain) that wine is a 'yuppie' drink. It was as described by Sönke a huge cultural success, encouraging many members of St. Pauli's active fan scene to drink and socialise together. However, the reality of running a wine bar, turning a profit and also dealing with complaints from neighbouring tenants meant that this original venue was forced to close in November 2011.

However, the original Weinbar Sankt Pauli was never far from this group of fans' minds, in fact one friend of Sönke remarked, "Whenever you guys sit down together and get drunk, you always start talking about the old wine bar – you should do something about it." It seems most good ideas at St. Pauli are born out of getting drunk. So, when the Museum acquired the space in the Gegengerade (following the successful campaign to stop the police station being located there) it seemed the natural venue for a wine bar. It was also a great way of keeping the Museum project visible and in the public eye, during the long process of fundraising and the gradual repurposing and rebuilding of the space.

Over time, the 1910-Weinbar itself has become a great source of revenue for the Museum project, with around 700 people visiting every home game. In 2018, before the Covid-19 pandemic, the 1910-Weinbar sold over 10,000 bottles of wine on matchdays and at events over the course of the year.

Heiko's wine bar was definitely an inspiration, but wine also made perfect commercial sense. Sönke said they started with the rule that, at St. Pauli, 'drinking always works' and saw wine as the right focus as it doesn't put them in competition with the Fanräume next door (which sells beer) or the official club caterer. In fact, the only place you could get wine in the stadium on matchdays was in corporate hospitality, and even they stop serving after the game, so there was no direct competition.

A wine bar in the Museum was also relatively cheap and easy to set up. Initially, it was a temporary structure built by volunteers – all they really had to do was buy a fridge. Almost immediately, the place was packed out before and after home games. It was also perfect – alongside temporary exhibitions – for keeping the Museum in people's consciousness. Especially as Sönke puts it, "drinking gives people positive feelings, except – perhaps – the next morning!" Even so, he is incredibly proud of what the temporary wine bar achieved in such a short space of time. He continued by saying that he was delighted that people from different countries come over to enjoy the wine bar and sometimes end up crawling out of it. At this point, you can't help wondering if he's referencing some of Yorkshire St. Pauli erstwhile membership who have enjoyed some spectacular nights in the 1910-Weinbar's environs, singing along to Billy Bragg at the top of their voices before staggering off in the direction of the Jolly Roger pub.

With that last point in mind, is it possible that the 1910-Weinbar caters for a slightly more mature (in years at least) St. Pauli fan? It does have a slightly older demographic, but it is also true there's a good mix of people of all ages on matchdays. Sönke is keen to point out that the place should be accessible to all and that the wine remains affordable: one of the key principles being that nobody should be priced out.

There's another little-known fact about the 1910-Weinbar: its re-opening as a permanent space coincided with St. Pauli's incredible run of form at the back end of the 2016/17 season. So whilst much of the credit for the club's turnaround in fortunes went to then manager, Ewald Lienen and his coach, Olaf Janßen, was it the availability of reasonably priced wines that saved the club from the oblivion of 3. Liga?

It is well known amongst St. Pauli's international fanbase that whisky is Sönke's first love. Indeed, he has long harboured dreams of opening a whisky bar. However, he admits he has learnt a lot about wine in the last couple of years. He also has a pretty convincing counterargument for the demonisation of wine as a yuppie drink. An argument which is more international in outlook than the narrow British mindset: the guys who set up the original wine bar had strong links with friends in the Basque country where drinking wine is a way of life, free from the class conceptions that we tend to hold onto in Britain. In fact, wine is the drink of the masses across France, Spain, Italy and even southern Germany. In these places, wine is a normal companion to everyday life; it carries none of the prejudices of the United Kingdom, where beer is king, and wine is viewed as a bit, well, fancy.

Not content with offering wine on matchdays and at other functions, the team behind the 1910-Weinbar launched their own wine festival in 2017. The event was officially titled as the 'Wine Festival Against Racism' offering visitors the opportunity to sample over 100 different wines. The festival was a success and returned every year until Covid-19 hit, forcing the cancellation of the 2020 and 2021 events. The festival even managed to combine stadium tours and wine tasting. The 75-minute tour of the Millerntor included three strategically placed wine-tasting stops. Of course, the most important aspect of the wine festival is the raising of funds and awareness in the ongoing fight against racism. More than 40,000 Euros have been raised through the festival which has enabled the 1910-Weinbar to financially support a variety of local anti-racism projects including refugee team, FC Lampedusa St. Pauli; providing legal advice for refugees and Sea-Watch (which helps rescue migrants at sea). The funds also supported 'Football for All' initiatives developed by international St. Pauli fan groups in Leeds and Glasgow.

This is the real St. Pauli. There's no gentrification here, no social climbing, as Sönke puts it, this is a 'working class wine bar'. The only barrier to participation is dodgy politics, hence, both the wine glasses (cavernous bowl like things) and the champagne flutes carry the inscription, 'No Wine/Champagne for Fascists!' And that's exactly how it should be.

Hopefully, the 1910-Weinbar has a long and profitable future ahead; it's become another important social space on the St. Pauli fan scene; a must-visit attraction for fans attending a game at the Millerntor. The only note of caution Sönke offers is that, "it sometimes feels it's more about the 1910-Weinbar than the Museum and, actually, it should be the other way round." He has a point. Although, as mentioned previously, the wine bar does a pretty good job keeping the Museum itself in people's consciousness. It does, however, lead into the next chapter, which focusses specifically on the 1910 - Museum für den FC St. Pauli e.V. project – the challenges it faces and the exhibitions that have, thus far, occupied the space.

In conclusion, the 1910-Weinbar provides further evidence that – *as if we didn't know this already* – St. Pauli is a mass of contradictions. We're used to being accused of being a commercial juggernaut masquerading as a rebel club, of being capitalists, not pirates. Now, despite the reality being very different, St. Pauli fans will no doubt be labelled as 'champagne socialists' in a working-class wine bar. But wine is political too. The 1910-Weinbar's mantra is that wine should be a 'democratic enjoyment beyond elitist exaggeration' – actively promoting fairly-priced wine for the masses.

Chapter 16:
A Museum that is Part of St. Pauli History

The idea of establishing a St. Pauli Museum was a by-product of the club's centenary celebrations in 2010. Historians Christoph Nagel and Michael Pahl were approached by the publishing company Hoffmann and Campe to write *FC St. Pauli. Das Buch* – a comprehensive history of the club published to celebrate the club's centenary. To complement the book and further celebrate this landmark moment in the history of the club an exhibition was established – curated by Diana Schmies – and was housed in a series of interconnected shipping containers in front of the Südkurve on Millerntorplatz. Three-containers-high in places, it was an impressive construction, a symbolic nod to the district's maritime history and the huge, mechanised container port on the opposite bank of The Elbe, but also important in bringing together objects and photographs in a public place that – for the first time – told the story of the district's football club.

The book and exhibition had ignited something within historian Michael Pahl. Straightaway he said, "I want to continue with the museum after the anniversary book." However, Pahl was quick to acknowledge that he wasn't the first person to think along these lines. Michael Pahl and others were aware that Dieter Rittmeyer (then Chairman of the Football Department at the club) had been pondering the idea of a museum for the last 20-25 years, collecting numerous artefacts along the way.

However, the research and publication of *FC St. Pauli. Das Buch* had given Christoph Nagel and Michael Pahl access to many different individuals connected to the club who were interested in donating or loaning items for a museum. Dieter Rittmeyer's role as the 'unofficial archivist' combined with his collection of artefacts formed the basis of the Centenary exhibition in 2010. Subsequently, the FC St. Pauli-Museum Archive has been named the 'Dieter Rittmeyer Archive' in his honour. Of course, when a historical archive is described, it is often artefacts, documents and ephemera that spring to mind. However, one of the important parts of developing an archive is to record digitally the memories and opinions of contemporary witnesses – something the FC St. Pauli-Museum has striven to do since its earliest exhibitions.

Michael Pahl together with Roger Hasenbein and Bernd-Georg Spies got together to form a support organisation, initially to help with the temporary exhibition on the Millerntorplatz in 2010, but perhaps more significantly planting the seeds for a more permanent home for an FC St. Pauli-Museum and Archive.

It took the release of the plans for the redevelopment of the Gegengerade stand to give focus and urgency to the establishment of a museum. There was so much that was good news for St. Pauli fans regarding the redevelopment of the Gegengerade side of the ground. The old – uncovered – shallow terracing was to be replaced by a steep 10,000 capacity covered standing area; the stand unlike the Hauptribune opposite would house no executive boxes or corporate seating. This was a stand built for the fans, a construction that recognised the significance of this section of the stadium to the development of St. Pauli as a 'kult-club' – it has been well-documented that the old Gegengerade terrace was the first place that the punks and anarchists of the Hafenstraße gathered to watch the football in the 1980s. The external concourse of the new stand would house the St. Pauli Fanladen, the Fanräume (once significant funds had been raised by supporters to finance the space) and the AFM, three significant fan-lead organisations integral to present-day supporter culture.

However, there was one glaring miscalculation that only became apparent when the plans for redevelopment were published. It was an error so huge that it threatened to undermine everything the club and its supporters stood for. The plans revealed that – at the North end of the Gegengerade redevelopment – a huge area underneath the stand had been reserved for the construction of a police station. Sönke Goldbeck recalls how, up until this point, the plans had gone under the radar. Stefan Schatz from the Fanladen recalled how at the meeting, "Our faces fell and we were relatively horrified." Had the proposal been implemented it would've become the biggest in-stadium police station in all of Germany. The plans seemed almost sacrilegious to the generation of fans that had stood on the old Gegengerade – a betrayal of everything they stood for.

Sönke Goldbeck, member of the Executive Board at FC St. Pauli-Museum, recalls that – at the time – the club itself had no real interest in looking at other options for housing the police station that is a requirement at all Bundesliga and 2. Liga clubs. Gernot Stenger, Vice-President of the club, did at least release the funds for the design of an external police station. However, most of the club employees involved favoured the simple option of including the police cells within the new stand.

Maarten Thiele of the active fan scene remembers the feeling of powerlessness amongst supporters. He said, "We always heard about negotiations that were going on in the background." Stefan Schatz confirmed this, "The mood in the fan scene was a bit disillusioned because the club management had signalled there was no way to change it." Sönke Goldbeck offered perhaps the bleakest summation of the situation, "At the end of 2011, all hope was really gone."

However, events that occurred during the winterpause of January 2012 changed everything. It is perhaps the perfect example of something positive – a silver-lining – emerging out of a dangerous and damaging situation. The Schweinske Cup was an indoor tournament being played at the Alsterdorf Sports Hall in Hamburg during the winter break. It had become traditional for large numbers of St. Pauli fans to attend, loudly and vociferously supporting the team. However, in January 2012, hooligans from VfB Lübeck and HSV joined together in a premeditated attack against St. Pauli fans inside the arena.

Instead of moving to arrest the perpetrators, the police launched a baton attack on St. Pauli fans who were also pepper-sprayed within the confinements of the concourse underneath the stands – this resulted in many completely innocent bystanders being injured. This latest police mistreatment of St. Pauli fans was to be the catalyst for moving the FC St. Pauli-Museum project forward as an alternative to the police station. There was no way, after the treatment of St. Pauli supporters at the Schweinske Cup, that the club or its fans could countenance the thought of a permanent police presence within the Millerntor. As Michael Pahl said, "I also thought it would be even more helpful if you could offer an alternative. So, you are not only against something (the police station) but at the same time can also be for something else and say, 'wouldn't it be a great idea to realise a museum in the stadium instead?'"

In September 2012, at a packed meeting of around 200 fans in the Centro Sociale a manifesto was written and the slogan *Museum instead of Goliathwache* was thought of by St. Pauli fan Gegengeraden-Gerd which succeeded in planting the idea in many people's consciousness.

By FC St. Pauli's game with VfR Aalen on 25 September 2012, significant momentum had gathered amongst supporters and the Millerntor was, once again, bedecked in the red and black of the Jolly Rouge. This reprise of the protest movement last seen in January 2010 was a significant stadium-wide signal of support for the Museum campaign which included those supporters on the half-built Gegengerade holding up thousands of red cards bearing the 'Jolly Rouge' symbol.

On 21 November 2012, the first general meeting of FC St. Pauli-Museum took place. Events moved quickly and before long FC St. Pauli-Museum had submitted a business plan that would allow both the club and the supporters to benefit.

During this period, FC St. Pauli-Museum continued to organise events to stay in the public eye. The most high-profile of these being the first *Fußball & Liebe* (Football & Love) festival that took place at the Millerntor in September 2013. The festival – part of the district's wider Reeperbahn Festival – comprised of a programme of events that included talks, children's events and live music. Former striker Marius Ebbers and rapper Sookee were part of a panel that discussed homophobia and sexism in football. *Fußball & Liebe* showcased what the Museum could do. Over 3,000 people took part and it was repeated in 2015 with even more success and over 5,000 visitors.

There was no turning back. The club agreed that the Museum could rent the space under the Gegengerade that had seemingly been destined to fall into the hands of the Hamburg police. The FC St. Pauli-Museum joined the Fanladen, Fanräume and AFM on the back-straight, making that area of the stadium completely supporter-centric. The new police station was eventually housed on the site of its predecessor: outside the stadium on the corner of the Heiligengeistfeld between the Gegengerade and the North Stand. It was a victory for both the supporters of St. Pauli and for common sense.

By the summer of 2014, the Museum was ready to put on its first exhibition. On the 26 July, *F*ck You, Freudenhaus!* opened its doors for the first time on the Gegengerade. A bold name for a bold new museum that didn't want to adhere to the stuffy cliches of a 'typical' football museum. The exhibition title, in English, *Fuck*

You, Whorehouse! was deliberately tongue-in-cheek, a subversion of the stereotypical view of St. Pauli and its red-light district.

For those people familiar with the grey concrete innards of a newly constructed football stand, there may have been some apprehension about how such a cold, functional 600 square-metre space could be transformed into an absorbing exhibition? A lot of credit had to go to the team from exhibition specialists, Bontempo. From the moment supporters entered the exhibition via a reconstructed players' tunnel, the scene was set. A highlight of the exhibition was the incredible 'Miniature Millerntor' a 1:100 scale model of the modern stadium built by Veronika and Holger Tribian. The first exhibition inside the stadium was about the stadium itself. Natalie Bugs one of the driving forces behind the *F*ck You, Freudenhaus!* exhibition recalled how this was important for supporters who themselves were in the midst of seeing their home transformed from the tumbledown ground of the 1980s and '90s into the new modern-day version. In a way, the exhibition was an important bridge between the new and the old: reassuring fans that the Millerntor is about so much more than bricks and mortar. The exhibition itself included a 'Condolence Book' where supporters could write their own memories of what they loved about the 'beloved dump' of the Millerntor that existed almost unchanged between 1961 and 2006.

A number of temporary exhibitions continued to grace the Museum space underneath the Gegengerade most notably 2017's *Football in Ruins. FC St. Pauli in the 'Third Reich'* – which is referenced extensively in the following chapter. In 2019, the Museum launched a new education-focused project *BAM! Education at the Millerntor*. Building on the success of local schools visiting the *Football in Ruins* exhibition, the museum runs workshops about the club and its role in the Nazi regime alongside other educational options for young people. These include understanding and tackling prejudice and discrimination as well as the environmental issues that are amplified by textile production and 'fast-fashion'. Central to the *BAM! Education at the Millerntor* project is linking these educational topics to some of the core values central to the St. Pauli ethos: fighting fascism, racism and homophobia and – increasingly – becoming more conscious of the role a football club can play in sustainability. The workshop on textile production dovetailing with the club's decision to produce an entirely sustainable playing kit and training range through the establishment of the in-house *Di!Y* sportswear brand.

Of course, the Covid-19 pandemic put a strain on Museum finances. Between March and May 2020 and again from November 2020 to July 2021, exhibitions were closed and, just as importantly, the Museum and the Wine Bar were not able to welcome fans on matchdays. It was a difficult time, but it did allow for a period of reflection for those involved in the running of the Museum. Instead of a series of temporary exhibitions, the Museum had (pre-Covid) decided to establish a permanent exhibition space entitled *Kiezbeben 2.0* (Neighbourhood 2.0). Essentially, a permanent exhibition dedicated to the period of history that has come to define the club: the period of time when football, politics and punk rock coalesced on the steps of the Gegengerade and transformed FC St. Pauli forever.

Alongside the permanent display, the FC St. Pauli-Museum also has the capacity to run temporary exhibitions. Towards the end of 2022, the Museum celebrated *20 Years of Ultrà Sankt Pauli,* an exhibition charting the birth and evolution of USP. The exhibition was mostly curated by members of the USP with the Museum providing the physical space and any additional expertise.

Whilst the Museum in the Gegengerade is an important physical space for St. Pauli fans, the Museum has also been at the forefront of developing virtual exhibitions. Not only was this important during the recent Covid lockdowns but a sophisticated virtual presence also expands the reach of the Museum, providing access to St. Pauli fans worldwide. As technology has advanced, the online museum can offer virtual reality walkthroughs of exhibitions providing both past and present. This interactive resource is particularly poignant and important in the context of the online version of *Football in Ruins. FC St. Pauli in the 'Third Reich',* which has allowed the continued availability of the information regarding the club's involvement with the Nazi regime.

Following on from these web-based online exhibitions, the Museum has also launched its own App. This has given people the ability to scan both QR codes and images to bring up additional information or resources on their phones – something that has been utilised in this book at the beginning of each chapter.

The Museum is certainly future-proofed and has made a commitment to the virtual experience, however, like those institutions – the Fanladen, Fanräume and AFM – that it shares the Gegengerade with, bringing people together as a community on both match and non-matchdays remains central to its success. The Museum and Wine Bar are about so much more than just documenting history. They represent a vibrant, activist community where a great deal of time, energy and effort are devoted to preserving FC St. Pauli's legacy in both historical terms but – as importantly – through ongoing action and activism. The Museum and Wine Bar rely heavily on a dedicated group of volunteers who have worked tirelessly to grow the FC St. Pauli-Museum from the germ of an idea into one of the St. Pauli fans' most treasured institutions. Visit the Museum at any time during the week and you will be assured of a warm welcome. Visit on matchdays and the Wine Bar will be packed with supporters enjoying the wine but more importantly enjoying the company of fellow fans, regardless of the result on the pitch. Undoubtedly, the wine helps, especially after another single-goal defeat at the hands of someone like SV Sandhausen but, the Museum has a greater value because of the bonds of friendship and solidarity that it has created amongst those who frequent it.

Undoubtedly, the FC St. Pauli-Museum established to document the history of the club has itself – over the intervening years – become an important part of that history.

Chapter 17:
FC St. Pauli in the Third Reich

Pirates, Punks & Politics examined the impact of World War Two on the city of Hamburg and the district of St. Pauli. It also attempted to understand the football club's association with the Nazi regime during the period. Sources were scarce and definitive information was inconclusive regarding FC St. Pauli's complicity with the Nazis. In 2017, the FC St. Pauli-Museum hosted an exhibition *Football in Ruins. FC St. Pauli and the 'Third Reich'*. The research associated with the exhibition alongside the work of Gregor Backes (*With A German Sports Greeting: FC St. Pauli under National Socialism, Gregor Backes, Unrast Verlag, 1 September 2017*) added further clarity to the involvement of the football club as an organisation and of its prominent members in the rise of National Socialism in the 1930s and '40s. This exhibition is available – in English as well as in German – as an interactive, 3D walkthrough on the museum website. This chapter serves as a summary of that exhibition.

As such, this chapter is divided into two distinct sections. First, is a chronological outline of the events and their impact on the city, district and club. The second section focusses on the lives of seven individuals connected to FC St. Pauli and their personal involvement in the mechanisms of the Third Reich. These case studies can only ever provide a snapshot of personal attitudes *towards* and complicity *with* the regime – even from this sample of seven representatives of the club it is clear to see that different attitudes prevailed.

On 15 April 1945 – fifteen days before Adolf Hitler took his own life in his bunker in Berlin – SC Victoria and FC St. Pauli played out the club's final league game to take place during the war. It ended in a 4:3 win for St. Pauli. Football in Hamburg had continued – albeit intermittently – during the war.

During the Third Reich, FC St. Pauli spent four seasons in the Second Division and eight in the First Division. However, these divisions were much smaller and more regionalised, meaning they never had to face the two German powerhouses of the day: Schalke 04 or Dresdner SC. And, even during this period, it was HSV that usually finished top of the local division, meaning they progressed to the final round of the German championship. FC St. Pauli managed two fourth place finishes (1936/37 and 1942/43) and third place in 1944/45. Football in Hamburg may have continued throughout the Third Reich, preserving a degree of familiarity, but life for residents of the city was to change dramatically.

Adolf Hitler was appointed Chancellor on 30 January 1933. It was a pivotal year in German politics and one that would have ramifications all around the world. Hitler and the NSDAP dispensed with democracy. The Enabling Act, passed on 23 March 1933, turned Germany into a one-party state and a dictatorship.

The elimination of opposition was swift and systematic. In Hamburg, by the end of April 1933, more than 1,700 people had been taken into 'Schutzhaft' (protective custody). In the predominantly Jewish neighbourhood of Grindelviertel, just a mile or so north of St. Pauli, Storm Troopers chased Jewish people through the streets. It was a sign of what was to come. In May 1933, Karl Kaufmann was appointed as the Governor of Hamburg. In the September of the same year, the Fuhlsbüttel concentration camp was established within the grounds of the existing prison (situated in the northern suburbs of the city close to the modern-day location of Hamburg Airport). Between 1933 and 1945 thousands of prisoners were interned at Fuhlsbüttel and over 500 died there. The prison known as 'KolaFu' was one of the most brutal in Nazi Germany. Towards the end of the Second World War, the prison became a satellite camp of the Neuengamme concentration camp – housing prisoners that had been displaced by the Allied bombing campaign. These prisoners were put to work clearing debris and corpses from the city and the port as well as fortifying anti-tank defences around Hamburg.

In 1934, Hitler further consolidated his power. In January, the Law for the Prevention of Genetically Diseased Offspring was passed – it would see over 400,000 people sterilised by 1945. Following the death of President Hindenburg on 2 August, Hitler assumed the title of Führer and Chancellor. Later that month, on 17 August 1934, a large crowd assembled in Hamburg at Rathausmarkt to again welcome Adolf Hitler to the city. Despite rulings to the contrary, a variety of Nazi souvenirs and mementos were sold by street hawkers in the city. These included cushions adorned with swastikas, Hitler figurines and handkerchiefs with his image printed on them. There was an undeniable appetite for these trinkets amongst the Hamburg population. Between 1925 and 1939, Hitler visited Hamburg on at least 33 occasions.

Life and football continued through this period: during 1933 and 1934, workers and volunteers continued to build a new St. Pauli sports ground at the Millerntor.

However, the shadow of the National Socialist regime was never far away. Also in 1934, persecution of additional groups not befitting of the NSDAP's 'Volksgemeinschaft' (people's community) was extended to include homosexuals and the unemployed. In the September of 1935, the 'Nuremberg Laws' were passed which forbade marriage between Jews and non-Jews and stripped the Jewish population of the right to vote. This followed on from the compulsory teaching of 'race and genetics theory' in all German schools.

It was often thought that FC St. Pauli officials were well-connected to the emergent Nazi regime, as they were able to push through the building of a new ground. However, shortly after the turf had been laid and the stadium was completed, the NSDAP commandeered the arena for a farming and horticulture exhibition under the banner 'Blood and Soil'. The grass at the Millerntor proved to be the perfect surface to demonstrate the latest advances in ploughing techniques. Photos show that ditches were also dug on the pitch and horses were stabled in the ground. Over 500,000 visitors also walked across the turf during the course of the exhibition.

It took more than a year for the pitch to recover. However, on 23 August 1936, the new FC St. Pauli stadium was inaugurated with a match against Victoria Hamburg in front of an enthusiastic crowd. Club President, Wilhelm Koch, led the formalities although the opening ceremony was used as a propaganda event by the NSDAP.

In 1936, former FC St. Pauli player, Otto Wolff (see biography at the end of this chapter) was appointed as an economic adviser to the Hamburg region. As such, he oversaw the confiscation of Jewish properties and their handover to Germans.

In 1937, approximately 15,000 Jewish people still resided in Hamburg despite continuing oppression and tightening of restrictions. Despite this ongoing persecution, less than one fifth of the Jewish population had emigrated from Hamburg since 1935. From July 1938, all Jewish citizens were required to adopt Sara or Israel as an additional forename. In October of the same year, all passports belonging to Jewish people were stamped with a red 'J'.

On 9 November 1938 at 23:55, the local Gestapo headquarters received a telegram from Berlin. It signalled the start of a new level of oppression against the Jewish population throughout Germany. The operation became known as Kristallnacht (the Night of the Broken Glass). In Hamburg, the SS were uncontactable by telephone that evening, but the SA were alerted and began to gather outside the Rathausmarkt before breaking off into small groups and smashing windows and damaging Jewish-owned properties in the city. Due to the delay in communication, the most brutal attacks on Jewish property in Hamburg didn't take place until the late afternoon or evening on Thursday, 10 November . At about 19:00 that evening, the mortuary at the Jewish cemetery in Harburg was set on fire, with onlookers preventing the fire brigade from extinguishing the flames. The New Dammtor synagogue was also destroyed and Hamburg's main synagogue in Bornplatz was also set ablaze. A contemporary eyewitness told the *Hamburger Abendblatt* newspaper in an interview in 1988: "I saw the flames erupting from the Grindelhof synagogue. In front of it, a pile of Jewish prayer books and Torah scrolls were burning. I found the faces of the SA men, illuminated by the burning synagogue, most repulsive. I had the impression that the men were convinced that they were doing something particularly good." The Gestapo arrested 879 Jewish people in Hamburg during Kristallnacht.

Six months later, in the spring of 1939, orders were given to tear down the synagogue at Bornplatz as it had been badly damaged by fire during the November pogrom. The Jewish community were forced to remove the rubble at their own expense.

In June 1937, Reich Governor Kaufmann announced that Hamburg was to be one of five, newly created, *Führerstädte* (Führer cities). Under the plans, Hamburg was to become 'Elb-Manhattan' due to the number of planned skyscrapers that included the 'Gau-Hochhaus' a proposed 250-metre tower block on the banks of the Elbe.

These were the architectural plans for St. Pauli and the Elbe, but what of the occupants of the district? A study by sociologist Andreas Walther published in 1935, described St. Pauli as: "an area of decay of the most left-wing, radical parts of Hamburg" where "many people maintain a covert hatred against the government."

Joseph Goebbels was less charitable describing the residents of the district of St. Pauli as, "sub-humans all."

As a consequence of the plans to make Hamburg a Führer city, Deutsche Erd - und Steinwerke GmbH, an SS-owned company purchased the old brick factory in Neuengamme on the outskirts of the city with the purpose of resuming production using conscripted labour. Initially, the site was opened as a satellite of the concentration camp at Sachsenhausen with around 100 prisoners transferred to Neuengamme to begin the production of bricks needed for Hamburg's building projects.

By 1940 Neuengamme had become a concentration camp in its own right. Neuengamme and its satellite camps processed over 100,000 prisoners – making it the largest concentration camp in Northwest Germany. Over 42,000 people who had resided at the camps died, with over 26,000 souls perishing in the camps themselves and another 16,000 who died in the death marches and bombings that occurred in the final stages of the war. This figure included the 9,000 prisoners who had been removed from the main camp as part of the evacuation process that began on 20 April 1945 and who were held on four ships – including the Cap Arcona – in cramped conditions and without access to food or water. Many of these prisoners died from hunger or disease. British Intelligence concluded the ships were bound for Norway and were full of retreating troops and Nazi officials. On 3 May 1945, the British bombed the ships killing the majority of those onboard – hundreds of dead bodies were washed ashore in the days that followed.

Interviewed in 1983, Walter Felgner, Second Officer of one the ships (the Thielbek) recounted the arrival of prisoners aboard his doomed vessel: "And then the people came. We knew there were concentration camps in Germany. I believe almost everyone knew that [...] But what we didn't know was how these people looked. That was a shock for us [...] There were people that were only skin and bones."

As Allied bombing raids on Hamburg became more frequent, Jewish people were forced to vacate their properties so that they could house those Germans who had been made homeless by the bombing. In 1940, Governor Karl Kaufman had ordered the deportation of all Jews still living in Hamburg. In May of the same year, deportation of Sinti and Roma people from Hamburg also commenced. Much later, in May 1944, the Gestapo also carried out mass raids on St. Pauli's Chinese community, arresting 130 people.

In July 1943, 'Operation Gomorrah' began (a detailed recount of the destruction can be found in *Pirates, Punks & Politics* Chapter 2). The bombardment of the city lasted until 3 August. During that time, it is estimated that 37,000 people were killed and 180,000 injured. Over half of Hamburg's residential buildings were destroyed.

As documented above, in the spring of 1945, SS Officers began to evacuate the concentration camp at Neuengamme in a bid to cover up their crimes. However, on 20 April 1945, twenty Jewish children were found hanged in a cellar at Bullenhuser Damm. It was later discovered that they had been subjected to a series of horrendous medical tests. The school on the street had operated as an additional facility for the Neuengamme camp. Just thirteen days after this horrific discovery, on 3 May 1945, Governor Kaufmann handed the city over to British control making Hamburg the last major German city to surrender.

Hamburg and its population had suffered immeasurably during the war. The city lay in ruins – ariel photographs from the time have an apocalyptic feel, with most buildings raised to the ground. Over 900,000 people were made homeless as a result of the Allied bombing raids. When the city was liberated by British troops it was in ruins and its people hungry.

Hamburg would, of course, recover but it would take time and the National Socialist regime and the events of World War Two would cast a long and dark shadow over the city and its inhabitants.

Beyond the requestion of FC St. Pauli's stadium for the "Blood and Soil" horticultural show in 1935 and the briefest of outlines of the club's on-the-field performance during the Third Reich, there is not much new information that relates directly to the club and its relationship with the Nazi regime in the above summary of Hamburg's war. However, the second part of this chapter takes seven individual members of FC St. Pauli and their experience (and involvement) of life under National Socialism.

Otto and Paul Lang

In the spring of 1933, after being expelled from SV St. Georg, the Jewish brothers Otto and Paul Lang lobbied FC St. Pauli to form a rugby department within the club. They were successful and the St. Pauli rugby department was established in March 1933. Otto and Paul Lang were both members of the team when they played their first ever game against Eimsbütteler TV on 3 September 1933.

In December 1934, an order by the Reich Sports Leader required Paul Lang to stop his sports teacher training and forbade him to work as a coach.

In October 1935, FC St. Pauli celebrated its 25th Year Anniversary. There is no mention of Otto and Paul Lang in the commemorative journal, nor do they feature in a team photograph published in the autumn of 1934. It would appear the brothers' departure from St. Pauli was almost as swift as their arrival – there is no further surviving archival evidence of their involvement with the club after this point.

Following this, the brothers' futures took very different paths. Before the end of 1935 – and following a confrontation with a member of the SS – Otto Lang left Germany and headed to Antwerp. From there he travelled by boat to Panama. Eventually, Otto Lang was granted entry into the United States and settled in New York.

By contrast, his brother remained in Hamburg with his 'Aryan' wife, Lieselotte. In May 1942, both Paul Lang and his wife were moved to the 'Judenhaus' in Heinrich-Barth-Straße 17, under orders from the Gestapo. In February 1945, with the war entering its closing stages, Paul Lang was deported to the Theresienstadt 'family camp' in Czechoslovakia. Theresienstadt itself formed a section of Auschwitz-Birkenau but had only been established in September 1943 in an apparent attempt to disguise the mass executions of prisoners taking place at Auschwitz. Those prisoners transferred to Theresienstadt were instructed to write letters to family members not yet deported to help cover up the genocide. Three months later, the camp was liberated by the Soviets and Paul Lang was able to return to Hamburg. Both brothers – who spent the remainder of their lives on different continents – died in 2003. They are commemorated and remembered on a memorial stone that sits outside the main entrance to the Millerntor Stadion.

That the brothers – who had been expelled from SV St. Georg in 1933 – were able to join St. Pauli and establish the club's rugby department that same year, could be an indication that St. Pauli were taking a more tolerant approach to Jewish membership of their organisation. However, Otto and Paul Lang are the only recorded example of this stance and, after late-1933, evidence of the brothers' continued involvement with the rugby department dries up.

Wilhelm Koch

Perhaps the most prominent and widely known of members of FC St. Pauli with a connection to the National Socialist regime is former President, Wilhelm Koch. After all, until as recently as 1998 the Millerntor Stadion was known as the 'Wilhelm Koch Stadion'.

Koch was born in Hamburg on 13 February 1900. He became a member of the club at the age of twelve – first as an active member of the gymnastic department and, later, as a goalkeeper.

By 1922 Wilhelm Koch was working for two Jewish businessmen, Emil Arensberg and Jaques Sekkel who ran an import/export business dealing in animal skins and furs.

In 1931, FC St. Pauli president, Henry Rehder moved to Berlin triggering an election. Koch put himself forward for the vacant position and won by 55-37 votes despite the former chairman backing the opposing candidate. However, Koch did have the support of another influential club official, Otto Wolff, who was already a member of the Nazi Party by this time.

Two years later, Koch's position was consolidated following a re-election by members and approval from the Commissioner of the Reich Sport as 'Club Leader'.

In 1937, despite it not yet being mandatory Koch joined the Nazi Party. However, aside from his membership application, the surviving records in Koch's NSDAP file are empty. This would suggest that he took part in no additional party or political activities. This was seemingly confirmed by members of FC St. Pauli that his membership of the NSDAP 'was never felt' inside the club and that he never wore the party badge. However, he must've had a degree of influence and good relationships with those in power. It is noted that under the Third Reich, FC St. Pauli continued to prosper at a time when many other local clubs ceased to exist.

Koch continued to benefit from Nazi policies outside of his involvement with the club. In 1933, along with his colleague, Hugo Scharff, Koch took control of Arensberg & Sekkel benefitting from the 'aryanisation' of Jewish businesses. Correspondence supports the fact that he remained on good terms with the original owners who had fled to Sweden.

Immediately following the end of the war, in 1945, Wilhelm Koch was relinquished of his role as 'Club Leader' due to his membership of the Nazi Party.

However, on 18 June 1948, he was re-elected as president of FC St. Pauli – a position he held until his death in 1969. On his death, he was owed a substantial amount of money by the club.

However, his heirs decided to waive the repayment of money in return for the Millerntor Stadion being named the 'Wilhelm Koch Stadion'. The ground remained named after Koch until 1998, when members voted for it to revert to Millerntor-Stadion following the publication of René Marten's research that made known Koch's membership of the NSDAP.

Dr Otto Wolff

In 1920, after moving to Hamburg with his family, Otto Wolff joined FC St. Pauli. Five years later he made his debut for the first team. He played for the club over a ten-year period from 1925 to 1935. Playing on the right wing, Wolff won the District League in 1929/30. He returned to play for St. Pauli again in 1939/40 but only briefly.

In 1928, following the completion of his A-Levels, Wolff began his career by taking a job working for the German Railways. On 1 December 1930, Wolff joined the Nazi Party. He continued his studies and eventually gained a doctorate in economics.

In 1936, Wolff was appointed as a clerk to Carlo Otte, the economic advisor to the Gau in Hamburg (the Nazi Party organised Germany into administrative districts known as 'Gau'). He was subsequently involved in the programme of 'aryanisation' of Jewish businesses. When the Jewish heritage of a company owner was doubted, Wolff is reported to have suggested that the NSDAP official in question take a closer look at his ears to see that he really was a Jew. Wolff personally benefited from the 'aryanisation' process, purchasing a building in Harvestehude that was confiscated from its Jewish owners. He went on to purchase another building in the same manner.

In 1940, Wolff was promoted to acting Gau economic advisor. As part of this appointment, he became a member of the SS where he was given the rank of Lieutenant Colonel. He continued to gain prominence, eventually becoming the Director of the Economy for the entire Hamburg region. As such, he was heavily involved in the organisation of forced labour and a role that necessitated working closely with the commander of the concentration camp at Neuengamme.

At the end of the war, Wolff was taken into custody. He was released from prison in 1948 and returned to FC St. Pauli who welcomed him back.

Wolff was described by Hamburg's Senator of Culture in 1951 as being: "One of the worst and most brutal henchmen of absolute anti-Semitism in the economy." However, over 20 years later in 1972, he was described in an FC St. Pauli journal in positive terms: "In the last war, in particular, FC St. Pauli would feel the very helpful and beneficial hands of our dear Otto."

When he died on 8 November 1991, he was given a glowing obituary in the FC St. Pauli newspaper. However, in November 2010, members voted to rescind Wolff's golden club badge of honour. His engagement with the Nazi regime and his involvement in the 'aryanisation' of Jewish businesses is beyond doubt.

Walter Koehler

Walter Koehler joined FC St. Pauli in his early teens. He played football, later becoming a referee and youth coach. In 1932, Koehler became a member of the paramilitary, Sturmabteilung (SA) in order to conduct sports operations (coaching) within an SA unit in Hamburg.

A year later, at the recommendation of club leader Wilhelm Koch, Koehler took over the post of youth leader within FC St. Pauli. He continued to oversee the youth department when they became affiliated with the Hamburg division of Hitler Youth in 1938.

However, in February 1939, the 'Gaunachrichten' newspaper published an article that criticised discipline within FC St. Pauli. It is thought that Koehler himself championed the article (although he denied this). It included the provocative question: 'How long will FC St. Pauli continue to allow individual club members of young age to play cards and table tennis, to smoke cigarettes and doing pub politics in the clubhouse?'

Of all the groups that resisted the compulsory membership of Hitler Youth, perhaps the most famous were the 'Swing Youth'. This was the name given to the many young people who continued to enjoy 'Swing' dance and music (a movement that began in the Afro-American communities in Harlem in the 1920s), despite its official ban that had come into force in 1938. There was an active Swing scene in Hamburg who met regularly at the ice-skating rink on the Heiligeneistfeld or in Café Heinze on the Reeperbahn. It was also rumoured that future member of FC St. Pauli's 'Wunderelf', Harald Stender was a member of a Swing group. It is only conjecture, but it might have been fear of a Swing group with connections to FC St. Pauli that led Walter Koehler to leak information of activities within the clubhouse to Gau News. As a result of the article in the Gau News, Wilhelm Koch relieved Koehler of his duties at the club. Walter Koehler had no further involvement with FC St. Pauli. He died in 1975.

Karl Miller

Karl Miller was born in Hamburg in October 1913, the son of Karl Miller Sr., whose butcher's shop was located in Wexstraße in the neighbouring district of Neustadt.

In 1926 Miller's school team won the Hamburg school championship with an 8:1 victory over Barmbek. As a result of his exploits in schools' football, Karl Miller joined the FC St. Pauli youth set up, but in secret, as his father did not approve of his football activities. Legend has it that it was only after a victory over HSV that he learned of his son's involvement with FC St. Pauli youth team. In 1933, Miller made first team debut.

In 1939, after the outbreak of war, Miller was drafted into the Luftwaffe as an ant-aircraft gunner, stationed in Hamburg. On 6 April 1940, he made his international debut for Germany in the 7:0 win over Hungary.

In the early stages of the war Miller was transferred to Saxony. His commanding officer – recognising his footballing ability – stationed him at an anti-aircraft position sited on the roof of Dresden SC's grandstand. Miller played for Dresden SC winning the German Cup in both 1940 and 1941. In 1942, he was used as an extra in the propaganda film 'The Big Game'. A year later, Miller was posted to Russia. After returning to Hamburg on leave, people at the Air Force Sports Cub ensured that Miller did not have to return to Russia and was instead stationed at the flak tower on Heiligeneistfeld.

In 1945, after the peaceful transfer of power in Hamburg, Karl Miller returned home to Wexstraße. Once again, he worked in his father's butcher's shop. It is reported that he was able to tempt players from across Germany with the promise of sausages and meat (at a time where they were scarce) and as such was responsible for assembling FC St. Pauli's 'Wunderelf' side that competed for the German championship (although never won it) between 1948-51. Miller was appointed an honorary member of the club in 1966. Sadly, he died just one year later, aged 54.

Herbert Müller

In the early 1920s, a young Müller regularly played street football around St. Pauli and Altona with his friends Günter Peine and Harald Stender.

In 1931, Herbert showed an interest in joining the Hitler Youth. But his politically left-wing father gave him a pair of football boots and instead Müller joined the FC St. Pauli youth team. Müller is quoted as saying: "My dad did it right. At St. Pauli, he distracted me."

In 1937 Müller started work at the Blohm & Voss shipyard. Eventually he progressed to work as a draughtsman, focussing on motor parts. During the war he worked on technical drawings for battleships, including the Bismarck as well as a variety of U-boats. Due to his specialist skills, he was able to evade military conscription on five occasions.

Despite laws that stipulated you could only play competitive sports if you were a signed-up member of Hitler Youth, Müller did not comply and maintained his interest in the sport through training and street football, until he turned 18.

The 1938/39 season saw Müller join the FC St. Pauli first team, initially as a substitute. He ended up making over 150 appearances for FC St. Pauli. In July 1944 Müller was finally conscripted, he served as a loader and driver for flak-cannons. At the end of the war, with his unit disbanded, Müller removed his uniform and walked home from the Netherlands to Hamburg.

After the war, Müller continued to be involved with football. He completed his coaching licence in 1954 and worked as a volunteer for various clubs in Hamburg. He was responsible for discovering St. Pauli legend Holger Stanislawski and German international, Stefan Effenberg.

Peter Jürs

Peter Jürs – the son of an innkeeper – was born in Hamburg in 1895. He played youth football for FC St. Pauli. Later in life, he became part of the youth team management and even had a short stint as treasurer.

He had been injured in World War One, suffering permanent damage to his left hand which meant he couldn't return to his old job as a printer.

In 1937, he began a new job in military administration. In this new position he began to forge documents that enabled many local people to evade conscription. In June 1940 he was arrested on suspicion of document forgery. At his trial in 1941 he was initially sentenced to death, although the penalty was later reduced to 15 years in prison. In 1943 he was transferred to the Neuengamme concentration camp on the outskirts of Hamburg. He remained in the camp but was evacuated shortly before the end of the war. He was among the prisoners transferred to the ship 'Cap Arkona' that was later bombed by the RAF – Jürs was one of the 4,600 people to be killed in the attack which took place just five days before the end of the war.

–

These seven individual stories show how each person's experience of National Socialist varied. They remain just that – individual stories – they can't be used to generalise about FC St. Pauli's role in the regime. Within this handful of biographies, there are stories of compliance and resistance to the Nazi regime. Some such as Dr Otto Wolf and Walter Koehler personally benefitted and ideologically believed in the Nazification of Hamburg. Others, like Peter Jürs, resisted.

Of course, it was the city's Jewish population – including Otto and Paul Lang – that suffered most. It is believed that over 7,800 Jewish residents of Hamburg died during the Holocaust, although – sadly – only 6,150 of those names could be determined. In 2017, a memorial was unveiled at the site of the former Hannoverscher Bahnhof train station that transported 8,071 Jewish and Roma residents of the city who were sent to ghettos and concentration camps between 1940 and 1945. Their suffering will never be forgotten.

Football. Escape. Exile.

Football. Escape. Exile. is the title of the exhibition honouring the life of Max Kulik. It was researched and written by a team from

FC St. Pauli-Museum which included Celina Albertz, Christopher Radke and Thomas Glöy. What follows below is a summary of their research.

Max Kulik was a Jewish physician and footballer who was a member of Hamburg-St. Pauli Turnverein, the direct predecessor of FC St. Pauli. The meticulous research into Kulik's life is of particular interest as his connection with St. Pauli predates – quite considerably – that of Otto and Paul Lang, previously the first players of Jewish heritage with an active involvement in the club (in the rugby department) as confirmed by historical archives.

Max Kulik was born in St. Pauli in 1898. Back then, the district was cramped with over 70,000 people (twice as many as today) living in densely populated blocks. Kulik's father was a craftsman and as such earned enough that he and his family could live in the north of the district removed from the squalor and bustle of the docks and the Reeperbahn. At the time, just 2.58 percent of the population of the St. Pauli district were Jewish.

In 1909, Max Kulik's older brother, Leon, played for Hamburg-St. Pauli Turnverein in the first friendly match at the Millerntor against FC Schwerin. In the summer of 1913, the 15-year-old Max Kulik joined the football section of Hamburg-St. Pauli Turnverein. He made his way quickly from the youth team to the reserves, playing at right-half. In March 1914 he was called up to the first team for the first time. With the outbreak of war in August 1914, many of the older players joined the army. This further cemented Kulik's position in the first team. The following May, the team achieved promotion to the B-Class with Max scoring the final goal in a 4:0 win over Hermannia Veddel that sealed the promotion. His commitment extended beyond the pitch – Max was a regular attendee at club committee meetings. From December 1916 to March 1917, Kulik's family home in Annenstraße even served as the official address of the club's football department – Max was organising the team's fixtures from home.

Having turned 18, Kulik registered at medical school in Berlin and signed up for military service. In June 1917, Max Kulik was transferred to the Western Front spending that summer and autumn as a grenadier in the trenches. But in the October, thanks to his medical studies, he became a medic and spent the rest of the war moving from field hospital to field hospital – relatively removed from frontline action but having to deal with a constant flow of soldiers suffering horrific injuries. In November 1918, the war ended and the drafted players from Hamburg-St. Pauli Turnverein slowly returned to Hamburg. Of the 60 or so players who went to war from the club, 30 did not return but both Max and Leon Kulik were amongst those that did. A total of around two million German soldiers lost their lives in The Great War – among them 12,000 men of Jewish faith.

In 1920, Max Kulik enrolled at the University of Hamburg, returning to live with his parents in St. Pauli. However, he did not return to play for Hamburg-St. Pauli Turnverein. Instead, he joined Eimsbütteler TV. This turned out to be a successful sporting decision. Max was a regular starter for Eimsbüttel and was widely regarded as one of the most talented players in the city – something that was confirmed by his selection for a Hamburg representative side in a city match against Kiel. Kulik also played when Eimsbütteler TV beat Austrian champions Rapid Vienna 2:1 in July 1921.

However, just a few months later, on 27 November 1921, Max Kulik learned of his father's death whilst playing a match. He left the field and went to be with his family. He never played for the Eimsbütteler first team again. Further tragedy struck the Kulik family in July 1923 when Max's older brother Leon died unexpectedly at the age of 36. In November of the same year, Max Kulik qualified as a doctor and began work at a hospital in Sternschanze. In May 1926, he opened his own practice in Eimsbüttel.

Following the conclusion of the First World War, the social climate changed significantly. Large parts of the population blamed

Jewish people for the Germany's defeat in the war, antisemitism was on the rise.

On 30 January 1933 Adolf Hitler was appointed as Chancellor. The antisemitism that had been bubbling away was now state doctrine. The government-sanctioned terror campaign against the Jewish population began on 1 April 1933. There were nationwide riots targeting Jewish businesses. Almost overnight, Max Kulik lost most of his non-Jewish patients at his practice in Eimsbüttel.

Sport was impacted too. Slowly, sports clubs across the country stopped admitting new Jewish members and started to exclude existing ones. In April 1933, Max Kulik wrote his last article for the Eimsbütteler TV club newspaper and by 1934 he was forced to leave the club.

In 1935, several Nazi functionaries moved into the building where Max was running his medical practice. One of them – Ernst Jensen – who Kulik later described as a "very bitter antisemite" did everything he could to harm Kulik's business. On 26 August 1936 in Nice, Kulik married his French-born wife Louise Charlotte Hübner. Such marriages between Jewish and non-Jewish people had been banned in Germany since September 1935.

By 1937, Max and his wife were already planning their escape to France. This was a complicated and expensive process, the so-called *Reichfluchtsteuer* (Reich escape tax) costing the couple 15,000 Reichsmarks.

On 4 February 1938, Max Kulik was taken into 'protective custody' by the Gestapo and taken to the Fuhlsbüttel concentration camp. It was only the fact that he had a valid visa to France that he was released – on the condition that he left Germany immediately.

On 1 April 1938, the couple fled to France by car. However, they found work hard to come by as to practice as a doctor in Paris required him to repeat parts of his studies.

The outbreak of the Second World War on 3 September 1939 saw Max Kulik along with 10,000 other 'enemy aliens' interned in camps across the French capital. The only way out of the camps was to 'volunteer' for the French Foreign Legion, something Kulik undertook and that resulted in his posting to North Africa. However, this was only temporary as the armistice signed between France and Germany in June 1940 saw the demobilisation of the Foreign Legion. It is not known how Kulik returned to France, but in the spring of 1941, he and his wife were trying to get a visa for the United States via the 'Marseille-Martinique corridor' – the last legal escape route from Vichy France.

On 6 May 1941, Max Kulik boarded the SS Winnipeg without his wife who had not received her visa. Later that month the SS Winnipeg was intercepted by a Dutch warship and diverted to Trinidad. After a few weeks, those with valid visas were able to continue their journey to New York – this included Max Kulik.

In January 1943, Max Kulik opened his own medical office in Manhattan, by this time Max's marriage to Louise had broken up. She had escaped to Baltimore via Portugal and was remarried by the summer of 1945. Max's younger brother Siegfried – who had settled with his family in Gloversville, New York State – died by suicide in 1946. The Kulik's had also lost their mother in 1942 who had remained behind in Hamburg.

Max applied and was eventually granted US citizenship and split his time between New York and his holiday home in East Hampton. He died in New York on 8 September 1959, aged 61.

With so little known about Jewish members of FC St. Pauli and its predecessor Hamburg-St. Pauli Turnverein, each biography that is researched sheds new light on both the early years of the club and the contribution of those people of Jewish heritage. This work is important; raising both historical understanding and contemporary awareness of the suffering and persecution faced by Jewish people during the Nazi regime.

With antisemitism, racism and far-right violence on the rise in Germany and across the world it is important to recognise and learn from the horrors of the past. This is especially important as we begin to lose the generation that were the last witnesses and survivors of National Socialism.

It seems prescient to finish with the words of Max Kulik's niece Ruth: "All those Holocaust deniers, they're just waiting for the last of us witnesses to die."

It is the job of all of us to keep their memories alive and to never again allow society to succumb to the horrors of fascism.

Chapter 18:
Derbysieger! Derbysieger! Hey! Hey!

Derby games form the emotional epicentre of watching football. The Hamburg derby is no different: it is a conduit for the city's sporting emotions. In recent years, the days and weeks leading up to the Hamburg derby have become increasingly fractious with fans from both sides of the divide ratcheting up the tension through proactive graffiti, physical attacks on rival fans and even the hanging of effigies from bridges.

The two clubs not only represent different districts within the city of Hamburg (some would argue that Hamburger SV are based outside of the city and are, thus, a team of the suburbs) but also a very different supporter demographic. HSV are the storied club with a trophy cabinet bursting with national and European trophies. FC St. Pauli's trophy cabinet remains the domain of regional league titles. HSV are judged by their achievements, FC St. Pauli defined by their activism. Historically, the rivalry hasn't always been as intense. In the late 1970s and early '80s many HSV fans would cross the city to watch St. Pauli games at the Millerntor when their team was playing elsewhere in Germany. Watching a city's two sides was common amongst football fans until large numbers of fans began to travel to away games in the late 1970s – it was common for those living in Manchester to watch both City and United, the same was true on Merseyside.

Importantly, since *Pirates, Punks & Politics* was published in 2014, HSV have lost their status as the only German club to have been a permanent fixture in the Bundesliga. The clock at the club's Volksparkstadion that signified the number of years, days, hours, minutes and seconds that the club had been in the Bundesliga since the league's inception in August 1963 finally stopped ticking on Sunday 12 May 2018 after 54 years, 261 days, 0 hours, 36 minutes and 2 seconds. The home fans had bought the club an extra 15-minutes of time by letting off a series of pyro that blanketed the end of the pitch in front of the Nordtribüne in a thick covering of black smoke causing the referee to take the teams into the dressing rooms. As a football fan, you could understand their supporters' frustration and disappointment, but the TV images beamed around the world just seemed to confirm that some HSV supporters had decided to go down disgracefully. The Hamburger SV team had done their bit on the final day of the season, beating Borussia Mönchengladbach 2:1. Unfortunately, avoiding relegation relied on Wolfsburg losing at home to 1. FC Köln. At the interval in that game, there was still hope as Wolfsburg and Köln were tied 1:1. However, the home side racked up three further goals in the second period to defeat Köln 4:1 and condemn HSV to Bundesliga 2.

HSV had flirted with relegation from the top division on so many occasions in recent years – it almost felt like they couldn't be relegated. But in 2018 they finally succumbed. The stadium clock was eventually dismantled as the club set about looking to the future and trying to return to the Bundesliga. Most onlookers probably anticipated an immediate return. However, five seasons later – as of 2022/23 – the once proud champions of Europe were still languishing in Germany's second tier. Indeed, the glory years of the 1970s and '80s are starting to feel like a very long time ago. Even Hamburger SV's last silverware – the 2003 League Cup – is covered in a thick layer of metaphorical dust that has accumulated over the intervening two decades (it is also a trophy that has since been abolished).

The by-product of HSV's longer than expected stay in Bundesliga 2 has been an increase in the frequency of FC St. Pauli v HSV derbies. Until Hamburger SV's 2018 relegation derby games had been few and far between only coinciding with FC St. Pauli's rare sojourns into the German top-flight. In the five years between September 2018 and April 2023, the two teams played each other ten times.

For St. Pauli fans, the renewed opportunity to take on their local rivals was always going to be an exciting prospect. However, whatever way you tried to interpret the statistics they could never favour FC St. Pauli.

If we stop the clock at the 100th competitive encounter between St. Pauli and Hamburger SV (a 0:0 draw at the Volksparkstadion on 30 September 2018) we get a handy percentage breakdown of the results over almost a century of matches. If you are an FC St. Pauli fan it doesn't make great reading: Hamburger SV victories number 66%; FC St. Pauli win just 19% with 15% of games drawn.

The rivalry didn't begin well either. The first ever encounter on 7 December 1919 resulted in a 9:0 victory for Hamburger SV. The game took place at the sports ground in Rothenbaum (which remained home to HSV's amateur side until its demolition in 1997). At the time, the St. Pauli side were still a division of St. Pauli Turn-Verein (St. Pauli TV) as a separate FC St. Pauli football department was not established until 1924. St. Pauli TV didn't fare much better in the next meeting of the two sides – three years later – on 15 January 1922 in the Alster District League. They lost 7:0.

In fact, St. Pauli lost the first fourteen encounters with HSV conceding 85 goals and scoring only eight. It wasn't until the 1930/31 season – competing in the Hamburg Oberliga – that St. Pauli recorded their first win over their local rivals – a narrow 1:0 victory at the Rothenbaum sports ground. Typically, FC St. Pauli wins ended up being like buses – having waited 14 games and 11 years for their first victory – they did the double over HSV, beating them 2:1 in the return Oberliga fixture on 21 December 1930. However, although Hamburger SV lost twice to their neighbours, they went on to win the North German Football Championship that season. St. Pauli, despite finishing sixth in the ten-team, Hamburg Oberliga won a play-off game against Eimsbüttel TV to qualify for the last 16 of the Championship where they duly lost 3:4 at home to Lübecker BV Phönix.

Hamburger SV continued to dominate during the National Socialist regime including during the war years when regional league was further sub-divided into three smaller divisions. However, FC St. Pauli's record win over their rivals did occur during this period – an 8:1 away victory played in front of around 4,000 spectators on 3 October 1943.

As football began to reorganise after the war, St. Pauli recorded some tangible success in relation to their neighbours. During the 1946/47, in the Stadtliga Hamburg, a 3:2 away win and a 2:2 home draw contributed to St. Pauli beating HSV to the league title by three points.

It was the start of a period where FC St. Pauli, whilst not exactly eclipsing the achievements of HSV, were able to at least punch their weight. Even more remarkably, legend has it that it was all to do with sausages. Whilst this was an over-simplification, sausages, meatballs and other sundry meat products did play a part in the club's post-war success.

The story centres around Hamburg-born Karl Miller and his butcher shop-owning father Karl Miller Senior. Karl had made his St. Pauli debut in 1935. During the war he was stationed in Dresden where he began playing his football with Dresden SC and being part of their Tschammerpokal's (predecessor to the DFB Pokal) winning team two years running. However, after the war, he was keen to return to Hamburg (and thus out of the Russian-controlled zone), returning to live above his father's butcher's shop. From there, with the promise of a plentiful supply of meat in a country where food was scarce and heavily rationed, Miller was able to persuade many former teammates to join him in the city. Amongst those who followed Miller to Hamburg were former international Alfred 'Coppi' Beck and future national coach Helmut Schön. Another of St. Pauli's favourite sons, Harald Stender substantiated the myth in the documentary *Mythos of St. Pauli*. Stender said, "He told me once that I should come to the shop. Karl Miller and Karl senior were both butchers. And when I came to the shop Karl took me to this little room at the back of the store. And he gave me sausages."

From these unlikely beginnings perhaps FC St. Pauli's most famous side were born – 'Die Wunder-Elf' or 'The Miracle Eleven'.

The 1947/48 Oberliga Nord season saw FC St. Pauli record 22 wins, two draws and just three defeats. Incredibly, Hamburger SV's record was identical. St. Pauli had won 1:0 in the away game but lost 2:0 in their new stadium on the *Heiligengeistfeld. On 2 May 1948, the two teams met at a neutral venue (SC Victoria's Stadion Hoheluft) in a match to decide the championship. Despite the game being goalless at the break, Hamburger SV emerged 2:1 winners. Just over a month later, on 13 June 1948, the two sides met again at Station Hohrluft, this time in the final of the British Zone Championship with HSV running out comfortable winners, 6:1 in front of a crowd of over 30,000 spectators.*

However, second place in the Oberliga Nord was still good enough for FC St. Pauli to qualify for the first National Championship since the Second World War. The club then faced late heartbreak in the semi-final against 1. FC Nürnberg, losing to a goal in extra-time. It was a golden period for the St. Pauli – at least in terms of reaching the National Championships, a feat they managed each season between 1948 and 1951. Although the club enjoyed further successes against HSV in the Oberliga Nord during this period, they once again found themselves defeated in another championship-deciding game on 22 May 1949, this time losing 5:3 in Altona – after the two sides once again finished the season level on points.

There was a notable 5:0 victory for FC St. Pauli at the Millerntor on 6 April 1951. It was a game where over 30,000 people crammed into the stadium. As a result of the over-crowding there was trouble between supporters: fans stormed the pitch, and many were injured. St. Pauli's five goals were all scored in the second half. However, in the first-half, St. Pauli had a bizarre goal ruled out. Supporters had spilled over the boundary wall onto the perimeter of the pitch, one supporter returned a ball that was going out for a goal-kick into the path of Alfred 'Coppi' Beck who gratefully fired it past the HSV keeper. The referee, not realising what had happened, gave the goal before a discussion with his linesman had the decision overturned.

The two rivals continued to face each other twice a season in the Oberliga Nord until the formation of the Bundesliga at the start of the 1963/64 campaign. HSV were accepted into the newly formed national league – St. Pauli were not because the league didn't want two teams from the same city. It represented something of a parting of ways for the local rivals. They wouldn't meet again for nine years until they were drawn together in the preliminary round of the DFB League Cup at the start of the 1972/73 season. Normal service was quickly resumed with HSV beating St. Pauli 4:1 at the Millerntor although some respectability was restored when St. Pauli kept the game goalless in the return-leg at the Volksparkstaion.

Another five years elapsed before the next Hamburg city derby. However, it did become perhaps the most famous derby of them all (at least in the brown and white half of the city). Following FC St. Pauli's historic first promotion to the Bundesliga in May 1977, the two teams met at the Volksparkstadion on 3 September 1977 in front of a crowd of 48,000 fans. It was a true David versus Goliath moment. HSV were the holders of the European Cup Winners' Cup, their team contained the German midfield legend, Felix Magath and England's own 'Mighty Mouse' – Kevin Keegan.

Franz Gerber opened the scoring on the half-hour, slotting the ball past Rudi Kargus in the HSV goal to stun the Volksparkstadion into silence. The visitors then rode their luck to keep Hamburger SV at bay, before Wolfgang Kulka fired a rebounded shot into the net on 87 minutes to seal the victory for St. Pauli. Maybe it was fitting that St. Pauli who would become Hamburg's punk team carried out their landmark smash and grab raid on their big city rivals in 1977 of all years (although some punk purists would argue the scene was already over by then, whilst the common consensus is that St. Pauli's own punk following didn't begin to emerge at the Millerntor until the 1980s). However, the 2:0 win at the Volksparkstaion in September 1977 was something of a highwater mark for the club who lost the return fixture (also played at HSV's ground) 3:2 the following January and not long after found themselves consigned to relegation back to Bundesliga 2.

It wasn't to be known at the time, but FC St. Pauli wouldn't play against HSV at the Millerntor Stadion for an incredible 38 years. The club's continued to meet each other during that period, whenever St. Pauli experienced their – brief – flirtations with the Bundesliga. Although there was also the humiliating 6:0 defeat at the Volksparkstadion in the DFB Cup on 19 November 1986 (HSV went on to win the cup that season, beating Stuttgart Kickers in the final).

St. Pauli's longest stay in the German top-flight lasted for three seasons between 1988/89 and 1990/91. They were promoted once more in 1995 and survived for two seasons – 1995/96 and 1996/97. The club also experienced a solitary season in the Bundesliga in 2001/02. Incredibly, all the derby games played during that period were hosted at HSV's Volksparkstadion. FC St. Pauli were beset with financial problems during these years and looked to maximise their gate-revenue for their matches against HSV by playing them at a bigger venue. Security reasons also played their part – hooliganism was still a major problem in German football in the 1980s and '90s, with St. Pauli fans' overt anti-fascist stance providing a flashpoint with right-wing fans from other clubs (including HSV). Surrendering home advantage against their local rivals may have brought in some extra revenue, but the on-the-field results were predictably disastrous. Of the 14 consecutive derby games played at the Volksparkstadion between 1978 and 2002, St. Pauli lost nine and drew five. There were no victories on enemy turf. In 1995, HSV and St. Pauli also met in the final of a pre-season tournament in Bavaria. Competing for the impressively large – in physical terms, if not stature – Biller Cup, the two sides played-out a 1:1 draw. St. Pauli lost 7:6 on penalties in a game more remembered for the fact that St. Pauli manager, Uli Maslo, had bricks and concrete thrown at him by HSV supporters.

However, FC St. Pauli can – for the foreseeable future – claim bragging rights in the most recent set of top-flight Hamburg derbies. The two clubs came face-to-face again after St. Pauli were promoted to the top division for the 2010/11 campaign. By this point, the club were on a more secure financial footing and the Millerntor Stadion itself had two new stands. Finally, St. Pauli were able to host the derby again. The atmosphere that greeted the teams was electric with confetti and streamers raining down from the Südkurve. The game was tense, with Carsten Rothenbach going closest for the home side early on, when he fired a shot just wide of the post.

In the 77th minute, Fabian Boll received a pass inside the area and kept calm to fire this shot past Frank Rost in the Hamburg goal to put St. Pauli ahead. The clock counted down, the St. Pauli fans started to believe but, with two minutes left, the Croatian striker Mladen Petric unleashed an unstoppable shot from outside the box to equalise. The brown and white half of Hamburg was going to have to wait a little longer to claim another victory over their rivals.

Most observers didn't give St. Pauli much of a chance when they ventured across the city to the Volksparkstadion on Wednesday 16 February 2011. The game had already been re-scheduled once due to HSV suffering problems with their pitch and St. Pauli were in the familiar process of their slide towards the relegation places. The night before the postponed game, both sets of fans had clashed on the Reeperrbahn and in the surrounding streets, the atmosphere in the city was tense. For the re-arranged game, the visitors took to the field in their distinctive metallic-copper shirts (that could be turned inside out and worn as a more regular brown top) designed to commemorate the club's centenary. The team featured reserve goalkeeper Bene Pliquett – a fan of the club and thought to be a member of Ultrà Sankt Pauli. It was Pliquett that was the busier of the keepers on the night, going on to form an impenetrable barrier between the ball and his net. Victory was secured in the 59th minute with Gerald Asamoah etching his name in the history books nodding home a corner that had been flicked-on at the near post. Asamoah ran to the corner-flag to celebrate with his teammates and fans in that corner of the ground, a process that was repeated when the final whistle eventually sounded, and St. Pauli had claimed the three points. Perhaps the most iconic celebration of the night belonged to Bene Pliquett, as he donned a 'Derbysieger' t-shirt and karate-kicked the corner flag in a moment of sheer elation.

FC St. Pauli's imminent relegation meant that they would be able to keep the title of 'Derbysieger' for just over eight years. The next set of derby games would be played in a different division altogether.

The HSV clock had stopped, but their relegation to Bundesliga 2 in May 2018, meant that local hostilities were about to be more frequently renewed. The first Hamburg derby in the second tier of German football took place on 30 September 2018. The game – an HSV home fixture at the Volksparkstadion – finished goalless. As mentioned at the beginning of this chapter, the build-up to this latest round of derby games had a more sinister undercurrent to it.

The events surrounding the return fixture at the Millerntor on 10 March 2019 are discussed in detail in the next chapter, which also provides a good excuse to gloss over the score line: a comprehensive 4:0 away victory for HSV. But as fans trooped despondently out of the Millerntor having been thumped by their local rivals, it seemed unlikely that the team was about to embark on its most successful run of results against Hamburger SV in its history. At that stage, it was assumed that HSV would return automatically to the Bundesliga and that the derby would once again go on hiatus. It didn't turn out like that.

Hamburger SV developed an unfortunate knack of messing-up promotion from various positions of invincibility. Whether that involved capitulating spectacularly in the run-in after having led the table for much of the season or by scrapping into the relegation play-off match in 2021/22, going to Hertha Berlin and securing a 1:0 first-leg away victory, only to lose 2:0 in front of their own fans a week later (to make matters worse, managing Hertha was former HSV legend, Felix Magath).

What these missed promotions did mean was an extended run of derbies – five season's worth at the time of writing. And – for once – FC St. Pauli had the upper hand. On 16 September 2019, St. Pauli embarked on a five-game unbeaten streak against their rivals which included four wins and a draw. St. Pauli began their run winning 2:0 in front of a packed Millerntor. On 18 minutes, Marin Knoll crashed a header against the upright and Dimitrios Diamantakos reacted quickest to the rebound, diving to meet the ball and heading it over the line. It was Knoll who created the decisive second goal on 62 minutes, his cross forcing HSV defender, Rick van Drongelen to turn the ball into his own net.

Even more incredibly, the return game in front of 57,000 spectators at the Volksparkstadion also finished 2:0 to FC St. Pauli. Henk Veerman opened the scoring after twenty minutes, the big striker coolly chipping the keeper to send the 5,586 away fans into a state of delirium. Henk's derby goal and his all-round contribution to St. Pauli even resulted in a dog being named after him!

Just nine minutes after taking the lead St. Pauli doubled it! The ball broke to Matt Penney on the edge of the penalty area, and he sent a low shot curling into the far corner. Penney had a short but explosive spell at St. Pauli on loan from Sheffield Wednesday. He was sent-off on his debut and then became the first English player to score for St. Pauli in the Hamburg derby. The team from the banks of the Elbe had done the double over their illustrious rivals – Hamburg was truly 'Braun-Weiß'. At full-time, the players once again rushed to the segment of visiting fans in the corner of the stadium, celebrating profusely as the guest-block was ablaze with pyro.

The scene was to be very different the following season. When the teams met on a Friday night at the end of October 2020 at the Volksparkstadion, there were only 1,000 supporters in attendance. Covid-19 restrictions had hit. There were no away fans (officially) present, with empty blue seats providing a disheartening backdrop in the cavernous arena. The game swung back and forth like a pendulum. HSV took the lead early on before Rodrigo Zalazar fired home an equaliser on 35 minutes. The second half only really came to life in the closing stages when Simon Makienok toe-poked the ball past the HSV keeper to have those St. Pauli fans watching at home on their televisions dreaming of another win at the ground they refer to as Mordor. However, the lead lasted just two minutes with Simon Terrode getting his second of the game to leave honours even at the final whistle.

By the time of the return derby at the Millerntor in March 2021, the Covid situation had worsened, and no supporters were allowed inside the Millerntor for the Monday night game against HSV. The atmosphere was even more eerie than it had been at the previous match where the 1,000 or so HSV supporters were able to create some noise. It was left to our imagination to picture how a packed Millerntor would've exploded when Daniel-Kofi Kyereh fired home the winner two minutes from time. As it was, the television broadcast clearly captured the clink of the ball as it rattled the goalframe before it nestled in the back of the net. St. Pauli fans were left watching endless replays of both the goal and Kyereh's iconic summersault celebration.

The 2021/22 season saw St. Pauli extended their unbeaten run to five games, winning an exciting early season encounter 3:2

in August 2021. Crowds were slowly being allowed to return to football, with 10,003 spectators inside the Millerntor to witness Finn Ole Becker open the scoring after exchanging passes with Guido Burgstaller. Sonny Kittel levelled for the visitors just before the break, leaving the second half balanced on a knife edge.

Derby games are all about the emergence of new heroes and FC St. Pauli were about to add another to their pantheon in the lanky form of Simon Makienok. On 56 minutes the striker burst into the penalty area down the left side, cutting a low shot into the net from a tight angle. Two minutes later he repeated the trick, his brace firing the home side into a 3:1 lead. It is unclear how many dogs in the Hamburg area have been named Simon in his honour. HSV pulled a goal back on 77 minutes which added a degree of tension to the finale, but St. Pauli saw the game out – much to the delight of the restricted but vocal crowd inside the Millerntor. St. Pauli were five games unbeaten against their rivals.

Covid restrictions had tightened further by the return game at the Volksparkstadion on 21 January 2022. Only 3,000 fans watched as HSV claimed a 2:1 victory, coming from behind after Guido Burgstaller had opened the scoring for the visitors. St. Pauli's period of dominance was over, if only temporarily. The supporters had certainly enjoyed the period of three years where they could repeatedly chant, 'Derbysieger! Derbysieger! Hey! Hey!'

The 2022/23 season saw return of a sold-out Millerntor for the derby game on 14 October. After a series of summer departures that included all the recent derby goalscoring heroes – Finn Ole Becker (to 1899 Hoffenheim), Daniel-Kofi Kyereh (SC Freiburg), Simon Makienok (AC Horsens) and Guido Burgstaller (Rapid Wien) – St. Pauli fans could've been forgiven for wondering where the goals were going to come from. This was compounded by a shaky start to the season that left the club in the lower reaches of the 2. Bundesliga table, whilst rivals HSV blazed a trail at the top. It is fair to say that, going into the game, expectations were low, with the more pessimistic of the St. Pauli following fearing another home rout like the one HSV dished out in 2019. However, with the right attitude anything is possible in a Hamburg derby and manager Timo Schultz certainly had his players fired-up from the start. The first half was goalless, but the game's momentum swung in St. Pauli's favour when HSV defender Sebastian Schonlau pulled down Etienne Amenyido as he raced through on goal – red card! The away side would have to play the remaining hour with ten men.

The second half kicked off under a blanket of smoke as both sets of fans put on an impressive display of pyro as the teams re-emerged from the tunnel. The hosts took the lead when Eric Smith rose to head home from a corner on 61 minutes. The Millerntor erupted! A goal to the good and with a man advantage, St. Paul tormented the visitors and on 74 minutes Marcel Hartel side-footed home a deserved second goal. In the final minute, substitute David Otto met the ball under the crossbar to nod home a third, putting the icing on the cake of a convincing performance.

Unfortunately, events on the pitch were somewhat overshadowed by police violence outside the stadium prior to the match. Many people both at the Millerntor and following the build-up to the game online were first alerted to the brutal policing via a video circulating on *Twitter* that clearly showed two police officers pinning an individual to the floor, with one officer kneeling on the man's neck whilst rabbit punching him repeatedly in the kidneys. There is no excuse or justification for such an unmitigated violent response from the police. Police reports and those of the St. Pauli fans in the vicinity of the violence differ considerably – as you would expect. However, the fact that there were no visiting supporters in the area and the fact that this brutality took place outside the Fanladen on the Gegengerade only seems to confirm a massively prejudiced and unjust action on behalf of the police. It has subsequently come to light that the unit believed to be responsible for the violent attack on St. Pauli fans were a specialist riot unit (BFE) from the Blumberg Federal Police who have a reputation build on brutality. There is clearly something wrong with the authorities' approach to policing in the district, something that stretches back past the G20 to the Hafenstraße demonstrations in the 1980s and '90s. The fact that such flagrant abuses of power were caught on camera only reinforces the view amongst St. Pauli fans (and the wider left) that the police are an out-of-control instrument of state repression. The incidents also took the gloss of what had been a very impressive derby victory for St. Pauli – some things are more important than football. The return fixture at the Volksparkstadion in April 2023, was an entertaining goal-fest. St. Pauli stunned the home crowd taking the lead through Greek fullback Manolis Saliakas with HSV levelling just before the half-time break. The home team then accelerated into a 3:1 lead before Elias Saad pulled one back. HSV scored again before Jackson Irvine gave St. Pauli hope of a comeback with a headed goal. It wasn't to be – HSV hung on and claimed three points in a 4:3 victory.

Chapter 19:
The Toxic Masculinity of Derby Day (Match)

FC St. Pauli 0 Hamburger SV 4
Bundesliga 2
13:30, Sunday 10 March 2019, Millerntor Stadion

My first ever Hamburg derby. This is partly because I'm not a massive fan of derbies and the animosity that goes with them. Maybe this has something to do with my first ever derby experience – aged ten – when my dad took me to Kenilworth Road for Luton versus Watford on what I remember as being Boxing Day 1982 (a quick fact check has the date as 27th December 1982). We stood on the open terrace as bricks, coins and bits of broken concrete rained down on us from the adjacent section occupied by home fans. It was a miserable experience, compounded by a 1:0 loss to our arch-rivals. But the main reason this was my first St. Pauli/HSV derby was because the two sides had been in different divisions for so long – there hasn't been the opportunity.

It's been a long time – nearly a decade in fact – since the last derby at the Millerntor a 1:1 draw back in September 2010 where

Fabian Boll had fired the home side ahead before Mladen Petric equalized for HSV two minutes from time. The line of commentary documenting Boll's goal was used to good effect as a sample in Le Fly's song *We Love St. Pauli*.

This game was certainly (like the reverse fixture in the suburbs, earlier in the season) relentlessly hyped online. A kind of slow, drawn-out goading of each other's fans over the internet, that caused tensions to bubble and simmer weeks before the actual game. As far as I am aware, there were no effigies hanging from bridges this time, and no choreos were sabotaged in advance as had been the case at the first fixture in the Volksparkstadion in September 2019 (a relatively uneventful, on the pitch at least, 0:0 draw). But – in the run up to the game at the Millerntor – there was a lot of testosterone and machismo flying around on social media. It is this aspect of derby games that doesn't sit comfortably with me. I am also aware this makes me something of the exception as a football fan. I understand that football is built on rivalries, that they form an intrinsic part of the game and supporter culture. Perhaps it is because I am an outsider, not a Hamburg resident? I have no real animosity towards HSV, other than them being the big sporting and commercial behemoth to St. Pauli's perennial outsider/underdog. I prefer to save dislike for teams where there is a clear political divide between supporters such as Hansa Rostock or teams like RB Leipzig who have bought their way to the top. I know HSV had a problem with right-wing hooligans in the past and that a certain minority of their fans are all too fond of vandalizing our club and district, but I just don't have that innate hatred hard-wired into me. Maybe, I can blame Kevin Keegan? His move to the Volksparkstadion in the 1980s gave the club an almost exotic feel in an era when so few English players plied their trade abroad. For additional context, I never really hated Luton either – despite the flying bricks. I even had something of a soft spot for players like Ricky Hill and Brian Stein, not to mention the beautiful adidas kit they wore back in the early 1980s. I guess what I am trying to articulate here is: I am not an ultra! I am not part of that demographic of – mostly – young men who feel the need to physically confront or defend themselves against opposition fans. My instinct is to run, not to fight and I understand that this impulse puts me at odds with many of the people I would be sharing a terrace with later in the day. I am simply not fuelled by testosterone, but I am aware of the role it plays (and has always played) in football culture. It is just not my fight.

I arrived in Hamburg early Sunday morning. I bumped into Dave from Manchester St. Pauli whilst queuing to buy tickets for the S-Bahn at the airport. He was still on a high from Blackpool fans' emotional return to Bloomfield Road the day before, and it was nice to have some company on the train. The crew from Yorkshire St. Pauli were also over. As was Shawn Roggenkamp who had flown in from New York. This was a game nobody wanted to miss.

Alighting at Reeperbahn (as 'instructed' by the police), the place was eerily quiet, even for a Sunday morning. There'd been much more of a police presence when Holstein Kiel came to town last year. The whole place was calm. In fact, aside from the police helicopter frequently buzzing the district, it didn't feel too tense.

The only thing we saw on the way to the ground was one St. Pauli fan bleeding profusely from the head whilst at the same time holding a friendly conversation with the police officers standing nearby – hard to tell if he'd experienced any football-related trouble or was still recovering from the night before. The mood outside the Gegengerade was pretty good too, more limited to the nerves of playing HSV rather than worrying about potential off-the-pitch complications.

I decided to get in the ground earlier than usual and managed to time my walk back to the Südkurve just as the HSV team bus pulled-up. Some burly police officers pushed us back to let the coach through. As they did, the coach was pelted with eggs, beer and plastic cups (no bottles or glass as far as I could see). For me it was the first moment we – as St. Pauli fans – crossed the line. I know, a lot worse has happened at other clubs: we've seen it at Anfield and elsewhere. We know where it can lead, when the spiral of hate builds, and it plays out to its logical conclusion: the Boca Juniors versus River Plate in the Copa Libertadores Final of 2018 saw the second leg moved to Madrid after the Boca coach was attacked by fans on the way to River's Monumental Stadium, hospitalizing several Boca players. Of course, throwing some beer and eggs at the HSV bus wasn't comparable to Boca-River, you could even argue it is almost an expected, acceptable part of derby day. But then again, we can't claim to be different and then do the same stupid shit as everyone else. Also, we can't in anyway blame this behaviour on the ultras. It wasn't them lobbing stuff at the coach, it was regular St. Pauli fans. So, before other sections of our support get 'holier-than-thou' about things, we might need to check our behaviours too.

There were positive aspects of derby day: the pre-match choreo inside the ground was astonishing. It was well thought out, constructed, and delivered. I liked the fact it had multiple stages to it: just as you thought that it was over, another massive flag appeared. The roar from all sides of the ground at the start of the game was also befitting of the Millerntor. I'm pro-pyro, so I didn't have a problem with the initial use of smoke and flares – it adds to the atmosphere, and nobody really expected the derby to be smoke and pyro free! However, before too long, it felt like the flares and the pyro were just being exchanged tit-for-tat between the two sets of supporters at either end of the stadium. "Oh look, they've randomly lit some flares, we better randomly light even more." It was an action with no point, except for looking good on Instagram. Crucially, it was coupled with an over-zealous referee, who set his stall out early by stopping play at any sign of smoke.

I haven't mentioned the identically dressed group of supporters who rocked up – theatrically – through the side entrances of the Südkurve about 20 minutes before kick-off. According to friends in the queue outside, they just simply barged their way through and stormed their own block. Again, I can cut them a little slack, it's almost expected 'fan-behaviour' to move en masse but it is not especially courteous to your own fans, is it? This group must've placed a hell of an order at Millets. They were all dressed identically in sensible black hooded raincoats (itself, a reasonable precaution against the inevitable Hamburger Wetter). They were also all wearing red bandanas, balaclavas, or face masks. I understand the various reasons and history behind this: acting as a collective and recognisable group; stopping the individuals involved being identified by far-right extremists or by the police spotters in the stadium or those reviewing the footage on CCTV. I also know this is an accepted and acknowledged part of anti-fascist culture. But it changed the dynamic and the atmosphere on the Südkurve for those not directly involved in the action, and later it became a source of tension between St. Pauli fans in the stadium. Obviously, these were the designated pyro-guys. They remained on the fence all game, periodically lighting more flares or smoke bombs. In moderation – okay, but all the time, with this ref? It was a recipe for trouble.

I lost track of events, but I think the first long stoppage occurred shortly after halftime. It felt like the whole of the Südkurve was ablaze. It no doubt looked impressive on the television and in subsequent social media posts, but it resulted in a lengthy stoppage and the referee sending the captains of both sides to talk to their respective supporters.

The game continued. We shipped more goals. I think on about 81 minutes, flares were repeatedly fired from the Südkurve onto the pitch, drawing boos and whistles from the rest of the stadium, most notably the Gegengerade. Shortly afterwards, the referee took the players off the pitch. The benches left too. For all we knew the game was abandoned (I had a hunch it wouldn't be, but at that point we genuinely didn't know).

The Gegengerade turned on the Südkurve; the Südkurve turned on itself, with fans shouting at the masked men on the fence who rebuffed the insults with their macho 'we don't give a fuck' posturing. It was ugly. My mind went back to the end of the previous season and HSV's final home game that confirmed their relegation. How we all laughed at them for stopping the game with their bonfire of black smoke! Not only had they been relegated, but they couldn't even go down with dignity. We had all felt doubly good, morally superior: the HSV team had embarrassed themselves and their fans had lost all credibility. But fast-forward six months and here we were doing the same thing: being bad losers. *We can't claim to be different and then do the same stupid shit as everyone else.*

The teams came back out, the match finished. At some point before that, the red and black bandanas on the fence presented some stolen HSV banners. The St. Pauli fans on the Gegengerade sang something along the lines of, "You're shit, just like HSV" at the guys on the fence. There were more flares. Pretty much everyone who wasn't dressed in red and black had stopped following the Vorsänger on the fence– no one was singing. It was embarrassing. It was horrible.

As the HSV players and fans celebrated an historic derby victory, our players were left to wander forlornly around the pitch. They still stopped in front of the Südkurve, a move that drew more booing and consternation from the Gegengerade. It was a grim ending. Oh, and it was raining.

The Südkurve emptied quickly, leaving a cluster of fans behind the goal, who decided in one final act of machismo, that they would create a bonfire with stolen HSV flags. My lasting memory of derby day is just that: a fire burning on the terrace and a plume of acrid black smoke filling the sky. The blaze forced the fire service to come and extinguish it with a hose, it felt like a metaphor of sorts.

Looking back objectively: the pre-match choreography was great; but the constant pyro; firing rockets onto the pitch (again, how we howled indignantly when Rostock fans did the same at their stadium a few years back – okay, so we didn't fire them at the away fans, but it's not much different, really); parading and burning stolen flags; and worst of all, our own fans turning on each other is just plain stupid.

So how did it come to this? I can understand the expectations that our ultra-minded fans need to live up to. After all, they are one of the most renowned and respected ultra-groups in Europe, perhaps even, the world? This was their first home derby match in nearly a decade. They had to make a marquee statement – something that would be recognized and remembered, something that would attract attention around the globe. That, of course, is pressure. What I just don't get is, why did they choose to sink to their opponents' level? Why did they copy their rivals' juvenile actions? Why was it all about machismo? Could we not have used humour, satire or surrealism to make our point? Isn't that the St. Pauli way?

I don't have the answers, I can only speculate. And who am I – a middle-aged man, trying to live out his football days being part of a club that follows a distinct left-wing, progressive ethos that itself is probably a product of my youth nearly thirty years ago – to lecture these youngsters on how active support should manifest itself? In many ways, this is their time, not mine. They'd be within their rights just to say, "Fuck off, Grandad! It's not the 1980s anymore!" In addition, despite my love of the club, I am still really a casual observer – a tourist – citing my objections from outside of the active fan-scene. I am definitely not an ultra. I was called out on Twitter for not 'knowing or understanding' the ultra-mentality. This is a fair criticism. I am not part of that culture.

It is so hard not to let your own prejudices get in the way. I don't want to be one of those old guys who tell you it was better in their day. It wasn't. I don't want to tell them how they should do things. I am conscious that I am projecting my safe middle-class value judgements on a working-class, antifascist movement that has had to physically fight on the streets against the far-right. Who am I to cast judgement? Yet, from the moment the red and black hooded representatives took their place at the front of the terrace, the whole thing reeked of toxic masculinity. Of young men, with too much testosterone. There was arrogance, an air of aggression and a self-importance among these young men that was unpleasant. But maybe, that was the point.

They obviously see their youth as their strength (it may well be), but it can also be a weakness. It is one thing having your own ideas about what constitutes active support, but it is another to undermine the values that have defined our club for the best part of three decades. My personal feeling is that they need to massively dial down the machismo. Perhaps more than that, they need to diversify a little. How come virtually everyone in a bandana or balaclava was a young, white male? Maybe we need more female representation on our curve. Although compared to other ultra-groups at different clubs USP has a much higher number of women actively involved in the running of the group. I know that USP recognize these shortcomings. I also know that we can rely on them to be there to actually fight fascism when it rears its head. For this we should be grateful. We need them.

As the fan scene continues to evolve, it looks like there's an another 'new breed' of supporters that is trying to gain recognition and influence. While that group might still be there to fight fascism when it rears its head, there's too much macho-posturing, attitude and, of course, the needless flag-stealing and burning nonsense inside the stadium.

One of the saddest sights for me – aside from the pyre of burning flags – was seeing Oke Göttlich, FC St. Pauli President, pitch side, in front of the Südkurve looking on with a worried expression. Everything about St. Pauli exists on a tightrope: from balancing commercial opportunities with an ethical stance to results on-the-pitch. Oke has been the most sympathetic and supportive of the FCSP presidents to the active fan-scene that I have seen in my time watching the club. He understands fan culture and is sympathetic towards it. It is a shame that he now must consider how to measure and balance the club's response.

Perhaps I am over-reacting. Being way too sensitive. In a few days it would all be forgotten, part of the derby-day experience.

Nobody outside the fanbase will remember the stoppages to the game and the nasty atmosphere in the stands. The St. Pauli brand will be undiminished. Perhaps, ironically, all the pyro and the smoke will make us even more appealing in the eyes of some fans who want nothing more than to buy a hoodie, to buy into the identity? But, for me, this match left a taste in the mouth as acrid as the smoke that filled the stadium.

But, because we are St. Pauli, we will discuss what happened. We will overcome this impasse. The wounds will heal. And I hope that we can all learn from it. That we can truly understand that to be different, to be progressive, to be an alternative to all the crap, beer drinking, insult hurling, male dominated bullshit that exists in football, we simply can't do the same stupid shit as everyone else. We must do better.

Of course, the HSV fans don't get off completely free-of-charge on this one either. They too, were complicit in too much pyro. And don't think we didn't notice the provocative Union Jacks and the 'No Surrender' flags in the guest-bloc.

That was my take on things. I can't claim to be right, or even close to being right. Even by being as objective as possible, my opinions are still a product of my experiences and unconscious biases. I love St. Pauli, but I am still an outsider, I cannot claim to be part of the 'ultra' fan-culture or even to completely understand it. As such, this recollection of events remains purely personal. The only way we can move on from this successfully is to listen and understand other St. Pauli fans' viewpoints. Or maybe, I should just steer clear of derby games.

Chapter 20:
If You've Got A Blacklist,
I Want To Be On It...

On Friday 17 January 2020, *The Guardian* published an article that was headlined, *Greenpeace included with neo-Nazis on UK counter-terror list*. Essentially, *The Guardian's* scoop revealed that British Counter Terrorism Police had issued a document which gave equivalence to Greenpeace and neo-Nazi groups such as Combat 18 and the National Front. The report also caused quite a stir among British-based St. Pauli supporters.

As we have seen, in previous chapters, St. Pauli's Totenkopf has become a global symbol around which individuals and groups with left-wing or anarchist tendencies can coalesce. We have looked in detail at the proliferation of American-based FC St. Pauli groups that formed in direct response to Donald Trump's election as President in 2016. This symbolism is important. Simply wearing a St. Pauli hoodie out-and-about in any major town or city is likely to result in a few knowing nods from passers-by. Most of us can recall times when strangers have stopped and exchanged greetings when wearing a piece of club merchandise. The Totenkopf has come to stand for so much more than being a supporter of a Hamburg-based football club. It has become both a political statement and a symbol of rebellion.

Of course, being in the wrong place at the wrong time wearing a skull and crossbones t-shirt can also put the wearer at significant risk. This goes beyond not wearing your colours on your way to an away ground. Supporting St. Pauli isn't just about football. Getting caught wearing a St. Pauli top could be problematic if you stumbled across any group with differing political opinions. In both Germany and Britian, far-right groups wouldn't hesitate to attack an individual wearing the St. Pauli skull and crossbones.

Whilst being targeted by neo-Nazis for wearing the Totenkopf doesn't come as a surprise to St. Pauli fans, *The Guardian's* discovery was certainly a shock to followers of the club. In short, FC St. Pauli's Totenkopf logo was included in a visual guide issued by British Counter Terrorism Police under the heading *Left Wing Signs & Symbols Aid*. It would appear that this document was distributed among medical staff and teachers as part of the government's 'Prevent' anti-radicalisation scheme.

There was certainly some significant disparity between the groups listed under *Right Wing Signs & Symbols Aid* – that included numerous fascist, neo-Nazi and white supremacist groups with a long history of violence Britain – and those listed under the aforementioned *Left Wing Signs & Symbols Aid*. This included groups such as Greenpeace, CND, Critical Mass and – FC St. Pauli – habitual residents of Germany's second division.

There are several ways of looking at this surprise development. First, it is worth considering the caveat listed in the document itself:

> *"Please note that not all of the symbols noted within this document are of counter terrorism interest and should be viewed in context."*

This serves as a convenient get-out clause on behalf of the Counter Terrorism Police, but it doesn't get them off the hook entirely. It certainly doesn't explain why they chose to equate violent, right-wing extremist groups whose purpose is to spread violence and hatred with a series of anti-fascist, anarchist and environmental groups whose aims – broadly speaking – are all about peaceful co-existence.

The whole document smacks of some middle-aged terrorism 'expert' sitting down at his computer and googling vaguely left-wing organisations and groups that they don't like the sound of. The list was that pathetic.

It is, of course, possible to laugh at these claims and St. Pauli fans were certainly quick to respond. Within hours there was a 'Counter Terrorism St. Pauli' Twitter account in operation. Social media was awash with memes. Fans even used the official police document to play a game of 'Left-Wing-Bingo' – seeing how many of the named organisations people belonged to or have tattooed about their person! However, beyond the parodies, sinister forces were at work.

The document was leaked just a month or so after the December 2019 election of Boris Johnson's hard-line Conservative government. A healthy parliamentary majority meant that Johnson had already felt confident enough to renege on election promises by closing A&E departments and by offering tax-breaks to anyone earning over £120,000. And – although the Counter Terrorism document was officially dated June 2019 when the Conservative Party were governing the nation, albeit relying on a 'confidence and supply' deal with Northern Ireland's Democratic Unionist Party – the intent was there for all to see. The Conservatives were planning on coming down hard on left-wing dissent to the point of equating peaceful protest groups with neo-Nazi terrorist organisations. It was hard not to conclude that the counter terrorism document wasn't another weapon on their well-publicised 'War on Woke'.

The Tories and their powerful friends in the media were fresh from spending the previous four years slandering and lying about the most committed anti-racist, pacifist in modern British politics. The relentless campaign of lies and the weaponization of anti-Semitism that Jeremy Corbyn endured should go down in history as one of the most shameful distortions of truth of the new millennium. However, this was bigger than Corbyn; his treatment was a shot across the bows of any individual or organisation who dared to challenge the neo-liberal status quo.

Anyone on the left was now fair game. The Tories had begun prepping the next wave of groups to be scapegoated. With Brexit nearing completion they were in need of a different target: new groups to demonise (providing them with cover as they continued to siphon public money and resources into the hands of private individuals). The 'left' fitted the bill perfectly. It seemed like 'reds under the bed' all over again. A perfect McCarthy-esque witch-hunt that was – by that point – already being successfully trialled by the Donald Trump administration in the United States.

The violence that flared at the 'Unite the Right' rally in Charlottesville, Virginia on 12 August 2017, resulted in the death of anti-fascist protestor Heather Heyer. She was killed when far-right sympathiser, James Alex Fileds Jr. drove his Dodge Challenger at speed into a crowd of anti-fascist counter-protesters. The purpose of the original protest had been a coming together of white supremacists, neo-Nazis, Klansmen and neo-Confederate groups. The rally itself was a response to the removal of prominent confederate statues and monuments that itself was a response to the Charleston mass shooting in 2015. In the shooting, a white supremacist had killed nine black members of the church and injured many more. In the immediate aftermath of the far-right violence in Charlottesville, Donald Trump tweeted that there were 'very fine people on both sides' of the protest, once again drawing a false equivalence between violent right-wing groups that included the Ku Klux Clan and various neo-Nazis and left-wing antifascist counter-protestors. Then, in August 2019, ahead of a demonstration in Portland he tweeted, 'Major consideration is being given to naming ANTIFA an 'ORGANIZATION OF TERROR''. The intent was clear: equate the antifascist with the fascist. There were direct links to football too. The 2019 Major League Soccer season was dominated by supporter-led protests about the authority's decision to ban the antifascist Iron Front symbol from being displayed in stadiums. The new season's MLS 'Code of Conduct' initially banned the use of this antifascist symbol but coordinated fan protests saw the ban revoked on 24 September 2019.

You can't help thinking that Johnson, Cummings et al., took note. The left, anti-racists and environmental campaigners were being softened up as the next public enemy No.1. The press treatment of Corbyn, Abbott and a Labour Party who fought the 2017 and 2019 elections on a (vaguely) socialist manifesto had primed readers of the *Daily Mail* and *The Sun* to lay the blame of society's ills at the door of 'snowflake' left-wingers. It was the perfect storm for the Tories.

On a personal note, as a teacher, the development was particularly worrying. It was also incredibly disingenuous. Outside of the classroom, I make no bones about my politics. I'm proud to be left-wing, proud to be anti-fascist. But listing FC St. Pauli and other organisations on the left on a 'terror' document was unacceptable. In my professional role, I would never dream of imposing my politics on my students. It is my duty to be politically neutral in an educational context – something I take very seriously. Kids are often very idealistic and perhaps more naturally 'left' thinking than most adults. Perhaps this is why Greta Thunberg has touched such a nerve with them. They fear the direction in which the planet is heading. Most kids are astute enough to – independently – view characters like Donald Trump as simply ridiculous. So, in the rare instances that a discussion takes a political turn, I often find myself trying to balance their 'youthful idealism' by pointing out the other side of the debate (the side that runs directly counter to my own personal beliefs). However, this is the kind of nuance that the government can't seem to understand: I am quite capable of holding my own left-wing views without feeling the need to indoctrinate the next generation. Most of the time it is a struggle to get them to underline the date and title, let alone organise them in the pursuit of a glorious socialist utopia!

It's especially hard in education because – without question – the government is pushing an ideological and political agenda in schools. The curriculum has been re-written to promote 'knowledge' or unquestionable 'facts' over critical thinking. Policy-makers want a narrow, controlled curriculum that produces a narrow, controlled populace. They are pushing draconian punishments, zero-tolerance environments that include isolation booths. Headteachers are also deliberately off-rolling 'troublesome' students to inflate results. And, most blatantly, schools are being given away to the Conservatives' mates in business – in plain sight – as late-capitalism scrabbles to squeeze the last drops of private profit from public institutions.

But this is where we are now. In football, in education, in society we are well and truly through the looking glass. We live in a world, where the anti-racists are branded as racist. Where inclusive, welcoming organisations on the left of the political spectrum are now directly equated to violent, right-wing fascist groups.

We can't let this narrative succeed. Journalist Owen Jones, speaking after a court ruling that an attack on him was indeed a politically motivated and homophobic assault, published a series of tweets that perfectly sums up the current situation:

> *"The far right is growing in Britain and across the Western world and beyond. We need to unite to defeat this menace. There is no judicial solution to fascism: it has to be defeated through popular struggle."*

> *"Much of the British press and the ruling Conservative party have systematically and deliberately whipped up hatred and bigotry against minorities and have viciously demonised the left."*

Jones concluded: *"Both sides' rhetoric must be abandoned: we have to focus on the fact that it's the far right who are the chief violent political menace - they've killed and maimed and are viciously targeting minorities and the left. That means holding media and politicians accountable, too."*

On this, Jones is 100% correct. There is no both sides to this argument. There is only fascism and antifascism.

Fascism is wrong; racism is wrong, sexism and homophobia are wrong. Being anti-fascist, anti-racist, anti-sexist and anti-homophobic are the only options. There is no grey zone.

FC St. Pauli being placed on a British terror list was at once ludicrous, humorous and outrageous. The government can put St. Pauli fans on as many blacklists as it likes, but we are not going to change. Being antifascist is at the core of the club's identity. It goes back to the very beginnings of the FC St. Pauli 'kult-club' phenomenon, when the Gegengerade terrace at the Millerntor became a gathering place for those squatters, punks, anarchists and antifascists in the mid-1980s. It continued through countless physical confrontations with fascist supporters from other clubs. And today it is writ large on the wall of the redeveloped Gegengerade terrace where it states, in four-foot-high lettering: 'NO FOOTBALL FOR FASCISTS'.

The rest of the world might've looked on with amusement or indifference but, perhaps, for St. Pauli fans in Britain the episode was a validation that we were doing something right. As Billy Bragg first sang back in 1988, "Here comes the future and you can't run from it, if you've got a blacklist I want to be on it". He was right.

Chapter 21:
Nothing Compares to FC St. Pauli (Match)

FC St. Pauli 4 Hansa Rostock 0
Bundesliga 2
13:30, Sunday 24 October 2021, Millerntor Stadion

In March 2020 the world ground to a halt. We all have our own stories of what happened next. The pandemic touched everyone – in every corner of the globe.

Football – at that point in time – seemed insignificant. Whilst across most of Europe, governments led the way closing schools, restricting movement of people and banning mass gatherings (including crowds at football matches), in Britian, Boris Johnson's Conservative government dithered. They stalled or, floundered or, both. They were defined only by their sheer incompetence.

On the morning of Friday 13 March 2020, when it was becoming clear that the government wasn't going to make the decision for them (and with virtually every other major sporting league in the world already suspended) the Premier League finally called off top-flight fixtures. And perhaps only then because Arsenal manager Mikel Arteta had tested positive and was forced to self-isolate. You got the feeling that if the players and coaching staff hadn't started to come down with the virus, the Premier League would've soldiered on regardless, wringing every last penny out of each 'customer' – encouraged by Boris Johnson and his cronies' denial that anything was wrong.

Football was about to enter a new era. For the first time since the World War Two the season was placed on pause. These were historic times.

Whilst professional football had its hand forced by events, the British government continued to dally. It was another 13 days from the cancellation of Premier League games to the commencement of the first national lockdown on 26 March 2020 (randomly, the Conservatives decided to begin lockdown on a Thursday).

The Tories' position on this isn't surprising. Their raison d'être is to protect private wealth, this will always be put before prioritising public health. The last 10 years of austerity politics have claimed hundreds of thousands of lives and the Tories haven't batted an eyelid. It's even more ideological than that: it's by design not accident that society's most vulnerable – the elderly, those with health issues – have died as a direct result of government policy. It is the flip side of Johnson's 'herd-mentality' – thin out the herd, by letting the weakest be picked off by predators (Iain Duncan-Smith and the DWP, anyone?) and disease. The Coronavirus was manna from heaven for the Tories. It has enabled them to fast-track their policies. It is no coincidence that Johnson and Cummings sought council from eugenicists like Andrew Sabinsky. This thinking was at the heart of government. The virus was most fatal in old people and those with underlying illnesses. It targets those that – in the eyes of the Tories – don't make a 'useful' contribution to the economy, but instead drain money and resources. You could imagine Boris Johnson and Dominic Cummings rubbing their hands with glee at the prospect of wiping billions off the pension bill and saving a fortune in benefit payments.

That wasn't the only rationale behind Britian taking a different approach to tackling Covid-19 to the rest of the world – of flying in the face of advice from the World Health Organisation. The Conservatives were trying to protect the economy, protect their mates in big business and minimise the financial impact. This was far more important to them than the health of the people. Virtually every other European nation went into lockdown earlier.

The level of arrogance was (and continues to be) almost unbelievable, until you realise this was (at this stage before they fell out) the *Johnson & Cummings Show*. Two men with a perverse sense of arrogant entitlement, who – seemingly – would rather throw the whole country under the bus than admit they were wrong. Their policies were a reckless gamble at best, but it was no surprise that these chancers were prepared to play fast and loose with people's lives. Let us not forget, Johnson is the sort of bloke that has trashed a pub and got away with it; a man who had no compunction about setting fire to £20 notes in front of the homeless. He's a posh-boy sociopath who has spent his entire life thinking he is better than everyone else.

In Britain, the remainder of March, April and May 2020 drifted by with no professional football. Time slowed down and only a prolonged spell of warm weather stopped the nation going completely crazy. Then, whispers started to circulate of something called 'Project Restart'. It was the Premier League's plan to see out the remainder of the 2019/20 football season.

The impetus had come from Germany. The Bundesliga was the first European professional league to resume after the outbreak of the pandemic. On 16 May 2020, German professional football resumed playing under tight safety guidelines in empty stadiums. A day later, at the Millerntor Stadion, FC St. Pauli beat 1. FC Nürnberg 1:0 in an eerie contest that saw Viktor Gyökeres score a late winner in front of a deserted Nordkurve. This – spectator-less football – was for the foreseeable future at least to become the 'new normal'. Of course, football is big business, so fans were able to watch games from their own homes on TVs and laptops. They were even given the option of watching the match that was sophisticatedly over-dubbed with crowd noise. At the most elite levels of the game, matches during lockdown brought into focus how irrelevant supporters in a stadium have become to proceedings– financially at least. In the Premier League the money generated through the turnstiles is dwarfed by income from broadcasting rights and sponsorship. Lockdown was a reminder how insignificant fans had become to the whole pantomime.

Of course, this is only true at the highest echelons of the game. You get the feeling that along with cockroaches and rats, the Premier League, Champions League, UEFA and FIFA would be the only things to survive Armageddon. Further down the football pyramid, the pandemic posed a real threat to the very fabric of football culture. The lack of gate receipts left some clubs on the verge of bankruptcy.

It is probably appropriate to zoom in on FC St. Pauli here. The club has been on a stable financial footing in recent years. But inevitably, the pandemic placed a financial strain on the club. At the start of the lockdown, St. Pauli seemed relatively well positioned to ride out the crisis. However, this is viewing things in purely financial terms. St. Pauli is about so much more than the bottom line. It is the activism of core supporters and the fan culture that surrounds the club (not just on matchdays in the stadium) that makes St. Pauli special. Watching matches play out in an empty stadium hammered this point home. The Millerntor is a magical stadium, but shorn of the fans who occupy its terraces it was just another concrete shell (albeit an impeccably graffitied and stickered one).

In some ways we were lucky. Thanks to advances in technology, we were still able to watch every game – if we chose to do so. This would not have been possible even 10 years ago. In theory at least, we weren't missing a single minute. The reality of course was much different. Many St. Pauli fans chose not to watch the games online. A blog post from *Magischer FC* lamented the absence of those familiar matchday routines. Commenting on that first game against Nürnberg the blog read, "they'd never looked forward to a game so little and that included long away trips to Heidenheim!" Those of us that did tune in to watch games online, even sporadically, soon realised it wasn't the same without the fans in the stadium. The club realised this to. President Oke Göttlich and other prominent club officials were photographed (socially distanced of course) holding up a banner that read, 'Ohne Euch Ist Alles Nix' which translates as 'Without you (supporters) it is nothing'. Behind that on the Haupttribüne was a much larger banner that remained in place for all subsequent 'ghost games' which stated, 'Football Lives Through Its Fans – Reforms Now!' This banner not only acknowledged the absence of supporters, but it called on the football authorities to use the pandemic as an opportunity to rethink its priorities; to move away from decisions made purely for financial reasons and to consider the impact on the game's supporters.

I'm not sure anybody really got used to games without supporters in the stadium, but we adapted. We had no choice. The 2020/21 2. Bundesliga season started with a handful of games that had a very limited number of spectators in stadiums. 2,226 fans watched the home game against Heidenheim in September 2020, a month later there were only 1,000 souls in the Volksparkstadion to watch HSV and FC St. Pauli draw 2:2. It was to be the last round of fixtures that season with fans present in the stadium. Covid cases were on the rise and games were once again played behind closed doors. As a result, the 2020/21 season was largely unforgettable with St. Pauli finishing in a respectable 10th place. Probably the most memorable moment was the return fixture in the Hamburg derby at the Millerntor in March. Daniel-Kofi Kyereh scored the only goal in the defeat of rivals HSV and celebrated with a spectacular summersault. The win secured St. Pauli's status as Derbysieger (derby winner) and Stadtmeister (city champion) for yet another season.

The start of the 2021/22 season saw the return of fans to stadiums across Europe. In Britain, despite much higher infection rates, stadiums were back at full capacity immediately. Germany took a more cautious approach, gradually increasing capacity as the season unfolded. There were 8,900 supporters at the Millerntor for Matchday 1 of the 2021/22 campaign – a 3:0 win over Holstein Kiel. That number had crept up to 13,917 by St. Pauli's 4:1 win over FC Ingolstadt 04 on Matchday 7 in mid-September.

Things were starting to look up. Rules on international travel also started to relax, and my return to the Millerntor began to look more like a possibility than a pipedream. This dream took a huge step closer to reality when the Fanladen announced that a limited number of tickets would – once again – be made available for international supporters beginning with the home match against Dynamo Dresden at the start of October 2021. It was time for me to choose a suitable fixture and book my flights to Hamburg. I chose the game against regional (and ideological) rivals, Hansa Rostock.

It had been 675 days.

Or 1 year, 10 months, 25 days.

Or 22 months, 25 days.

Or 1 completely missed football season: 2020/2021.

Or 67 games (64 2. Bundesliga; 3 DFB Pokal).

It had got to the point – sometime in the middle of 2020 – where it didn't even matter about watching a game. I just wanted to be *in* St. Pauli. To walk the streets. To stand in the shadow of the Millerntor. To inhale the strange mixture of beer and piss that envelops you when you get off the train at Reeperbahn. But first it hadn't been possible, and then it didn't feel right.

To be honest, even towards the end of October 2021, it still didn't feel right. Covid cases were going through the roof again on Plague Island; the government didn't give a fuck anymore; and the majority of the weary (and misguided) populace had all but given up following any Coronavirus safety measures, much less they be denied their 'individual liberties'. It was grim.

But I was double-vaccinated; I had spent 18-months surviving constant Covid exposure in a completely unprotected education setting: bottled-up with 30 kids all day with no PPE and just an open window for protection. Plus, it had been declared 'safe' to travel and – as mentioned before – the Fanladen were issuing tickets to international fans again. It really was time.

The Covid crisis and extended periods of lockdown had got me questioning everything. In a time of climate catastrophe should I be flying 500 miles to watch a game of football? How does supporting a football club so far away from home sit with the quality of life of future generations? Truth is, it doesn't. I was acting purely selfishly here. It's the conundrum the whole world is facing – compromising personal pleasure for the future of the planet. I'd already failed. The first chance I got I'm back on a plane sating my own personal need for radical leftist football, whilst at the same time pouring jet fuel all over what is probably a radical leftist rejection of unnecessary air travel.

Then I dig deeper. Being able to attend Clapton CFC games all through the pandemic (in my role as photographer) got me through the crisis. It kept me sane. It gave me focus from week to week. I would've really struggled to see the point of it all without a Clapton game to go to. It 100% softened the blow of not being able to visit the Millerntor. But in this time of environment crisis, should I even be making the 100-mile round trip to The Stray Dog each weekend? How can I justify that? Does my mental well-being justify or offset the fossil fuels burnt and emissions produced travelling by car? It's a total headfuck. It's a truism that those of us on the left of the political spectrum are bloody good at denying ourselves happiness. How far should we go? All I really know, half a century into this life, is that football has been my constant. I can't function (happily) without it. So that's my weak justification for all this.

I'd forgotten how beautiful Sankt Pauli is in autumn. I was blessed with clear blue skies that framed the yellow, orange, red and brown leaves on the district's trees, including those on Budapester Straße that looked like they had been earmarked for destruction in the ongoing wave of redevelopment that engulfs the area (see also, the massive new Premier Inn that has sprung up from a hole in the ground on the corner with Simon-von-Utrecht Straße).

I enjoyed walking the district, stopping at lamppost after lamppost to photograph sticker after sticker on my phone. The stickers! The graffiti! How I'd missed them all. The only place I didn't make it to was Rota Flora to witness the latest round in the paint-off between Rota Flora and the Hamburg Police Department as part of 'Pimmelgate'.

'Pimmelgate' could be seen either as a ridiculous over-reaction on the part of Hamburg Senator, Andy Grote and the Hamburg police or, more seriously, as a draconian clampdown on the right to protest. In short, a Twitter user had replied to a tweet from Grote, Hamburg's Interior and Sports Minister, describing him as a 'pimmel' – which basically translates as: a dick, a knob or, more formally, a penis. As a result of this post on social media, some six months after the tweet, the family home of the owner of the Twitter account was raided at dawn. "My house was searched at 06:00 this morning. Six officers in the apartment... they know there are two young children living in this household. Good morning, Germany," wrote @pauli_zoo in response to the raid. Of course, in a district as militant as St. Pauli, there was immediate kick-back to this over-reaction from the police. Bright yellow stickers proclaiming 'Andy, Du bist so 1 Pimmel' ('Andy, you are such a dick') have appeared all over the district. The billboard on the front of the Rota Flora community space turned into paint-based battleground between local activists and police. The activists painted a massive version of the sticker on the side of the building; the police came in the dead of night and painted over it. The game of graffiti cat-and-mouse continued.

Being from Plague Island, I had decided to keep social interaction to a minimum, partly because lockdown has made me even more reclusive than normal, partly because I was without my more sociable travel partner, Shaun, but mostly because I had calculated that *I* was the risk here. Even with a facemask, I was the one coming from a place of high infection (and the Delta variant) to a place with much lower infection rates. It seemed the correct thing to do.

Sven Brux had kindly granted me pitch-side accreditation for the match against Hansa Rostock so I could get some photos linked to this book, so I was even managing to avoid crowds during the game (all officials must wear masks inside the stadium as well as being double-vaccinated). It was a hell of an opportunity and an incredible experience.

On the morning of the match, there was a heavy police presence. I was wandering the district, and, on every corner, there seemed to be a squad of riot police. Strange, as Hansa Rostock had turned down their entire ticket allocation because they object to Hamburg's 2G entry policy which they claimed discriminated against those people not vaccinated (or recovered) from Covid (what is it about the right-wing and antivax?). Still, a number of Rostock hooligans had already travelled to Hamburg and left an intriguing selection of pigs' heads and graffiti for their St. Pauli foes in the days running up to the game. They'd also repainted the Davidtreppe steps in Hansa Rostock colours too (something HSV fans are fond of doing in the run up to derby-day). From the heavy police presence (and videos subsequently uploaded to You Tube) it looked like the visiting fans were kept to a bit of boisterous 'Scheiß Sankt Pauli' posturing on the Reeperbahn before being marshalled back onto the S-Bahn. In hindsight, they were probably grateful they didn't hang around until full-time.

Something dramatic has changed at FC St. Pauli in the 675 days and 67games between this and my last visit: we've actually got good.

Back in November 2019, I witness a standard, limp 0:1 defeat at the hands of Hannover 96. Today was a different story entirely.

I'll hold my hand up and say that I've not watched too many complete St. Pauli games this season. This is mostly because they are clashing with the set up for Clapton CFC games on a Saturday and Sunday. But I've seen the highlights – although even they don't do the transformation justice. What Timo Schultz has done is nothing short of incredible. We look like a team. We play with real attacking intent. And for perhaps the first time since Marius Ebbers back in 2010, we have a natural goal scorer up top in the shape of Guido Burgstaller. But more than that, we carry an attacking threat all over the pitch. From Paqarada to Kyereh via Dittgen. In fact, we look a lot like that 2009/10 promotion side managed by Stani where Ebbers, Kruse and Bruns ran riot supported by Takyi, Naki and Hennings. Of course, it's far too early to talk of promotion. We just need to enjoy the football we are being served up.

There has been a lot of focus on our attacking play, but I had been tipped-off the night before the game about the absolute monster at the back in the shape of Jakov Medic. I mean, he is a colossus. There was one moment, where he charged back from our corner to tackle a Hansa player as they threatened to break upfield. He slid in, won the ball and as he got up, let out a guttural victory yell that was part Viking warrior, part angry (& incredible) Hulk! He was immense.

I was lucky with the goals too. One of the good things about being a photographer (aside from being super-close to the action) is trying to second guess where to position yourself for the best pictures. I like to think years of watching football has given me some knowledge, but really, it's mostly down to luck.

Jackson Irvine's first goal for the club took the celebrations to the other side of the pitch, but I was in the right place for Daniel-Kofi Kyereh's header and goal celebrations. The second half played out in similar fashion. I thought I was out of luck with both of Guido Burgstaller identikit finishes (although only one counted, the other was chalked off by VAR). He celebrated to the Haupttribüne side of the Sud. However, I completely lucked out capturing Simon Makienok coming on (for Burgi) and scoring less than thirty-seconds later. I didn't quite realise how close I was to the celebrations until I momentarily looked up from the camera to see Makienok and most of the team inches from my face, just the other side of the advertising hoardings. That was a special moment.

Talking of special, I was lucky to witness not one but two Ultrà Sankt Pauli choreos. USP had been able to take over most of the seats in the South Stand, so were able to utilise the space with a two-tier choreo before kick-off. At the start of the second half, I was engulfed in the pyro that greeted the two teams returning to the pitch as *Antifa Hooligans* blasted out in the background. That was something else.

Also, being separate from the crowd (and being able to change ends at the interval) you really get a perspective on how bloody loud the Millerntor can be, especially when the whole stadium is singing in unison.

I've been spoilt over the last couple of years enjoying the interaction between Clapton players and the crowd post-match, but that didn't take anything away from watching the team celebrate with the fans in front of the Südkurve. I was lucky again, when Simon Makienok came to the fence right next to where I was positioned to thank the fans individually. How I'd love to photograph every game at the Millerntor! However, I'm eternally grateful to Sven Brux for allowing me to do it on this occasion.

All that was left for me was to hand in my photographer's bib and head back to the free Wi-Fi of the hotel and tune into the live stream of Clapton CFC Women's First Team's FA Cup win against Biggleswade United. It had been a hell of a day's football. It was good to be back.

Chapter 22:
Sexism in the St. Pauli Fan Scene

'No place for homophobia, fascism, sexism, (and) racism' is painted large on one of the entry points that leads from the concourse to the Gegengerade terrace.

On 28 October 1991, at the request of the *Fan-initiative St. Pauli-Hamburg* FC St. Pauli became the first club in Germany to publish stadium regulations that specifically prohibited racist, fascist, sexist and homophobic chanting inside the stadium.

The Millerntor Stadion having the highest percentage of female fans in the whole of the German football (approximately 30%) is frequently quoted by journalists in media overviews of the club.

For years the rainbow flag has held equal status with the club badge and the Totenkopf on the flag poles that fly above the South Stand. In August 2022, in time for Pride Week in Hamburg, this flag was updated to the more inclusive Progress Pride flag that represents transgender members of the community, intersex, people of colour and those living with HIV/AIDS. All of these actions and initiatives appear to reinforce the idea that FC St. Pauli welcomes *everyone* (except fascists) and that the Millerntor is a safe space for individuals, groups and communities who would normally feel vulnerable or at risk from verbal, physical or emotional abuse inside a football stadium. This is the utopia of St. Pauli that attracts many fans to the club in the first place.

Regular football has for generations been riddled with sexist, racist and homophobic behaviours. The stadium has been used by many as somewhere that legitimises and reinforces these prejudices either through the menacing acts of a terrace full of supporters making monkey noises at black players or chanting, 'Get your tits out for the lads' at any females that have the audacity to be present in this most male of domains. But it is also the less visible acts of sexism, racism and homophobia, the ones that take place more discretely that are just as disgusting, such as the casual use of the word 'gay' as a pejorative term in conversations on the terraces. Or it is giving a female spectator no choice but to squeeze uncomfortably past a group of men in a busy crowd – often accompanied by a sexualised comment. Any female who has attended a football match in the last 40 years will have experienced a scenario like this (and probably a whole lot worse). Most men too, won't have to dig deep into their memory bank to recall having witnessed and tolerated these behaviours. It's football, isn't it? It goes with the territory. It might've done, back in the last century. But it should have no place in the modern game.

Of course, sexism, racism and homophobia are still present in our stadiums today, although a lot more is being done to combat them. But there is a real danger that at St. Pauli we think it is a case of 'job done'. After all, we've got the stadium rules, we have painted the banners and we demonstrate our inclusivity every time we purchase and wear a club shirt with some element of rainbow detailing incorporated into the design. FC St. Pauli doesn't discriminate; the Milerntor is a safe space for everyone. Only it isn't.

Don't get me wrong, the vast majority of supporters inside the stadium agree with the message no tolerance of racism, sexism and homophobia in the ground. However, that doesn't mean that there aren't incidents in the Millerntor or that in some cases they go unchallenged and unpunished. Perhaps we have made more progress with racism or fascism? I don't think many people inside the Millerntor would be allowed to get away with shouting something racist or fascist. I am positive they would be called out by fans and ejected from the ground. For sexism and homophobia? I am not so sure...

I remember being at the game at home to FC Ingolstadt 04 in March 2014 where Bibiana Steinhaus was officiating. She is one of the finest referees in her generation, she has refereed in the Bundesliga, European competition and at a three Women's World Cup tournaments. The Ingolstadt game was a scrappy 0:0 that left everyone frustrated, Steinhaus was booed and jeered as she and her team went down the tunnel at full-time – and whilst scapegoating the referee for a poor team performance isn't particularly fair or sporting there was nothing too unusual there. However, earlier that afternoon, Steinhaus had sexist abuse shouted at her on several different occasions from the Gegengerade terrace. The fans I spoke to after the game were shocked. In some cases, fellow St. Pauli fans had intervened and told the perpetrators to shut up, but at other times they appeared to be able to shout their sexist insults unchecked. It leaves you wondering how the women standing nearby on the Gegengerade felt having to listen to the referee being abused because of her gender.

In a previous chapter that focused on the St. Pauli versus HSV derby at the Millerntor in 2019, I used the term 'toxic-masculinity' when describing the atmosphere on the terrace and around the stadium that day. It was one of those experiences where you realise that – despite St. Pauli's fabled high percentage of female supporters – terrace culture is still overwhelmingly male. This is especially true when things start to get heated. The machismo on display that day was off the scale. You could describe (even attempt a defence of it?) as a primal response of aggression fuelling counter aggression.

Perhaps, most of the time, these most toxic of male traits are kept in check. Perhaps, even those young, male St. Pauli fans are – most of the time – able to temper their machismo with the values they know the club adheres to. But, on derby day or on the streets when rival fans are in the vicinity, these aggressive behaviours cannot be held back.

Of course, there are occasions where a violent response is the only response. We have to remember that many of our most passionate supporters straddle the line between football and anti-fascist political activism – a divide that often requires actually fighting fascists on the streets or holding their own against the repressive state apparatus of the police.

But that is not always the case and all too frequently football grounds, even the Millerntor, can be foreboding places if you are not a white (cis) male.

Things at St. Pauli got more serious still. On 20 November 2021, an anonymous group of female St. Pauli supporters released a statement that accused members of Ultrà Sankt Pauli of a number of 'verbally and physically sexualised assaults'. Two days later, Ultrà Sankt Pauli published the women's statement on their website. The accusations were harrowing, they included:

- Significantly older men asking 18-year-old girls (or younger) if they could 'make out' with them
- Messages sent to women with inference to perform-ing sex acts, 'I saw you smoke, that requires good mouth motor skills'
- Unwanted physical contact, 'hands on backs or arms around the shoulders that stayed there for far too long'
- Older men providing alcohol to under-age girls
- Excusing sexual assault with the response, 'he's just like that'.

The authors explained that although these behaviours run through the entire St. Pauli fan scene, the specific accusations above related directly to members or associates of Ultrà Sankt Pauli.

The authors of the statement demanded that USP expel the accused people from their ranks and if not, to completely remove any reference to being an anti-sexist group from their vocabulary. The authors of the statement declared that these attitudes and actions are deeply rooted within the group and extend as far back as 2013.

Of course, these accusations are only one side of the story and those members of USP will have their own understanding of the incident. Events moved quickly, reverberating through the fan scene. USP addressed the allegations immediately promising to work through them and draw the appropriate conclusions. Debate and discussion continued amongst St. Pauli fans and the media picked up on it too. USP immediately withdrew from actively supporting the team inside the stadium through organised choreos and even stood down from orchestrating the singing on the Südkurve for two matches.

In January 2022, some seven weeks after the allegations were first made, Ultrà Sankt Pauli published their first written update on their website. It stated that members of USP had met with the accusers face-to-face in December 2021, although an agreed way forward relating to individual accusations had not been agreed.

USP completely acknowledged that 'shitty things happen in the Südkurve, on away trips and at events', acknowledging that they were 'not good enough'. In March 2022, USP provided a further update on the situation in a flyer handed out on a matchday. It went into more specific details about the accusations levelled against the group. There was a commitment to work with the Fanladen and the newly created *Awareness St. Pauli* (see below for more information) and to set up agreed procedures to deal with any future accusations of sexism or sexualised violence within the group (and the wider fan scene). There was a further update from Ultrà

Sankt Pauli in July 2022: the group had been proactive in evolving protocols for dealing with future incidents. The eight months since the publication of the accusation of verbal and physical sexualised assaults had been a period of sober reflection and constant appraisal of procedures on behalf of USP. As a group they had engaged with professionals who work with the victims of sexism and sexualised violence. There was also an event for members of USP that was led by Antje Grabenhorst from *Fußball gegen Sexismus* an organisation founded in 2019 specifically to raise awareness of the problem of sexualised violence within football.

Ultrà Sankt Pauli emphasised that they had made mistakes and that at times their handling of the situation had been insensitive and poorly communicated. They said, "It is important for us to emphasize again what should actually be self-evident: We stand by those affected by sexualized violence and take every allegation very seriously... We want to get better, keep learning and create safer spaces for everyone."

Whilst the specific allegations against Ultrà Sankt Pauli sent shockwaves through the St. Pauli fan scene, the reality remains that it is just one part of a broader problem that is endemic within football stadiums across the globe – and that is women continue to feel that watching football is an activity that carries considerable risk of verbal or physical sexual abuse.

One of the positive outcomes that emerged from the accusations at St. Paul was the establishment of *Awareness St. Pauli*. It is a working group comprised of different people connected to the club and the fan scene established to specifically deal with the issues of sexism, sexualised violence and discrimination within the FC St. Pauli environment. The guiding purposes and principles of *Awareness St. Pauli* is both to raise awareness of these problems within the fan scene and to actively support those victims of abuse in getting the support and resolutions they need.

Importantly, *Awareness St. Pauli* are committed to actively standing behind the victims of abuse, showing solidarity with them. The organisation recognises that 'a supposedly neutral attitude harms the person concerned and protects the person perpetrating violence'. The group also adheres to a feminist concept of violence that places violence against women in the context of existing structural power relations: Sexualised violence is expressed as those acts, words or deeds that are carried out against a person's will or without their consent. And, perhaps, even more crucially that 'the person concerned defines the sexualised violence and sexist discrimination inflicted on them. And only they can tell if something happened against their will'. This is crucial insomuch as it prioritises a woman's experience of a situation.

Between November and December 2021, *Awareness St. Pauli* conducted a survey amongst supporters to evaluate the prevalence of discriminatory behaviours and sexual violence within the St. Pauli fan scene. The results will hopefully be able to inform and educate everyone who steps foot inside the stadium. Whilst it will never be possible to completely irradicate sexism or sexist attitudes from the Millerntor, these measures will hopefully raise awareness and provide clear pathways and protocols for the victims of such behaviour to report it, bring the perpetrators to justice and make St. Pauli a safer space for future generations of women to watch football.

Whilst these issues were brought sharply into focus by the statement calling out behaviours within Ultrà Sankt Pauli, the problem reaches far beyond the USP's section of the Südkurve and out into the rest of the Millerntor Stadion.

There was another shameful incident of sexual assault conducted by a so-called St. Pauli fan at the away game against Greuther Fürth in August 2023. Online St. Pauli blog, *Magischer FC* gave space to the victims to report the incident first hand. The incident started with some basic mansplaining but, as the assailant became more inebriated, the behaviour worsened.

The words of the victims are extremely powerful as they describe events at the end of the game: "The drunk guy, who had been making us uncomfortable the whole time, pounced on a friend of ours, kissed her and wouldn't let her go. She tried to push him away and yelled repeatedly for him to let go of her. Then we pushed him away together. He then called us 'cunt, bitch, unfucked, fuck off' and didn't stop for several minutes. And from the people around us? Nothing. Quite the opposite. They agreed with him. Or looked away. We then stood trembling at the Fanladen and reported on our experience."

And this brings us to the heart of the problem. It could be described as 'bystander apathy' but that feels like a cop out. Other men on that terrace needed to stop looking the other way; to stop normalising and accepting this behaviour. The anger of the victims is completely justified: "We're tired of people who stand in our block, who think they're crazy left-wing, anti-sexist and feminist just because they wear a skull and crossbones on their t-shirt, and who then sexually harass drunk women."

The first and most important step is for male St. Pauli supporters to check and regulate not only their own behaviour but the actions and behaviours of their friends and those around them in the stadium. Not calling out a sly sexist comment made by an individual or friend only emboldens and normalises such behaviours. It is on every single male St. Pauli supporter to do their bit. Football and alcohol when mixed with testosterone often lowers inhibitions and slackens standards of behaviour. Nobody is advocating the banning of beer at football, but neither can sexualised violence or sexist comments be justified by perpetrators hiding behind being 'drunk' or unaware that they have crossed a boundary.

We can't hide behind our oft-held belief that St. Pauli is a left-wing utopia free of sexism, racism, and homophobia. Yes, we may proclaim to despise these behaviours, but it means nothing if we don't back it up with action. As men, we must recognise women's lived experiences within our own stadium, and we must stand with them in challenging these violations.

It won't be easy, and it is a battle that will probably never end. But we must keep learning, keep evolving and keep fighting to make the Millerntor live up to the words painted on the Gegengerade, that at St. Pauli there really is: 'No place for homophobia, fascism, sexism, (and) racism.'

Within the organisational structures of the club itself much is being done to address the balance between men and women in prominent positions in its hierarchy.

Sandra Schwedler has been a member of the club's supervisory board since her election in 2014, prior to her appointment she was a prominent and respected member of the active fan scene and has been an FC St. Pauli club member since 1997.

Similarly, Christiane Hollander has had a long association with the club and was the first woman to be elected to St. Pauli's executive board in 2017 when she took up the role of Vice-President.

In September 2021 she was formally joined by Esin Rager – a businesswoman and former journalist. She had held the position on a temporary basis from July 2021 but her position as a Vice-President was made formal when she was elected by a resounding margin at the club's AGM. Esin Rager has expertise in the fields of environmental protection and sustainability and her experience has proved important as the club look to reduce its carbon footprint and improve its sustainability. In an interview on the club website following her election she said, "As an entrepreneur, I am also involved in helping to shape a new, sustainable form of economy that focuses on social prosperity. My focus will be on bringing these areas of FC St. Pauli, i.e. economy, ecology and social issues into balance."

Another important step towards gender equality was ratified in a vote at the Annual General Meeting in September 2021. 441 out of the 449 members present at the meeting – held outside in the Gegengerade stand due to Corona restrictions – voted that in future at least thirty percent of the club's supervisory board, honorary council and election committee must be women.

At the next set of supervisory board elections in December 2022, a total of four women were elected – actually exceeding the club's quota by one. This was a first for German football – the first time the majority of members on a supervisory board were female (four out of seven). It was an outcome that President Oke Göttlich described as "a sensational result."

Sandra Schwedler was re-elected for her third term in office, and she was joined by Kathrin Deumelandt, Inga Schlegel and Anna-Maria Hass. All of these women bring considerable expertise and experience to the supervisory board. Inga Schlegel also brings a great deal of football experience. She was the deputy head of the women's and girl's football department as well as the former captain of FC St. Pauli Frauen 2 (the women's second team).

Whilst the newly adopted quotas are a positive step in the right direction, elsewhere at St. Pauli female representation in senior positions is also increasing. Stephanie Gonçalves Norberto (Education Director of the Youth Academy), Anne Kunze (Head of Media), Lara Becker (Head of Human Resources), Franziska Altenrath (Head of Strategy, Change and Sustainability) and Catharina Fricke (who is joint Head of Merchandising).

Of course, no number of quotas or appointments of women in senior roles at the club will dismantle the structural and institutional sexism that exists throughout society as a whole or in the traditionally masculine realm of professional football. However, FC St. Pauli are moving in the right direction. Female visibility in prominent positions within the club can only help with future appointments. Whilst the last few years have seen a significant shift in the profile of both women playing football and women's role within football there remains much work to do. FC St. Pauli need to be at the forefront of this push for change.

Chapter 23:
Such Great Heights (Match)

FC St. Pauli 2 SC Paderborn 07 2
Bundesliga 2
13:00, Saturday 27 August 2022, Millerntor Stadion

"But everything looks perfect from far away..."
– *Such Great Heights,* The Postal Service

I've got Sönke from the FC St. Pauli-Museum – and the liberating joy of drinking Prosecco at altitude – to thank for the success of this trip. I've been fairly reclusive on my last couple of visits to the Millerntor – mostly because I've had a camera full of pitch-side photos to go and edit on my laptop post-game, but also because I've not been drinking. I had a press pass for this game (thanks, Sven Brux) but I didn't get round to using it as I was diverted for a special mission to catch the game from high above the stadium on the roof of the Feldstraße Hochbunker.

The World War Two flak tower at the north end of the Heiligengeistfeld dominates the St. Pauli skyline (along with the television tower to its north). Even the redeveloped stadium is no match for the brutal grey concrete of the bunker that still manages to cast its sinister historical shadow even when the bright lights and sounds of the adjacent Hamburger Dom funfair are in full flow.

I've read a lot about the bunker over the years, it is a building that I have long wanted to go inside because it just stands there like a huge lump of immovable history, forever reminding the district of the horrors of National Socialism and the brutality of war.

The Feldstraße Hochbunker was one of a pair built in St. Pauli to help defend the dock area from Allied bombing raids. Its non-identical twin stood where the T-Mobile offices are now located to the south of the Millerntor. This slightly smaller bunker was destroyed in 1974 – although the discovery of tunnels connecting the two buildings temporarily hindered the building of the Millerntor's new South Stand in 2007. The decision to construct this type of air defence came in response to the heavy bombing of Berlin in August 1940. Hitler placed Albert Speer in charge of the overseeing architectural plans for anti-aircraft defences in strategic cities including Berlin, Vienna and Hamburg. The flak towers were usually constructed in pairs. A smaller tower to serve as the communications centre and the larger tower housing the majority of the anti-air defences.

The bunker to the north was completed in 1942 – in record speed – through the use of forced labour. Reports say it took less than 300 days to complete this massive concrete edifice – you can only imagine the grim conditions that the conscripts who constructed it were forced to endure. The labourers were viewed as disposable by the Nazi regime and were forced to work long hours with little or no medical care. The other terrible irony came during the bombing raids on the city – the bunker provided refuge for thousands of Hamburg's civilian population, but conscripted labourers were not offered that protection.

On its roof, in each corner, stood four massive anti-aircraft guns – the remnants of the guns' mountings and rotational hub can still be seen today. The building was made of reinforced concrete that is nearly four metres thick in places. As well, as being an important air defence, the building also served as a place of refuge during the sustained Allied bombing campaigns of World War Two. The bombing reached a horrendous intensity during 'Operation Gomorrah' which began on 24 July 1943 and lasted seven nights and eight days. The city was engulfed in a devastating firestorm that caused widespread destruction. The Hochbunker was designed to hold 18,000 inhabitants during air raids although it is thought that up to 25,000 people were able to find shelter within its walls. In a series of interviews carried out in June 2015 at St. Pauli church, several eyewitnesses told of the cramped conditions civilians experienced when sheltering from the bombing.

The building's footprint extends far beyond what is visible above ground. The foundations were designed to keep the building upright and functioning even in the event of massive damage to its outer walls or indeed the collapse of entire floors within.

The bunker survived the war, it also survived attempts to have it blown up as part of the post-war denazification. The building was simply too well constructed to be destroyed without causing significant damage to the surrounding area. As a result, it stands watch over St. Pauli to this day.

At the end of the Cold War, the use of the space as a potential emergency fall-out shelter became less obvious and there was once again talk of blowing it up. For some, the building is an ugly reminder of a dark period in German history and for that reason they think it should be destroyed. For others, its sheer hulking presence serves as a warning and a reminder from the not-so-distant past.

In recent years, the bunker has been something of a creative hub for Hamburg – containing recording and film studios, media start-ups and music shops. There was even a nightclub within its walls. It also used to feature regularly in the St. Pauli matchday experience. It was visible over the north end of the stadium. On many occasions, small groups of fans have gained access to it on matchdays – waving flags or lighting pyro from its roof. *Viva con Agua* even used the walls of the building to project images on to it.

But since the completion of the new North Stand, the bunker had disappeared from view, obscured by the much higher roofline of the newly rebuilt Millerntor Stadion. It was a shame; the bunker had become part of the backdrop to St. Pauli home games.

All that began to change when construction started on the controversial Hilldegarden project in 2019. Structurally, the project has seen the bunker gain another six floors raising it to a height of 58 metres – once again making it visible to those inside the stadium. The redevelopment has been controversial, with critics believing it is another step towards the gentrification of the district as well as a commercial landgrab. Concerns have also been raised about how the new space will commemorate and respect the building's history, the horrors of the Nazi regime and the suffering of those forced to work on the initial construction in 1942.

The redevelopment has divided opinion with many residents being vehemently against it, particularly its principal new use as a hotel. However, it is also going to be home to a unique new city park, covering over 8,000 square metres. The upper levels of the building are going to be filled with over 4,700 plants, creating an impressive expanse of green that will cap the bunker's previously grey concrete exterior. The building will be able to house 6,000 visitors at any one time; the park will be free-to-enter and accessed either by an external walkway that wraps itself around the outside of the building forming a planted mountain pathway to the roof, or via newly built lifts.

The plants have been carefully curated to withstand the unique microclimate and winds of the newly populated bunker. Even the soil used is a special substrate mix including compost and lava. The pockets of air in the lava make it much lighter than regular topsoil and also regulate the flow of water.

The artist visualisations of the completed project are stunning, creating an oasis of green in the sky that the marketing materials on the project's website somewhat predictably compared to the Hanging Gardens of Babylon. Whether the finished bunker lives up to these grandiose expectations remains to be seen.

One thing that is certain is the commitment to remembering the history of the Feldstraße flak tower. The Hilldegarden Association founded the *Arbeitsgruppe Gedenkstätte* (Memorial Working Group) to create a permanent memorial space to remember the victims of the National Socialist regime.

Covid has delayed the project that had originally planned to open in 2022, but work is gathering pace and there is talk of the building being completed in six months.

I've outlined some of the history of the bunker because I think it is important to contextualise it. However, there is a more personal question pertinent to this chapter: what the hell was I doing watching the match against Paderborn from its roof?

Our project was to capture the flyby of a light-aircraft chartered by Bayern Munich ultra-group, *Schickeria*, who were sending 20th birthday wishes to our own Ultrà Sankt Pauli as a surprise. The plane made enough swoops over the stadium that even an amateur photographer like me couldn't help but capture it. I hope my pictures managed to do the Millerntor and the district of St. Pauli justice. It looked beautiful.

It was an opportunity too good to turn down. As mentioned, I had long wished to visit the bunker. The stairwells and blast doors give you an eerie sense of the building's past as you make your way up through the internal structure before coming out into the more open space of the newly commissioned floors. It was still very much a building site, but one that is co-existing with the gun placements and original roof space to remind you of its history. There were a few workmen about also snapping photos of the stadium from their phones as kick-off approached.

We positioned ourselves and our cameras on the highest floor which offered a panoramic view of not just the stadium and the district but of the entire city. The sky was a little murky to start with, shrouding the cranes on the docks in mist, but as the afternoon went on the horizon started to brighten as the sun forced its way through the clouds.

Watching the game from the roof of the bunker was a surreal experience. You can only actually see the final quarter of the pitch and the goal at the south end of the stadium, along with a thin strip of action through the glass panels at the back of the North Stand. Frustratingly, 90% of the match seemed to be taking place under the Nordkurve's roof.

As a result, it was impossible to tell how the game was going or how well St. Pauli were playing. We just had to knock back another glass of wine and keep our fingers crossed that it was a better team performance than against Hansa Rostock a week ago.

We didn't see the goal that Paderborn scored a minute before the interval. But we did hear the silence that descended on the stadium. Yes, you really could *hear* it. The sound had been loud and non-stop up until that point, the non-stop support from the Südkurve finding its way up to us on the roof seemingly without a loss of decibels. Paderborn's goal silenced that momentarily.

For much of the second half we were distracted by the circling of the plane over the stadium as we tried to capture the perfect combination of light aircraft, banner and Millerntor. Etienne Amenyido's equaliser hit us in the difference in time it took for his shot to find the net and the roar to travel north to us on the breeze. The joy was short-lived as the stadium fell quiet again: first, Paderborn had a goal ruled-out by VAR and then they went ahead with seemingly the last kick of the game. Suffice to say we didn't see David Nemeth's stoppage-time leveller just a minute or so later. But we let out a pretty loud cheer of our own once we fully comprehended what had just happened.

Of course, we had no idea what sort of *performance* this had been, our vantage point giving us no real gauge of how well we'd played. But chatting to people who had been inside the stadium, this was one of those draws that due to the last-gasp nature of the equaliser felt like a win – and had everyone in a good mood post-match.

Back down at ground level with the game over, the 1910 e.V. Museum Wine Bar was filling up and by this point the only option was to carry on drinking.

After a while, everyone decided they were going to move on to the street festival in Paulienplatz, just behind the Jolly Roger. This was handy as I had been trying unsuccessfully by iPhone to direct Maev (of Derry and Clapton fame) from the Jolly to the wine bar. Instead, she stayed put and we met at the Jolly instead.

A couple of hours later, we were heading back to the Gegengerade, lured by the promise of food at a BBQ that was accompanying a film screening of the documentary about the Ukrainian ultras taking on the Russian army, *Frontline Hooligan*. However, with seemingly more emphasis on the drinking than food preparation our hungry stomachs soon took us back in the direction of *Kleine Pause* – where after an agonisingly long wait in the queue – we finally had some sustenance to start soaking up the alcohol.

The afternoon and evening had been what it always becomes in St. Pauli when you let the beer and wine take their course. I'd been able to reconnect with so many old Hamburg friends, most just randomly bumped into in the street or outside the stadium.

However, during the trip, there were moments that made me think of that line in The Postal Service's song. From atop the bunker – from *Such Great Heights* – everything at the Millerntor and in the district beyond, did look perfect – a perfection amplified by the roar emitted from the crowd when David Nemeth's 93rd minute equaliser hit the back of the net.

From that distance and height, the stadium – full of nearly 30,000 fans presented an image of a homogenous fanbase united in their support for the club. But back down on the ground, there are some worries in the St. Pauli fan scene. In many ways, this is perfectly normal. Beyond the immediate support for a football team, it is hard to imagine 30,000 people agreeing on anything (and even the actual football is a bubbling cauldron of differing opinions on performance, personnel, and tactics). So, to expect a singular voice on how the club is supported and what exactly that support stands for politically and socially is naïve at best.

There are, and not for the first time, concerns about the raised levels of machismo exhibited by certain sections of our fanbase. I'd been hearing stuff all week about how the behaviour of our fans at Rostock wasn't all that great. Yes, there was provocation both physically, verbally and in the form of the sunflower banner that was hung from the side of the home terrace facing the St. Pauli fans that was commemorating the anti-immigrant riots in the city thirty years earlier. But I'm not sure indiscriminately firing rockets at the Rostock support is a dignified response. Just like at my last game here against 1. FC Nürnberg in July, when there was violence *on* St. Pauli fans *by* St. Pauli fans in the Südkurve, at certain times you could taste the testosterone in the air around the Millerntor.

My feeling was that the film screening in the Fanräume was an event solely for a certain – exclusively young and male – type of St. Pauli fan.

It is the first time I have ever seen barriers put up around the Fanräume to section it off, and the first time that there's been some intimidating looking blokes stood at the entrance to this newly created private space. I imagine they have their reasons for this. And, also, it is also worth remembering that I hadn't been invited, I had just been drawn in by the lure of a free BBQ.

But – perhaps – it is another sign of a changing power-dynamic on the Südkurve? Anyway, I am getting involved in things that I don't fully understand and that are not mine to try and influence. But this does feel like a bit of a generational shift in fan culture, one where violence for violence's sake seems much more accepted. I remember this first hand (and first-time round) from football in England in the 1980s, and it wasn't great then. I am fully aware that violence is a very necessary part of the anti-fascist scene – but usually that it's saved for the actual fascists. Maybe, I'm just getting old. But truthfully, I've never been into the whole fetishization of 'hooligan' culture.

Then there were separate chats with good St. Pauli people who feel that – post Covid lockdowns – the whole vibe of St. Pauli both club and district is changing. That the 'touristification' of the district has changed the dynamic of the neighbourhood, pricing out working-class people and making this bit of Hamburg into what it has (via the lure of the Reeperbahn) often threatened to become – *Amsterdam 2.0*. It saddens me hearing people who have contributed so much to the community talk in this way. As an outsider, I am still prone to viewing St. Pauli as an oasis or a utopia, somewhere to escape the absolute dog shit of Tory Britain. Maybe that makes me part of the problem, although, in my defence I come to St. Pauli to recharge my political batteries; to be provided with the inspiration that things can be better, something that it is very easy to lose sight of back home.

This feeling of disillusionment in the left-wing scene in St. Pauli (as felt by some of those closest to it) also mirrors and pulls back into focus ongoing discussions that have been happening amongst those actively involved in Clapton Community FC. We too have been affected by the seemingly never-ending scourge of sexism and misogyny. There's a feeling held by some that we are not quite the alternative to modern football that we would like to think we are. This too saddens me enormously. At Clapton – as in St. Pauli – we are at risk of losing committed activists and good people; people who have put their heart and soul into the club and the community, if we don't improve.

It is too easy to put it all down to that age-old leftist problem of us all falling out as we battle to out-do each other with our earnest worthiness. This is not *Monty Python*. This is not a 'Judean People's Front/People's Front of Judea' dichotomy. This is a real risk of losing good people because they don't feel safe and welcome at football matches. We must do better. I don't know how, but we must.

The evening had one more trip back to the Gengengerade to collect some bags. And, despite getting on the U3 in the wrong (or the long) direction, Maev managed to make it to the Hauptbahnhof to get her overnight bus to Essen and I managed to navigate my way to my airport hotel to do some late-night photo editing.

A trip of such great heights (and not so good lows).

Chapter 24:
Women's Football Doesn't Exist

This chapter's heading was also the title of a discussion panel first held at the FC St. Pauli-Museum on International Women's Day, 8 March 2021 (and repeated the following year). It was deliberately provocative; a subversion of the worrying number of misogynist football fans who are unable to come to terms with the fact that women play football but also a deliberate nod to the nuance of linguistics.

Football – played by women – exists and has always existed, even when it was banned by various national football associations. In England, the Football Association's ban ran for 50 years from 1921 to 1971. In Germany, the Deutscher Fußball-Bund's ban ran from 30 June 1955 to 31 October 1970. Under this ban, men's clubs affiliated to the DFB were prohibited from establishing women's football teams, from making their pitches available for women's matches or for providing match officials for women's games. However, the DFB ban didn't signal the end of football for women. Instead, it is estimated that between 40-60,000 women carried on playing the sport outside of the auspices of the DFB. Businessmen and entrepreneurs recognised that there was still a market for the women's game. In 1958, the German Women's Football Association was established and helped to organise somewhere in the region of 150 international matches, sometimes drawing crowds in excess of 10,000.

Finally, in the third decade of the 21st Century, football – played by women – is beginning to get the recognition it deserves. At an elite level, international tournaments, prominent club sides and individual players are starting to receive a recognition and media exposure akin to their male counterparts. Attendance records are being broken as support for football – played by women – continues to grow.

These are all extremely positive developments. However, there is still a long way to go before women can experience anything approaching parity with men. The disparity in wages between men and women footballers is the most obvious example, but the unfairness doesn't stop there. There are much wider and more prevalent issues regarding access to pitches, training facilities and support for women playing the game either professionally or for the love of the sport. Significant barriers remain and prejudices still proliferate.

But first, back to the title of this chapter and the problematic term 'women's football'. During the panel discussion at the museum, former FC St. Pauli Frauen players Hagar Groeteke and Nico Appel powerfully put forward their dislike of the terminology. Hagar succinctly stated, "Gender has no effect on the sport." She continued, "Chess is chess. Football is football. Cycling is cycling. There's no such thing as gay cycling or women's football." Her friend and former teammate Nico Appel explained that she hated the term 'women's football'. She elaborated, "It is a discriminatory term and signals that there is a different kind of football." Nico continued, "When we use the term 'women's football' the first thing you have to ask yourself is, 'What kind of sport is this supposed to be?' I don't know this sport because I play *football*."

Perhaps there is some historical lag in the acceptance by many men that the game is now exactly the same regardless of whether it is played by men or women.

In Germany, throughout the 1970s, women's football had several rule variations that marked it out as distinct from the men's game. Matches were only 70-minutes long. Games were also suspended in the winter months between November and March. Women were not allowed to wear studs and had to play with Size 4 footballs. There was also a ruling that allowed 'intentional use of hands to prevent painful encounters with the ball'. It wasn't just Germany, even games in the first FIFA sanctioned Women's World Cup in 1991 (at the time referred to as Women's World Championship for the M&M's Cup) were only 80-minutes in length.

However, now, as Nico states, "We play football in the same way: twice for 45 minutes as normal. Which is something many referees still haven't understood and keep asking, 'How long are we playing?'" There is no women's football. There are women who play football.

The semantics are important. Used incorrectly such terminology fuels sexist and misogynistic attitudes, (us) men need to understand and action this shift in language.

The history of women playing football at FC St. Pauli has also been scandalously neglected. This is something that I have been equally guilty of. I am ashamed to say that writing about the history of the women's football department was not something I even considered whilst researching *Pirates, Punks & Politics*. I am even more ashamed to admit that, for most of my life, I never even questioned why football – in my personal experience – was an exclusively male activity. Throughout my formative years I never even considered that women would play the sport. I am hoping that it was just the ignorance of youth and not some latent sexism that formed my opinions. Growing up in the 1970s and '80s, there was a recognition of female athletes in individual sports like tennis, swimming, or athletics. Yet, when it came to team sports, it was as if there was a tacit acceptance that sport would be split along the gender lines established in a school setting i.e., boys and men would exclusively play football, cricket and rugby whilst girls would only ever have the option of playing hockey or netball. Fortunately, times have changed and there is now more fluidity in the options available for those who want to participate in team sports.

Over recent years, there has also been a considerable and long overdue sea change regarding the exposure that women playing football have received. This has also extended to the researching and retelling of the historical experience of women playing football. There is now a burgeoning field of books specifically about women's football. Books in English by academics and journalists such as Jean Williams, Carrie Dunn and Suzanne Wrack have raised the bar. Further afield, Gwendolyn Oxenham's *Under the Lights and in the Dark: Untold Stories of Women's Soccer* is a must-read from an American perspective. *Futbolera – A History of Women and Sports in Latin America* by historian Brenda Elsey is also enlightening. There are also German language books that look at the history of women's football in the country. *Frauenfußball in Deutschland: Anfänge – Verbote – Widerstände – Durchbruch* by Dr. Markwart Herzog and Sylvia Heudecker is one such resource – the title which translates to *Women's Football in Germany: Beginnings – Bans – Resistance – Breakthrough* succinctly outlines the common themes in the women's game. *Freigespielt: Frauenfußball im geteilten Deutschland* by Carina Sophia Linne documents the story of women's football in East Germany between 1960 and 1990. As far as I am aware, neither of these two books have been translated into English.

Herzog and Heudecker's subtitle of *Beginnings – Bans – Resistance – Breakthrough* is also true of women's experiences playing football at FC St. Pauli.

Shortly after the DFB begrudgingly lifted their ban on women's football in October 1970, a group of women began to think about getting a team together. They went to the FC St. Pauli board who said that the women could start a football department on the proviso that they could get a manager, coach and eleven players together. The team played for two years between 1971 and 1972. Monika Assmuteit (née Hoppe), one of the founders of the team, realised quickly that they would be pretty much left to their own devices, "We had hoped we would get some support (from FC St. Pauli), that there would be some publicity, but that didn't happen." This was a view echoed by her teammate, Regina Gronenberg, who emphasised, "We were dismissed at first and had to fight for everything." The newly established team faced barriers that remain familiar to women's teams in the present day. The team's kit was an ill-fitting cast off from the St. Pauli men's third team; they played on atrocious pitches at extremely unsociable times – men's and boy's teams had priority over pitch hire and training schedules. Gronenberg lamented, "We were training on a pitch that wasn't clay but reminiscent of a construction site in the post-war period."

There is an interesting music and football crossover connected to the formation of that first women's team at the start of the 1970s. Both Monika Assmuteit and Regina Gronenberg were members of a beat group called 'The Kids'. Increasingly they found that training sessions clashed with gigs and rehearsals. The antisocial hours didn't help, Assmuteit – in an interview with FC St. Pauli-Museum – explains how they struggled to get eleven players to attend training. So, they went to the Camelot Bar after the training session had finished and persuaded women to attend training the following morning even though many of them were working a night shift and had to train on no sleep.

Faced with such hardships and a lack of support and direction from FC St. Pauli itself, the women's team folded in 1972. It would be around 18 years before a new generation of women would pick up the baton.

The next women's team at FC St. Pauli had its roots in the Autonomous movement of the late 1980s, with many of the founding members coming from the punk and anarchist scene connected to the Hafenstraße. At the time, this next generation of women footballers had no knowledge of their predecessors in the 1970s. However, the patterns of resistance were all too familiar. The idea of a women's team was initially met with dismissal by the club itself, sighting the cost of building separate changing facilities for women. Initially, the women were forced to register with the club as part of the youth section which meant that the only training slots available to them were in the afternoons when they were still at work or studying. They were often completely ignored at meetings, almost as if the club believed the women were a temporary problem that would eventually go away.

The team were forced to register with the Hamburg Football Association in order to get pitches because FC St. Pauli were adamant, they didn't have enough available timeslots for the women to play at weekends. The early years felt like a constant battle. Their eventual success was down to the perseverance of founding members like Barbara Figge. Despite opposition they refused to be ignored. "Finally, we were allowed to make our own team, we didn't stop there. We became a department (of FC St. Pauli). We also had our own treasury which we were allowed to manage – although we always had to chase after Christian Hinzpeter (Vice President and Managing Director of the club between 1990 and 1997) to sign the cheques!"

If there was resistance from the club to this group of women establishing a football team, it wasn't entirely one way. Coming from the autonomous, punk scene on the Hafenstraße the women themselves rejected many of the traditional ways of running a football team. This was St. Pauli – by definition – it should not conform to established power structures. Hagar Groeteke takes up the story, "The structures, meetings and formality was a red rag to all of us. And the history of FC St. Pauli didn't really interest us. We just wanted to drink beer, wave our skull and crossbones flag, watch football, bawl around and then play football ourselves." Hagar started as a street-footballer in mixed teams, playing in

Schanzenpark and for FC Hafenstraße. Things only got more serious when the men playing for FC Hafenstraße decided to join forces with FC St. Pauli's 4th team, leaving the women high and dry. Groeteke remembers thinking, "Oh great! If you are all joining the men's 4th team and leaving us, then we'll just have to found our own team."

The plan had always been to do it differently to other women's teams in the area who all had their 'strict rules and timings and their old men coaches'. In the beginning, the team was open to everyone. It was not established just to recruit the most talented players. In line with their autonomous roots, money wasn't to be a barrier to participation either. Hagar remembers, "If you had no money, you could still play for a year on someone else's player pass."

Gabriele Kröger was the first coach of this newly formed women's team. She recalled the sexist and misogynistic attitudes the women faced at St. Pauli at the time. However, she also knew that it was the same at every club in Germany, "This negative treatment that you experienced from the board or from certain people I have experienced as a woman, if I am honest, almost always. It was no different at HSV. It wasn't all hunky-dory there either." She continued, "You had guys in every club who wanted to make you look ridiculous. They would say, 'Look at your league table, you've conceded 138 goals. You can't play football at all. Go home, go back to the kitchen.'"

Hagar Groeteke has similar memories of men's attitudes at the time, "There are no women at St. Pauli and you can't play football at all." She recalled that the women successfully subverted this message by paying the 15 Deutschmark monthly membership into the FC St. Pauli bank account so that it showed up on bank statements as 'There are no women at St. Pauli'.

The women's team had to show resilience, perseverance and even a little ingenuity in those early days. They weren't given the key to the box that switched on the floodlights, meaning that during the winter months they would've been left in the dark during their evening training slot. As a result, they went to training sessions with bolt-cutters to break into the box. They then completed their training before flicking the lights back off and returning the broken padlock to the box, so as not to be accused of stealing it. This went on for months before the men in charge of the pitches begrudgingly realised the women were serious about their football and gave them a key.

Nico Appel recalls a similar struggle with regards to changing facilities in the old Clubheim, "The changing rooms were initially around the corner by the doping room. We moved forward one cubicle at a time from season to season. In the end, we were allowed to use the away team dressing room." Progress was slow.

Suzann Edding who played for the St. Pauli women's team for more than 30 years and who is now a member of the Honorary Council of FC St. Pauli noted that in the beginning the women's department was focussed on grassroots football – on playing and enjoying the game. She recalled how, back then, St. Pauli would often lose good players to more ambitious local women's teams. In recent years, with the support of its members, the women's department has looked to become more competitive.

This is, perhaps, where modern day tensions could begin to intrude. With the phenomenal growth of women's football that has seen leagues around the world – including the Bundesliga – begin to professionalise, there is clamour in some quarters for FC St. Pauli to have a high-profile, successful women's team, competing at the top level of the sport. After all, what better way to promote diversity, inclusivity, and an anti-sexism message by investing in the club's women's team?

That is all very admirable, but it has the potential to undermine the independence and autonomy of the women's department that has grown organically over the last 30 years. For Christiane Hollander, Vice-President of FC St. Pauli this is the decisive point: the women's department's autonomy over their future is sacrosanct. There needs to be acknowledgement of the years of hard work put in by those women running the women's teams, there also needs to be respect shown for those players currently wearing the shirt. Talking about throwing money at the situation and parachuting in a ready-made Bundesliga side, Christiane Hollander said, "I think it would be very harmful for FC St. Pauli to graft something on from the outside. It would make a mockery of the department and the club in general." Inga Schlegel, deputy leader of the women and girl's football department at St. Pauli agrees, "You could make more out of it, but it would be super artificial. It would no longer be authentic, and it would destroy a lot of what we have actually created here in the last few years."

The women's department's autonomy to make their own decisions is paramount. In that respect, Inga Schlegel is grateful that the club allows them to set their own pace regarding progress towards the Bundesliga. She believes the club's mantra of "if you need help, we are here, otherwise do your own thing" is the correct call.

For the 2008/09 season, the women's department split into two sides, 1. Frauen and 2. Frauen with the first team looking to become more competitive. However, even with this change, not many people within the club imagined that less than ten years down the line, the first team would be playing in the third tier of women's football in Germany, the Regionalliga.

The 2015/16 season saw FC St. Pauli 1. Frauen finish top of the Oberliga Hamburg going 22 games unbeaten, winning 19 and drawing three and scoring 103 goals in the process. The team then went into a three-way 'relegation play-off' to claim a spot in the Regionalliga. A 1:1 draw against TuRa Meldorf was followed by a convincing 4:0 victory over TUS Schwachhausen. However, there was one fixture still to play in this triangular tournament. This meant an agonising wait of seven days before TuRa Meldorf faced off against TUS Schwachhausen with Meldorf knowing exactly what was required of them to secure promotion – they had to beat the opposition by five goals. When they only managed a 3:0 victory there was an explosion of joy and relief in the St. Pauli camp. Finally, they had made it to the third tier of women's football in Germany – the Regionalliga awaited.

However, the women and girls' department's autonomy had been seriously challenged just five years previously, in 2011, when the coach of the women's team went over the heads of the women's department and registered the team with the Hamburg Football Association in a different category – making the jump from a B-Girls team registration to the Women's level. The coach went directly to the board of the club to get his wish granted. The women's team were then registered with the Hamburg FA via St. Pauli's rugby department without the women's agreement. The women's football department then had to have many meetings with both the amateur board and the Honorary Council before the coach's decision was overturned and the women were able to decide their own futures.

This is why what happens next for FC St. Pauli 1. Frauen must be in the hands of the women's department themselves. Women's football in Germany is changing rapidly. The DFB statue that stipulated all Bundesliga clubs must have their own women's football team has accelerated this process. As a result, independent Frauen Football Clubs (FFC's) have been pushed out of the top two tiers of women's football in Germany. Where once these FFC's proliferated, they now find themselves playing either at the lower levels of the league system or swallowed up by professional men's clubs. For example, FFC Frankfurt changing their name to become the women's team of Eintracht Frankfurt. Many other Frauen Football Clubs simply don't exist anymore – even the increased popularity of women's football is not without its casualties. Growth and exposure of the women's game is valuable, but that shouldn't necessarily mean that it follows the established – and less than perfect – path of men's professional football. Yes, women's football – football played by women – is the exact same sport as that played by men, but there should be no preconceived idea that it must develop in exactly the same way. It doesn't have to suffer the same fate. There is a chance that, given the opportunity to develop in its own way, it could avoid the major pitfalls of modern capitalist, commercial sports.

Christiane Hollander understands that the development of FC St. Pauli's women's teams is a slow process. She recognises the importance of taking people with you on the journey – and that these developments must come from within the department. Ambitions and visions for women's football at St. Pauli aside, there are real, practical barriers in place that will slow down progress. Suzann Edding acknowledges this even at the Regionalliga level, she says, "There are problems even playing at the district league level. The pitch (at the FeldArena) is not designed for that, but it is difficult to build a grass pitch (in the district) and we need a certain standard of floodlights. It takes time."

FC St. Pauli 1. Frauen midfielder, Annie Kingman is realistic in the pursuit of the teams' goals and understanding of her teammates circumstances. She said, "We want to become a competitive Regionalliga team and fight for a spot in the upper half of the table. We have the talent and the right guidance to achieve this goal. Our team is full of players with various backgrounds, and some of our players have played 2. Bundesliga. Many of our players work full-time and would not be able to commit the time required for the 2nd league. Still, in the very long term, anything is possible as the club continues to develop and support its women's side."

This is a point backed up by coach, Jan-Philipp Kalla, who said, "We have seen we can play well and successfully. Now we have a little more time to train... and maybe, FC St. Pauli will soon be ready for the 2. Bundesliga." If – and how – that happens will be up to the women themselves, however, the team does benefit from a small but passionate supporter base, led by two fan groups Die üblichen Verdächtigen (The Usual Suspects) and Ey, die Hunde (Hey, the Dogs). Kingman was quick to acknowledge the role played by supporters, "The fans make an enormous difference. Our fan base sets us apart from other teams in the Regionalliga.

We are the only team that has that constant support, and it pushes us to perform each and every time. The fans travel hours to our away games and therefore we never want to disappoint them. It is an incredible feeling to be on the field and hear them singing and cheering for us."

As for playing games at the Millerntor, Kalla and Kingman would welcome the opportunity although both are aware of the logistical problems of both the men's and women's seasons running simultaneously. When asked if she could envisage a situation where – like FC Barcelona Femení – FC St. Pauli 1. Frauen could sell out the Millerntor, Kingman responded, "I think we will continue to see growth in support for the women's game, especially because of the community surrounding the team. It is within St. Pauli culture to support women's sports; thus, I think it will only continue to grow as our team improves and starts playing better and better. While I wouldn't expect to get crowds like Barcelona or other 1st league teams, we will get the most support in our league."

When the question of what should happen next was raised and whether the club should be doing more to advance women's football at St. Pauli, that word *autonomy* came up again, "We are very grateful for whatever support that we receive from the club and we hope that it continues to grow in the future. Historically, we have enjoyed having autonomy over the team as we are able to make our own goals and see them through. Therefore, it is a bit of a balancing act."

Football played by women is growing at a phenomenal rate. However, it is clear that at FC St. Pauli (and in the wider game) that growth and the pace of change should be dictated by those most impacted by it – the members of the women and girl's football department.

FC St. Pauli now have nine women and girls' teams and a much-improved working relationship with the club compared to the early days. Barbara Klawun another of the founding members of the women's department notes that there is still a significant gap in income and sponsorship when comparing the men's and women's game. Hagar Groeteke pointed out another area where change has yet to manifest itself. She noted that FC St. Pauli's 'Youth Academy' is something of a misnomer. There currently aren't any female youth players. Hagar states, "If there isn't a single girl... the Youth Academy should actually be called a Youth Academy for Boys." This is further proof that whilst some aspects of the women's game have progressed phenomenally in the last decade, in other areas that progress remains painfully slow.

We can hope that by the time the next generation of players are lacing up their boots that 'women's football' really doesn't exist, that instead there are women who play football. That football truly has no gender.

Chapter 25:
Even Kiel (Match)

Holstein Kiel Frauen 1 FC St. Pauli 1. Frauen 1
14:00, Sunday 18 September 2022, Waldwiese Stadion
Frauen Regionalliga Nord

I had originally planned to attend FC St. Pauli 1. Frauen's derby game with HSV the following weekend. However, a combination of factors created a perfect storm for me to bring things forward by seven days and attend a (Nord) derby of a different sort against Holstein Kiel.

First, the Queen died plunging Vainglorious Island into a prolonged period of hysterical, state-enforced mourning. All football – from the Premier League to kids matches – had been cancelled the week before and there was some uncertainty as to whether fixtures would go ahead on the weekend of the funeral. Plus, Monday 19 September was declared a Bank Holiday. So, I could avoid the whole nauseating spectacle by decamping to Hamburg and Kiel without using up any annual leave.

And, as much as I wanted to experience the Hamburg derby, I am not a massive fan of watching football in a glorified cage, especially on a playing surface as bad as the FeldArena – the two pitches sandwiched between the Nord Tribune and the bunker – where FC St. Pauli 1. Frauen play their home matches. The artificial turf is not even 3G, more a spongy carpet liberally dusted with sand. It is also bone-jarringly hard, like greengrocers' grass laid directly on concrete.

This game might not be the Hamburg derby, but FC St. Pauli and Holstein Kiel also have history. Whilst their fan base is not quite as right-wing as Hansa Rostock, this is a club whose fans regularly fly several Union Jack flags with 'Holstein Kiel' running through the middle. At the start of this current season, they were also caught up in more flag-based controversy when the design for their 2022/23 home shirt appeared to prominently feature the German Imperial flag across the chest: a flag with distinct historical associations that has also become a symbol of the modern far-right in Germany. It turned out that Kiel's kit was a trick of the light and that the flag was the blue/white/red of Schleswig-Holstein and not the Imperial black/white/red.

Then, there's perhaps the most famous flag-related incident of them all. During the pre-match warm-up in September 2017 at the Holstein-Stadion, a Kiel supporter stole a flag belonging to FCSP fans from the fence in the guest-bloc. I don't think this fan imagined he would be chased down by St. Pauli goalkeeping coach Matthias Hain and striker Sami Allagui and unceremoniously tackled to the ground. Allagui – who struggled to win fans over with his on-the-pitch goalscoring prowess – gained instant cult status by returning said flag to the St. Pauli end.

There had been some low-key chatter about the Kiel fans' dislike of all things St. Pauli spilling over into the frauen fixture at the end of last season and potentially again today. Fortunately, nothing came of it on either occasion, but it was enough of a concern that Eddy from the 1. Frauen coaching staff suggested that rather than make my own way to Kiel, I should travel with the rest of the St. Pauli fans.

As a result, I found myself meeting members of supporters' groups, Die üblichen Verdächtigen (The Usual Suspects) and Ey, die Hunde (Hey, the Dogs) outside Hamburg Hauptbahnhof. I'd last encountered this hardy bunch watching St. Pauli beat Walddörfer SV 1. Frauen at the FeldArena in October 2021. The Covid pandemic had been starting to ease and travel was once again possible. I was over for the following day's men's fixture at home but had arrived in Hamburg just in time to catch the second half of the women's match. Full credit to Die üblichen Verdächtigen and Ey, die Hunde, as at that point in time, Covid restrictions meant that they were only allowed to watch the game from outside of the pitches, meaning their support was lent to the team through the almost impenetrable green wire fence.

Whilst the number of fans that watch FC St. Pauli's women's teams is (at present) relatively small, what these supporters lack in numbers they make up for in passion and dedication. These fans were not swayed by the fact that FC St. Pauli men's team were also in action away at Jahn Regensburg – their support always prioritises the women. There's a nuanced issue at play here too: whilst everyone is keen for women's football to grow in popularity and exposure, you feel that these supporters' groups have been able to develop a tangible bond with this St. Pauli squad and coaching staff. Inevitably, as the women's game grows there is always the danger that this bond is weakened. But these are positive challenges: how to grow the game without losing that connection with supporters.

As it happened, there was no ambush by Kiel fans. The stadium was about half-an-hour's walk from the station, but the only thing we had to dodge en route were raindrops – on a day when we seemed to have brought the usual 'Hamburger Wetter' with us. In fact, one of my travel companions described the weather in Kiel as, "Like Hamburg, only worse!"

The Waldwiese Stadion that is home to Holstein Kiel Frauen belongs to VfB Kiel and is a modest ground set in a natural hollow that leads you from the entrance down a steep bank of terracing that runs the length of the pitch. There was a bustling Clubheim in one corner and a kiosk selling drinks and snacks behind the goal. Die üblichen Verdächtigen and Ey, die Hunde took up position on the opposite side of the pitch at the top of a steep grassy bank in the shadow of Kiel's impressive TV-tower. The hundred or so Kiel fans were scattered along the terrace on the opposite side; the stadium was a beautiful autumnal picture bathed in the warm glow of the low-hanging September sun. In short, it was a lovely place to watch a game of football.

I had brought my camera and nervously hung around pitch side awaiting kick-off. It is always fun to photograph football. But I tend to forget that it is a much harder gig when you aren't familiar with the playing style and strengths of the team you are trying to capture. With Clapton (who I have ended up covering on a weekly basis) it is easier as you get to know the team, tactics and formation that they prefer to use – so you can then position yourself accordingly. Even with the FC St. Pauli men's team, I've seen enough of them (in person and on dodgy internet match streams) to be able to second-guess where best to sit with my camera. I don't know this side at all and coupled with the fact I couldn't go behind either goal due to the massive fences, plus the eerie autumn light, I came away slightly disappointed with my photo haul.

However, I was – fortuitously – in the right place at the right time for St. Pauli's goal. The visitors had started brightly and there was barely two minutes on the clock when striker, Julia Hechtenberg burst through the middle before slotting the ball calmly past the advancing keeper. It was a goal of real quality – scored on her birthday. What a way to celebrate!

The opening exchanges set the tone for the entire first half. St. Pauli dominated, breaking quickly down either flank, setting players free with some lovely passing combinations and a favoured 'round-the-corner' pass to set the wingers free. The visitors should've added to their goal tally during the first 45. Failure to score when on top and creating chances has – apparently – been a bit of a reoccurring theme in the opening matches of this 2022/23 campaign.

There were notable standout performances from Anna Marie Born and Janice Hauschild in midfield. But the Player of the Match award would have to go to the returning Annie Kingman. She was everywhere in the middle of the park – just as likely to be troubling the Kiel defence with her forward runs as she was to be jumping into a tackle. There was one audacious moment of skill where her back heel set St. Pauli free down the left. Annie would seem capable of playing at a much higher level, let's hope she remains FCSP's best kept secret. She has pace, skill and tenacity in equal measure.

Holstein Kiel came out in the second half a different side. Suddenly, St. Pauli were no longer able to play the game in Kiel's half. The visitors were pegged back as Kiel went in search of an equaliser. FCSP also lost a couple of players to injury which may have disrupted their shape and gave coaches Kim Koschmieder and Jan-Philipp Kalla plenty to think about. But from my position at the other end of the pitch, I just had the feeling that Kiel weren't going to score. It was a feeling seemingly confirmed when St. Pauli keeper, Friedrike Ihle, pulled-off an impossible save, diving to her left to turn the ball round the post. It felt like all three points were heading back to Hamburg.

But, ultimately, what do I know about football? I should've remembered that there is always one last chance for the opposition. And, in stoppage time, Kiel got their equaliser. The St. Pauli defence were unable to deal with a corner and the home side fired home. It was gutting for St. Pauli. The Kiel players celebrated as if their lives had depended on it – and why not? A late equaliser always feels like a win for the side who score it. And for St. Pauli the draw sure felt like a defeat. It was difficult to take after an afternoon of such hard work.

FC St. Pauli 1. Frauen have never won in Kiel. Last season's game was even more dramatic. It was the final match of the season and St. Pauli needed a draw to avoid relegation and guarantee their place in the Regionalliga. St. Pauli gave away a late penalty to lose 3:2. It seemed that St. Pauli were relegated. American midfielder, Annie Kingman takes up the story: "Those of us on the field did not know how the other games were going, therefore we thought the last-minute penalty against us was going to be the deciding factor to send us down a league. We were heartbroken. Some of us already had tears in our eyes as we played out the last few seconds. After the final whistle, we found out that we had secured a spot despite the loss. I have never experienced such a quick transition from utter disappointment to pure joy. It literally made me dizzy."

At the end of last season, the despair turned to joy. This time round, the team held out for a full 90-minutes before conceding the equaliser in the 92nd minute and the joy turned to despair.

Perhaps, by attending my first FC St. Pauli 1. Frauen game I was looking for a moment – something significant that would affirm a narrative that men's and women's football are finally reaching parity; that there isn't 'men's football' and 'women's football' – instead – that *football is football,* it has no gender. I really hope that this is the case. Inadvertently though, I might've discovered that it doesn't matter about men or women – instead – *St. Pauli is St. Pauli*. Gender is not an issue, conceding heart-breaking, last-gasp goals is something embedded in the whole club's DNA.

That is the convenient narrative thread I was able to construct from my first trip to watch 1. Frauen. However, I am sure, I am doing these players a massive disservice. They all have an incredible future in front of them, it is a future that will hopefully give them an equal opportunity to shape and define what comes next in the history of our beloved club.

I am also aware that although I consider myself an ally of women's football, attending one St. Pauli 1. Frauen fixture doesn't really lend much weight or gravitas to my opinion. When formulating a series of interview questions for the St. Pauli 1. Frauen players and coaching staff, I did that thing typical of middle-aged men everywhere, I bulldozed my way through with my own preconceived opinions. In essence, I had just watched FC Barcelona Femeni break the women's attendance record in the Champions League at Camp Nou and excitedly proposed that a club as progressive as FC St. Pauli should be putting women's team games on at the Millerntor backed by 29,546 enthusiastic fans. My enthusiasm was genuine but my rationale naïve. The response back from the management team was that 1. Frauen (whilst wishing for an improved playing surface) actually like playing at the FeldArena. Coach Jan-Philipp Kalla noted the lack of alternative venues and the fact that supporters like the fact that games take place in the district, in the shadow of the stadium. Annie Kingman pointed out that the closeness of fans to the pitch can be beneficial to the team: "I do not think the FeldArena limits the support that we get at home games. In fact, having the small field right on the stadium makes you really feel a part of St. Pauli. When we have a lot of support, the fans fill the whole side-line, and it is extremely intimidating for our opponents." Women's football is in the ascendency, but it is important for all of us (even well-intentioned allies) that its development needs to be led by women. This is of particular importance at St. Pauli where the women's section has total autonomy over how they choose to progress their area of the club.

As for the St. Pauli-HSV frauen derby, I had to follow that from afar. It turned out, Sunday 25 September 2022 was actually the date of a double derby! Kicking off almost at the same time as the main event, HSV and St. Pauli's 2. Frauen teams battled it out beyond the airport in Norderstedt. HSV 2. Frauen recording an impressive 5:0 win over their rivals.

Back in the FeldArena, around 500 fans lined the side of the pitch (including several visiting fans). Tickets sold raised over €1,500 for Dunkelziffer e.V. – a local charity supporting children and young people who have been victims of sexual assault. The game itself was a typical close-fought derby. HSV took the lead early on before being pegged back just minutes later when Linal Jubel equalised for St. Pauli. However, it wasn't to be the brown and white half of Hamburg's day. HSV went ahead again just after half-time, and St. Pauli couldn't conjure an equaliser. But there was much heart to be taken from the performance. HSV remained joint league leaders having won four-out-of-four. St. Pauli were still searching for their first win. It took until the eighth round of matches for FC St. Pauli 1. Frauen to record their first league victory, but it was worth the wait – an impressive 5:1 win away at TV Jahn Delmenhorst that lifted them clear of the relegation places in a very competitive Regionalliga Nord.

However, FC St. Pauli 1. Frauen's 2022/23 campaign was to end in cup glory. After two defeats in the Hamburg Cup Final back in 2016 and 2018, it was to be third time lucky. The stunning 6:1 victory over Union Tornesch took place on a gloriously sunny afternoon at Stadion Hoheluft home of SC Victoria Hamburg. The match was a sell-out with 3,882 fans in attendance the vast majority of those supporters making the four-kilometre trek north from the Millerntor. For a sense of scale Bayern Munich Frauen had just celebrated winning the Bundesliga in front of 2,500 spectators in their stadium. The atmosphere at Stadion Hoheluft was electric, with a pre-match choreo and a rainbow pyro welcoming the teams onto the pitch. The singing was non-stop as Die üblichen Verdächtigen and Ey, die Hunde were joined by Ultrà Sankt Pauli, Supportblock Gegengrade and Nordsupport.

The victory wasn't just about lifting the trophy, winning the Hamburg Cup means that FC St. Pauli 1. Frauen qualify for the DFB Pokal (German Cup) for the first time in their history. For Kim Koschmieder there was an element of personal redemption too – she had been a player in the previous final defeats in 2016 and 2018. Now, as coach she had led the team to an historic victory. And, perhaps even more importantly than silverware and national cup qualification, the presence of nearly 4,000 supporters has set the bar for future games involving FC St. Pauli 1. Frauen.

Chapter 26:
Witnessing History (Matches)

FC St. Pauli 1. Frauen 4 Magdeburger FFC 4 (AET)
FC St. Pauli win 3:2 on penalties
DFB Pokal 2nd Round
14:00, Sunday 13 August 2023, Adolf Jäger Kampfbahn

Not only did FC St. Pauli 1. Frauen's 6:1 win over Union Tornesch in the Hamburg Cup Final on 29 May 2023 break attendance records, it also broke new ground. As winners of the Hamburg Cup, the team qualified for the DFB Pokal (the national German cup competition) for the first time in their history.

The reward was a first-round home-tie against Magdeburger FFC of the Regionalliga Nordost. Whilst both clubs play at the same level of the football pyramid – the regionalised third tier of German football – FC St. Pauli were conceding a significant amount of cup pedigree to their opposition from the east. Magdeburger Frauen Fußball Club – as the name suggests – are an independent women's club with no affiliation to a professional or amateur men's team. They qualified 14 times for the DFB Pokal since the club was founded in 1997 and spent six seasons in the 2. Bundesliga between

2009/10 and 2014/15. Despite 'home' advantage, this was going to be a tough fixture.

The game couldn't be played at 1. Frauen's usual home venue of the FeldArena, sandwiched between FC St. Pauli's stadium and the Hochbunker, as the venue doesn't meet the required ground grading for the DFB Pokal. There was some hushed talk of the game being played at the Millerntor, but St. Pauli's home stadium had been requisitioned for Teutonia Ottensen's (men's) DFB Pokal tie against Bayer Leverkusen the previous day. So, instead, the game was hosted at Altona 93's dilapidated but charming Adolf-Jäger-Kampfbahn.

It has long been a part of the 'Mythos of St. Pauli' that many of the original punks and squatters from the Hafenstraße who populated the terraces of the Millerntor in the mid-to-late 1980s – disillusioned with the increased commercialism of St. Pauli – decamped to Altona and the Adolf-Jäger-Kampfbahn. With my photo accreditation sorted and due to my predilection for arriving at matches way too early, I found myself able to wander freely around the empty stadium.

It was a joy to walk the terraces in the early August afternoon sunshine. Altona's Gegengerade had everything you could wish for in a nostalgic stroll back in time. The crumbling steps of the terrace were carpeted in lush green grass and meadow flowers. At the back, fruit was starting to ripen on the blackberry bushes that had overgrown the external fence. The entrance gates are adorned with wrought iron art deco lettering depicting the initials and foundation date of the club. The main stand is a basic corrugated iron structure with its bucket seats seemingly lifted directly from the Millerntor's old Haupttribüne. In fact, so much of Altona's ground gave me the feel of the Millerntor prior to its redevelopment in the early 2000s, that it became easy to understand why so many people had migrated the short distance north-west from St. Pauli to Altona to get their football kicks. Even when I attended my first St. Pauli game back in 2007, much of the old stadium was still intact and a big part of its initial charm was the crumbling terraces and the trees that lined both Gegengerade and the Nordkurve (which for big games would see fans perched precariously in their branches).

The Adolf-Jäger-Kampfbahn was an old-school football setting which extended to the old school changing rooms. None of the luxury of a modern Bundesliga stadium or even the changing facilities at the FeldArena. And, of course, the commercialism was also minimal. No merch booths or club shop just a few concessions stands dotted around serving drinks and sausages.

Soon the Gegengerade terrace I had freely wandered was filled with supporters. Ultrà Sankt Pauli had organised a march to the stadium and arrived en masse, instantly adding phenomenal noise and colour to the proceedings. The crowd of 1,840 was significantly lower than the attendance at the Hamburg Cup Final at the end of May. It is possible to speculate why: first, it was not a final but the first round – albeit a significant and historic one for the team. Then, there's the fact that August is still very much holiday season which tends to influence attendances unilaterally. Also, there was a full fixture schedule of DFB Pokal action for both men's and women's teams across the weekend, which for those people who can't dedicate both days to football necessitates a choice being made. But with USP in full force, there was a loud and lively atmosphere inside the Adolf-Jäger-Kampfbahn – and I am sure that the players were delighted that so many fans made the choice to attend their fixture.

Prior to kick-off, Eddy Dieckow (who'd organised my accreditation) mentioned that Magdeburger FFC's recent results were high scoring at both ends, his exact words were "like a basketball game." This turned out to be a very astute observation.

The game was indeed high scoring with the advantage swinging pendulum-like between the two teams. It made for an absorbing if nerve-shredding contest. The other constant was the timing of St. Pauli's goals. Late strikes at end of the first and second halves as well as at the end of extra-time highlighted the relentlessness of this team.

There were also some notable absentees for St. Pauli: Former Swiss international, Rachel Rinast was missing due to World Cup media duties; whilst Anna Marie Born was present but on crutches after suffering a knee injury. Also side-lined was influential fullback Midou Loubongo.

The more you watch a team the more different players standout. On the first few occasions: Annie Kingman and Julia Hechtenberg were my go-to reference points – Annie for her vision and slick passing in midfield and Julia for her goalscoring. But one of the joys of watching the team more regularly is noticing the contribution of others: like the role Vanessa Zawada plays both as captain and as the deep-lying midfield rock on which so many of Magdeburger's attacks floundered. Then, there was Tabea Schütt's phenomenal work rate – but more of that later.

This Magdeburger side were good. Organised in defence, quick on the counter, especially dangerous breaking down the left flank. They deservedly took the lead through their standout player Neele Abraham after 18 minutes. Julia Hechtenberg bundled home an equaliser just after the half-hour mark, before Annie Kingman shocked the visitors by side footing home in stoppage time at the end of the first half – there wasn't even time for the restart, the referee blew for the interval.

The basketball comparison really kicked in after the break. Magdeburger equalised on the hour before taking the lead with just six minutes of the ninety left on the clock – it was Neele Abraham completing her hattrick.

The St. Pauli crowd which had been boisterous throughout was momentarily silenced, allowing the handful of visiting fans to make themselves heard. However, just as the game seemed to be slipping away from St. Pauli, Paula Bodenstedt found the energy to burst down the left, getting her toe to the ball fractionally ahead of the advancing keeper guiding it into the vacant net. Pandemonium – in the stands and on the pitch!

Extra time was going to be a test both mentally and physically. Magdeburger rather than being deflated by conceding a last-gasp leveller, regrouped, and rallied. Three minutes later they were 3:4 ahead. The score remained the same as the game went into the second period of extra-time. The score was still unchanged with just two minutes left on the clock. Then, a hopeful ball was looped into the Magdeburger box and – from deep – Tabea Schütt burst through to get ahead of the defence and knock the ball past the keeper to level the tie at 4:4. It was no less than Tabea deserved. She hadn't stopped running all game. Add in that she had delayed her return to college in the United States to play in the fixture and you could see how much this cup tie had meant to her. Her flight rescheduled, she had very little time to enjoy the post-match celebrations as she was due to fly out to Florida at 06:30 the following morning. Given the shift she had put in, she would probably have got there quicker if she'd forgone the plane journey and just run all the way to the Sunshine State.

The game was going the distance – all the way to penalties. Magdeburger won the toss and went first. However, they missed their first two spot-kicks (Friederike Ihle brilliantly getting a hand to both, deflecting the first onto the bar and the second around the post) with St. Pauli converting theirs. The excellent visiting keeper did save one, but when a teammate fired wide the shootout finished 3:2 to St. Pauli.

For the penalties, I'd positioned myself between the two benches rather than directly behind the goal. As I attempted to take a picture of St. Pauli coach Kim Koschmieder kneeling anxiously on the touchline during the penalties, she shouted over, "No photos unless we win!" Fair enough. It was lovely, a few minutes later, to snap her and the rest of the coaching staff and substitutes as they burst onto the pitch to congratulate the players in their victory. The game had been full of drama and had ended in the most dramatic of ways. However, the drama would not be confined to Sunday on the pitch. The following evening the second-round draw – shown live on Sky Sports – paired FC St. Pauli 1. Frauen with their cross-city rivals HSV.

A couple of days later it was announced by the club that the game would be played at the Millerntor. The fixture would fall on a blank weekend in the men's domestic calendar (due to internationals). You would like to think that the decision to play the match in the main stadium was due to the magnitude of the occasion and the potential to break women's football out of the shadows at the club, putting them on a more even footing with the men. However, a cynic might argue that the club's hand was somewhat forced over potential security concerns of the two sets of rival fans meeting anywhere else (certainly Altona's ground appeared to have no viable segregation for fans). It would be a shame if it was due to worries over male supporters not being able to behave themselves that led to FC St. Pauli 1. Frauen's long overdue Millerntor debut, but whatever the reasons, the time had come. The women of FC St. Pauli would get to play at their home stadium in front of a record crowd for women's football in Hamburg. It was going to be historic.

FC St. Pauli 1. Frauen 1 HSV 1. Frauen 7

DFB Pokal 2nd Round

Friday 8 September 2023, 18:30 Millerntor Stadion

Sandwiched somewhere in between the playing of the HSV club anthem and *Hells Bells* the stadium DJ blasted out *Rebel Girl* by early '90s riot grrrls Bikini Kill. It was at that moment that I grasped – not just the enormity of the occasion – but most importantly its historical significance. It made me reflect on the generations of women that had fought for the right to play football at St. Pauli – as described in a previous chapter, *Women's Football Doesn't Exist*. From Monkia Assmuteit and Regina Gronenberg who pioneered St. Pauli's first – albeit short-lived – women's team back at the start of the 1970s; to my friends Hagar and Nico who were part of the group of women who established the department and strove for recognition of women's football at St. Pauli in the early 1990s. Add to them the 30 years' worth of women who played football between then and now – frequently having to train at anti-social times on sub-standard pitches wearing second-hand kit – and you can understand the significance of this game at the Millerntor. This moment was hard fought and a long, *long* time coming. Let's hope it is more than symbolic and is a catalyst for systemic change.

The attendance was 19,710, surpassing the record for a women's game in Hamburg which stood at 12,000 for a German national team game against Sweden in October 2011 – a game which nobody can seem to remember, let alone *remember attending**. It also broke the FC St. Pauli 1. Frauen's own attendance record of 3,882 which had only just been set back in May 2023 at the Hamburg Cup Final. Furthermore, it was also a new record attendance for the Frauen DFB Pokal outside of finals, beating the 17,302 who attended 1. FC Nürnberg against Wolfsburg in the 2022/23 season.

To their credit HSV brought with them 3,200 supporters almost selling out the guest-bloc. That left roughly 16,500 St. Pauli fans – an incredible feat for sure, yet I can't help feeling a tinge of disappointment. If you think about it, pretty much every men's first team game at the Millerntor is a 29,546 sell out. So, you'd assume that for an historic derby game against your local rivals, the entire stadium would be sold out. Season tickets didn't apply, so virtually anyone (with a ticket buying history on the club's database) could purchase a ticket. Yes, only the Gegengerade and the Haupttribüne were open for home fans, but you would've assumed that an overwhelming initial demand for tickets would have forced the club to open the South Stand as well.

As always, there are reasons that could explain this: we can't shy away from the number of corporate seats we sell for men's games in both the Haupttribüne and the South Stand which didn't apply for this fixture; then there was the fact that this was still the tail end of the holiday season and many regular St. Pauli fans had taken advantage of the gap in the (men's) calendar caused by the international break to go away for the weekend; it was also unseasonably hot, which could've prompted people to head for the coast making the most of the weather; and – of course – we can't completely rule out some plain old latent misogyny, it's just the women, why should I bother?

But rather than quibble, we should celebrate – 19,710 is an impressive number! We should also celebrate the nature of the support. Credit to both sets of fans, they didn't let the machismo of the men's derbies spoil the occasion. It was as if both sets of fans knew this wasn't about them, this was about celebrating the achievements of the women footballers of Hamburg, regardless of what side they were on. Having photographer's accreditation meant I entered the stadium via the Haupttribüne and I was pleasantly surprised by the amount of families with young children in attendance wearing both FCSP and HSV shirts seemingly in equal number. You can only hope that some of these young fans will have enjoyed their experience so much that they will be switched on to supporting FC St. Pauli 1. Frauen (or their suburban counterparts) at future games.

Across the pitch, in the Gegengerade, there was also a lot of talk about how young and vibrant the crowd was. There was much discussion about the ageing nature of the support in the regular – season ticket dominated – Gegengerade. The lengthy season ticket waiting list makes it difficult for the next generation of St. Pauli fans to experience a game on the stadium's largest terrace. The number of younger fans combined with what felt like a higher proportion of female supporters breathed new life into the Gegengerade terrace.

Then there was the impact of Ultrà Sankt Pauli repositioning themselves to the centre of the Gegengerade for this game. It made a hell of a difference; the noise level was insane. It felt much louder than regular home games, just by virtue of those making the most noise being at the centre of proceedings. Sometimes, with USP positioned down low in the Südkurve you feel like their incessant singing gets lost to the rest of the stadium – no such problems for this fixture!

Also, Ultrà Sankt Pauli deserve credit for the way they have managed their support for 1. Frauen over the course of these two DFP Pokal games. You could've expected them to steamroller in and take over due to their position as the largest organised supporters' group at the club. However, USP liaised with both FC St. Pauli 1. Frauen fan groups Die üblichen Verdächtigen and Ey, die Hunde to ensure that they were consulted with how the active support manifested itself for both this game and in the previous round at the Adolf-Jäger-Kampfbahn.

This cooperation and consideration extended to the display of pyro at the start of the game. The 2019 derby at the Millerntor was discussed previously in the chapter, *The Toxic Masculinity of Derby Day*. Much of the controversy and resentment focussed on the balaclava-wearing supporters who occupied the front fence, repeatedly setting off pyro that caused the match to be stopped on a couple of occasions. This time, the pre-match pyro display was done respectfully, courteously, and safely by those on the front fence. The space at the front had long been occupied by youngsters prior to kick off, but it was clearly explained that just for the short duration of the display, these young fans would need to move back a safe distance of a couple of metres or so as not to be impacted by the flares. Then, as soon as the display was over, they were able to return to their positions at the front. For me, this showed a welcome change of approach from all involved and an acknowledgement that even these male dominated supporters' groups can grow and change for the better.

The pyro and the noise that greeted the teams as they emerged from the tunnel was unreal. This was a Hamburg derby for sure; laden with the atmosphere that makes watching football at the Millerntor great but shorn of the unnecessary machismo. This needs to be a blueprint for future derbies irrespective of gender.

Causing mild confusion amongst the crowd and to the consternation of the match officials, Kim Koschmieder brought her team out early onto the Millerntor pitch. This was done to allow the players to soak up the atmosphere and quell any nerves the team may have been harbouring about playing in front of such a crowd. They disappeared back down the tunnel returning with the opposition for the traditional – always spinetingling – entrance to the opening chimes of ACDC's *Hells Bells*.

Whilst the two sides occupied the same division just last season, a lot has changed since then. HSV won promotion to Bundesliga 2 and have added some quality players to their roster. The gulf in class between Bundesliga 2 and Regionalliga was evident from the outset. St. Pauli found themselves 0:2 down after just six minutes. Nerves undoubtedly played a part, but the score line was no real surprise. When the two sides had met at the end of last season in the league, St. Pauli lost 0:5 to HSV. When FC St. Pauli *1. Frauen* played HSV *2. Frauen* in the Regionalliga a week before this game they lost 0:3. The visitors were a good side, relentless down the flanks and especially effective when channelling the play down the left through 16-year-old winger Lisa Baum (remember the name, she has the potential to be one of world football's future stars).

At 0:2, Joline Floeter came agonisingly close to pulling it back to 1:2, with the HSV keeper just managing to get something on her shot to divert it wide. HSV went straight up the other end and made it 0:3. It was 0:4 by half-time but the home support was still loud and unconditional.

The second half could've been disheartening but some excellent defending and superb goalkeeping from Friederike Ihle kept HSV from adding to their total until the 60th minute. As the clock ticked over into the 90th minute, the score stood at 0:7. St. Pauli had barely registered an effort on goal since Floeter's chance early in the first half.

However, it wasn't all HSV. There had been a moment of great skill from Annie Kingman in the centre of the park, Kingman turning out of a tight space that drew a massive cheer from the Gegengerade. Rachel Rinast, up front, had used all her experience both drawing and committing fouls tactically throughout the game.

And it was Rinast who broke into the area in the 90th minute. She held off the challenge of her defender and got a left foot shot away from a tight angle. The HSV keeper got a hand to it and the shot was deflected onto the underside of the bar. The stadium took a collective gasp. The ball bounced down – almost in slow-motion – and Joline Floeter was on hand to bundle it over the line. The team had their goal. The Millerntor went wild.

This was the moment the crowd had been waiting for. Make no mistake, Floeter's goal felt like the winner to everyone inside the Millerntor. *Song 2* rang out; people were in raptures. It was a celebration worthy of winning a championship or a cup final not just getting on the scoresheet despite being completely outclassed by a superior opposition. None of that mattered, this was the moment FC St. Pauli 1. Frauen etched their name in history and added themselves to the great pantheon of incredible Millerntor moments.

The final whistle blew seconds later. The noise level went even higher. St. Pauli's celebrations were in full flow. The fact that, over in the corner, the HSV players were celebrating their victory with their own support was an irrelevance. They couldn't be heard over the noise created by everyone on the Gegengerade, and nobody could take their eyes off the celebrations of the home team. The players and management were still on the pitch 20 minutes after the final whistle soaking up the adulation of the home fans – it felt like nobody wanted to leave.

This had been an historic occasion. The first time in over 33 years of the women's football department at FC St. Pauli that the team had got to play in the stadium. A one-off game is great, but what will be the legacy? It seems relatively easy for supporters to turn up once a season to a showpiece game at the Millerntor and shout about being committed to women's football. Even more so for the club hosting such an event – it's an easy win, one that looks great on social media. However, for the women's department to continue to grow and to strive towards parity with the men, there needs to be real, sustainable change.

There needs to be an equity in training facilities, training scheduled for more reasonable times. Home matches need to take place on better pitches than those at the FeldArena – an agreement to use Altona 93's new stadium when it is eventually built has been mooted. Maybe there is scope to redevelop the FeldArena into a mini-stadium and move the existing pitches to an expanded footprint on the Heiligengeistfeld? Additionally, all this needs to be done with the women's department maintaining their autonomy. It's a big ask. But, ultimately, both the men's and women's first team need to have access to same resources, facilities and youth development – even if that means the 1. Frauen costing the club money, in the short term, or even indefinitely. Only with equal access, resources, media exposure etc., can football truly have no gender. Repeatedly flashing the slogan across the Millerntor's electronic advertising hoardings is one thing, delivering on the message is another entirely.

> *My Hamburg-based friend Thomas Kozinowski has corrected me about the 2011 women's international that nobody seems to remember. Thomas and his niece were there – his first women's international and her very first football game, at age 10. According to Thomas, "the game itself was indeed rather dull, with Germany winning by a header from a young Alexandra Popp... but that's not what made an impact: long before the game was over, my niece asked if I'd take her to a St. Pauli game too, and I assume she did so because that experience might have inspired her. Aged 11, she became an FC St. Pauli club member, has held several season tickets since the age of 12 and keeps persuading her (non-football) friends to adopt the St. Pauli way of life." Thomas continued, "Let's hope and keep fingers-crossed that this DFB Pokal game has inspired many others and that it won't remain a stand-alone occasion, but the start of something exciting, lasting and durable."

Chapter 27:
Waiting for the Great Leap Forwards

A news story broke on 7 December 2022 that – whilst vaguely comical – was also another portent of the instability of 21st Century politics and of the serious spectre of conspiracy theories, fake news and falsehoods that so easily gather credence and followers in the social media age.

In the opening chapter of this book, there was a lot of focus on the rise of right-wing extremism that swept through Great Britain and the United States of America in the wake of Brexit and the Trump administration. Of how any modest gains in fairness and equality made in the post-war consensus had been first eroded by thirty years of neo-liberal economic policy, and then further undermined by the amplified voices of nationalism and xenophobia that have rushed to fill the void created by the failures of late capitalism.

As people woke up to the fact that they have been cheated by years of austerity (that began in earnest after the 2008 financial collapse), those with vested interests on the right were quick to blame foreigners, trade unions, nurses, public sector workers, 'lefty-snowflakes' and the 'wokerati' for declining living standards and increased wealth disparity. The right was waging a culture war and – due to their complete control of the mainstream media – waging it successfully. The modus operandi was to deflect blame away from themselves and sow division among those most impacted by their policies. It felt like we'd seen and heard it all before. It felt like history repeating.

Germany too wasn't immune from this process. We have already noted Alternative for Deutschland Party's (AfD) success at the polls, taking 10% of the vote share in 2021, giving them 83 seats in the Bundestag. And, as St. Pauli fans know, the country has had a long-standing problem with Neo-Nazis. But I don't know how many people predicted the events and arrests of early December 2022 unfolding in advance.

The planned coup d'état linked to the Reichsbürger Movement had hoped to overthrow the German Federal Government and replace it with a 71-year-old head of state, the aristocrat, Heinrich XIII. Prinz Reuß. They planned on returning the country to a German Reich like that of 1871-1918. It was bold as it was alarming. It was also slightly improbable, so much so that even far-right Alternative for Deutschland Party, MP Petr Bystron tweeted: 'A coup with 50 pensioners? They'd struggle to take over the town hall of San Marino'.

The planned coup felt very much like Germany's version of the storming of the United States Capitol in January 2021 – a collection of conspiracy theorists, antivaxxers and QAnon inspired radicals determined to undermine the legitimacy of a democratically elected government.

However, the sinister undertones and the level of planning and organisation involved had to be taken seriously. The Reichsbürger Movement clearly rejects modern democracy and – even more worrying – those at the heart of the planned coup included members of Kommando Spezialkräfte (KSK) and a former Lieutenant Colonel of the Paratrooper Battalion of the German army. Their number also included former police officers, AfD politicians and councillors, as well as a judge from Berlin, Birgit Malsack-Winkemann, who had already been designated the group's future 'Minister of Justice'. They had weapons and a sophisticated communications network. The planned putsch involved storming the Reichstag, taking politicians hostage, and forming an alternative government with Heinrich XIII at its head.

The German intelligence service are first thought to have got wind of the group's plans in April 2022 when they uncovered a plot to kidnap Karl Lauterbach, the German Health Minister. This tallies with the group's links to Covid conspirators who had been radicalised in response to Germany's lockdown restrictions and vaccination programme. German federal prosecutors believed that the group 'intended to cause conditions similar to civil war and ultimately to overthrow the democratic system in Germany'.

The arrests of 25 individuals in dawn raids on the morning of 7 December 2022 involved over 3,000 police officers, intelligence officials and members of the special forces. The raids mainly took place in the southern German states of Bavaria and Baden-Württemberg but also reached into Italy and Austria.

The random collection of individuals connected to the coup has a comedic value but not so the deep connections to the German special forces of the KSK. There have been long-standing connections between the far right and the KSK. So much so that a division of the KSK was disbanded after police seized weapons and ammunition during a raid on a soldier's home in Saxony. The threat of violence was real. In a video uploaded on 27 November 2022, one of the plotters had spoken of an "epochal upheaval" that would take place "in the coming weeks, hopefully before Christmas." The intervention of the German security services prevented this, but it doesn't stop people from wondering how far the rot spreads. Stephan Kramer, a senior member of the State Domestic Intelligence Service, speaking to the BBC in December 2022, said, "Today's extremists are not easily recognisable in public. We have Nazis wearing pinstriped suits, instead of sporting shaved heads; middle aged men wearing corduroy trousers – you wouldn't think were far right radicals." And this is the problem. Far-right, antisemitic, Islamophobic hostility has always been an issue in 21st Century Germany, however, violence and murder has usually been carried out by a very identifiable group of Neo-Nazis. But since the Covid-19 pandemic and the ease of access to conspiracy theorists like QAnon the risk has diversified. Nobody can be completely sure how deep their twisted ideology runs.

This is the point where a high-profile, visibly anti-fascist football club like FC St. Pauli remains important. Germany is fortunate that – in general – it has a widely-known and recognised anti-fascist scene, populated by activists and backed by a significant proportion of the population still traumatised and horrified by the actions of the Nazi regime.

However, St. Pauli with its passionate fan base, connections to other anti-fascist supporters' groups around Europe and the words 'No Football for Fascists' painted in six-foot high letters along the Gegengerade terrace contributes to the resistance and fights against the normalisation of right-wing viewpoints. Football in Britain doesn't really have an equivalent club – at least not with a comparable amount of exposure operating at a high level in the football pyramid. This is why so many anti-fascist, left-leaning fans from the British Isles have adopted FC St. Pauli as the team they support. The same is true in the United States where there was a definite correlation between the election of President Trump and the explosion of North American St. Pauli fan groups. Having a football club that represents people's politics is vital – it provides an outlet for opposition to the dominant narrative.

For as long as society remains at risk from the extreme right, FC St. Pauli will continue to attract anti-fascists from all over the globe. Sometimes an act of resistance can be attending a demonstration or confronting the far-right head on. Sometimes that resistance can be as simple as pulling on a St. Pauli shirt or Totenkopf hoodie and feeling part of something bigger than just yourself – of visibly demonstrating what side you are on. This is why the club is important.

On a personal level, here in 2023, my support for FC St. Pauli remains as strong as ever. I feel an enormous connection to not just the club but the entire district. It feels like home. More than the stadium and the streets of St. Pauli, it is the friends that I have made on my travels to Hamburg that mean the most. I'm quite insular and often prefer my own company, but during my 16 or so years of visiting the city (I say 'city' but aside from one sight-seeing tour and numerous meetings at the central station, I have almost exclusively spent my time in the district), I have met some inspirational activists and made life-long friends.

However, as we continue to live in an age of political, social and environmental uncertainty, I worry how my support of St. Pauli will manifest itself in the future.

It feels like freedom of movement will become increasingly more difficult as the century moves on – Brexit being, perhaps, the most obvious sign of nation states starting to become more insular and turn in on themselves. However, the ease of travel still currently possible for those of us from the global north was underlined to me during a friendly match between FC Lampedusa and Yorkshire St. Pauli at the FeldArena in May 2016. The match was being filmed for a US sports documentary series *Religion of Sports*. At the end of the match, I was interviewed. The ease and freedom in which I had decided to take part in the game by simply booking a flight, hopping on a plane, breezing through customs at the airport and taking the S-Bahn to the Millerntor was contrasted to the complex and circuitous journeys undertaken by the refugee players from FC Lampedusa. Their passage to Hamburg had been fraught with danger and uncertainty, and in some cases had taken months to complete. Even their arrival in Hamburg didn't bring with it the automatic right to remain – they lived under the constant threat of deportation. Unlike those refugee players on the opposing team, by virtue of birth and the 'right' passport, my journey was straightforward.

Gone too are the days of low-cost flights and cheap accommodation. And, more importantly, a huge environmental shadow hangs over my frequent trips to Germany. Is it really possible to justify being part of the problem of short-haul air-travel just because I want to continue supporting my football team? I could come full-circle and revert to going to Hamburg by train, but the reason I gave that up – and overcame my fear of flying – was due to the prohibitive cost of travelling by rail. This leaves me in something of a quandary – should I prioritise my personal desire to watch St. Pauli over immovable environmental problems? I probably know the answer to that.

I am fortunate that I have discovered – and become heavily involved – with Clapton Community Football Club, based a little closer to home in Forest Gate, east London. The club's anti-fascist stance draws on – but is not exclusive to – the St. Pauli template. The vibe around the club and the Old Spotted Dog ground has an awful lot in common with the fan scene at the Millerntor. Attending Clapton games as a photographer certainly got me through the Covid pandemic and helped reduce the amount of 'homesickness' for St. Pauli at a time when it was forbidden to travel. But I am not sure I could ever give up visiting Hamburg entirely. The football club, the district, the people of St. Pauli mean too much to me now, they are in my blood. They say you can't choose your football club, that it is handed down to you or determined by where you grew up, but that is bollocks. Choosing St. Pauli remains the best thing I have ever done. Finding a football club that reflects my ideals, beliefs and politics was paramount. In the next few years, I will have been attending matches at the Millerntor for a similar length of time that I grew up watching Watford games, yet I don't ever regret abandoning my boyhood team for St. Pauli. No matter how many times a season I get across to the Millerntor, FC St. Pauli will always be in my heart. Even if I am now attending more Clapton games, St.

Pauli can never be replaced. I feel enormously lucky that I now have both FCSP and CCFC in my life.

The world needs St. Pauli too. As resources become increasingly scarce, as the displacement of peoples becomes more commonplace due to war, famine, drought and continued environmental instability, the rhetoric from the racist, xenophobic right will only intensify. Border controls will tighten, attitudes to 'foreigners' will harden and division will grow. The left needs as many visible institutions as possible to act as rallying points for those of us on that side of the political spectrum. Football is a powerful force with an omnipresence in both people's consciousness and in society. It is through clubs like FC St. Pauli that football supporters can remain at the heart of the fightback.

Forza Sankt Pauli.
Siamo Tutti Antifascisti!

Epilogue:
Football Has No Gender (Match)

Clapton CFC 1 FC St. Pauli 1. Frauen 8
International Friendly
19:30, Tuesday 20 June 2023, Old Spotted Dog

In June 2023, something remarkable and unexpected happened. Something beyond my wildest football dreams. My two footballing worlds of FC St. Pauli and Clapton Community FC collided in the most wonderful of ways. How it happened, remains something of a blur, the pieces falling into place as if in a magical fever dream. I can't say it was my idea or that I made it happen, but I was a small part of facilitating the match and – for me – it was equivalent of fulfilling a lifelong ambition.

What made it more remarkable was that I don't think anybody thought the prospect of bringing St. Pauli 1. Frauen to Britain was even remotely viable. The previous summer I had been introduced to Eddy Dieckow who is part of the 1. Frauen set-up. Conversation turned to how good it would be to get the Clapton women's team over to play the St. Pauli 2. or 3. Frauen sides in Hamburg, perhaps during the winter break. At that point, there was no possibility that

St. Pauli would be able to visit London – it just wasn't financially possible.

So, when Christian Prüß, the club's Head of Creative Marketing messaged me to ask if we could meet prior to men's fixture against Greuther Fürth in March 2023, the prospect of a match between St. Pauli and Clapton wasn't even on my radar. Perhaps, it shouldn't have been such a surprise. The previous twelve months had seen a seismic shift in football. Women's football had been experiencing both unprecedented attendances and media exposure. It was as if the world had woken up to the fact that being a woman was no barrier to playing the game. Progress that for decades has been desperately hard fought for by those involved, suddenly seemed to accelerate. A successful European Championships in England in the summer of 2022 had ignited passions there, but the explosion was global. Attendance records were being smashed in every direction. It felt like the women's game was finally breaking free from decades of institutional sexism and the ever-present undercurrent of misogyny.

St. Pauli wanted to bring both the men's and women's first team on tour to Britain under the banner of 'Football Has No Gender'. The men were already confirmed to play against Dunfermline Athletic – who have German ownership and a connection with former St. Pauli player and manager Thomas Meggle – but the women were looking for opposition who shared a similar ethos.

Clapton women's first team had only been playing under the CCFC banner since 2019 when AFC Stoke Newington became part of the Clapton Community family. But in that time, they had secured a promotion and undertaken a history making run in the Women's FA Cup – that not only broke records but also helped facilitate a change in prize money available in the competition.

In 2021/22 Clapton's women's team became the lowest ranked side ever to reach the third round proper of the Women's FA Cup. In doing so, they had to win four ties all against higher opposition and *all* away from home. In the third round they were once again drawn away against Plymouth Argyle. The non-negotiable 13:00 kick-off required an overnight stay in Plymouth as well as a 500-mile round trip by coach from east London. The cost for fulfilling the fixture was going to be £3,000. This was just in excess of the £2,900 in FA prize money that the club had accrued for battling through four cup ties on their incredible run. There had been no gate-receipts either, as the entire cup campaign had been played away from the club's Old Spotted Dog ground – and in the women's FA Cup the gate money isn't shared between the home and away side. The club's success in the cup was coming at a considerable financial cost. As a result, Clapton organised a crowd-funder and in a matter of days fans had raised the money needed to get the team to Plymouth. The final amount raised was over £4,200. Clapton lost 5:0 against Plymouth, but the real victory was to occur off-the-pitch.

The FA announced an overhaul of FA Cup prize money and whilst they have still not reached financial parity with the men's competition, the money now available to the winners of each round should stop a repeat of clubs having to rely on the goodwill of supporters to be able to afford to get to fixtures. Clapton used their time in the spotlight well, garnering exposure in the national press. Captain Alice Nutman's quote in *The Observer* on Sunday 12 December 2021, echoed the passionate sentiment of Ewald Lienen's opening quote in this book. Alice stated: "Top-down development, trickle-down economics, we know they don't work, and the same is true in football. We're not asking for equal pay. That's a myth. We're asking for investment in grassroots and we're asking for space in which women and non-binary people are able to play football, which currently do not exist. Unfortunately, when the FA is the body that banned women's football for a 50-year period, you then need to do things to reverse that, and at the moment that's not happening. For anyone tier three and below that money makes a huge difference. It means that you're not living hand to mouth each month. We struggle to pay for our training pitch. That's the reality of grassroots football in this country as a woman."

Alice's statement confirmed that Clapton were indeed the fixture that St. Pauli were searching for: a similar, albeit much smaller, club with an ethos of speaking out against fascism, sexism and homophobia. A club as fiercely political as themselves.

Of course, both clubs still exist in the context of the capitalist system so, inevitably, it was thanks to corporate sponsorship that the game was able to be scheduled in the first place. It was only due to Levi's long-standing relationship with FC St. Pauli that the tour took place at all.

The St. Pauli Levi's Music School situated in one of the boxes in the South Stand and run by musician, Dave Doughman of the band Swearing At Motorists has been the cornerstone of Levi's relationship with the club. It provides the opportunities for youngsters and disadvantaged groups in the district to come together, develop their skills and share a love of music in a fully equipped music studio that overlooks the Millerntor pitch. Levi's were also one of the key sponsors of the club's tours to the United States in 2018 and 2019. In February 2020, Levi's extended the partnership by becoming shirt sponsors of FC St. Pauli 1. Frauen. The shirts were first worn in the semi-finals of the Hamburg Cup against arch-rivals, HSV. For Christian Weiß, Marketing Director of Levi's, the partnership expands their commitment to diversity and equality. It was also a shrewd bit of investment on behalf of Levi's, who were perhaps slightly ahead of the curve in anticipating the growth and commercial potential of the women's game. As a continuation of this partnership Levi's put up the money to spend three nights in London – the payback being lots of Levi's-related photo opportunities and a discussion panel on women's football hosted at Levi's London Haus on the eve of the game against Clapton.

However, FC St. Pauli's 'Football Has No Gender' tour didn't exactly roll into town on a wave of triumphant gender equality. Instead – thanks to EasyJet cancelling their Sunday evening Hamburg-Gatwick flight – the players, coaches and delegates from

St. Pauli arrived in dribs and drabs over the course of the following day. Maybe the nature of the team's arrival wasn't as planned but there was a steely-determinism and resilience that saw the group split into four and travel a variety of different routes and transport modes to our beleaguered island. It was mentioned several times that had the men's first team been faced with such obstacles they would've packed up and gone home, cancelling the match and tour.

The first group to depart were also the first to arrive in London just before lunch on Monday. Seven of the first team squad had taken the overnight train from Hamburg before catching the Eurostar from Brussels to St. Pancras. A gruelling trip and one with very little rest (no sleeper cabins for them, just standard seats). Other groups took the train to Bremen and Hannover before getting flights into Stansted and Heathrow respectively. The remaining members of the party able to get an early flight from Hamburg to Heathrow on the Monday morning. By about 19:30 that evening – 24 hours later than advertised – the entire squad was reunited at Levi's London HQ just off Carnaby Street.

The idea of taking both St. Pauli's men's and women's first team on a joint international tour is a noble one, progressive too. I don't know if any other club has done the same? However, the cynic could argue that whilst 'football has no gender' to misquote George Orwell it could also be stated that 'some genders are more equal than others'. Why? This can be put as succinctly as: *EasyJet versus private jet.*

Whilst 1. Frauen were booked on a budget airline, later in the week the FCSP men's first team flew by private jet (badged up with the club logo) from Hamburg to Edinburgh. No cancellations and complicated alternative travel arrangements for the men. It is up to you to decide if we are splitting hairs here. It's clearly progress that the club's women get to go on tour like the men, but the journey is far from complete. Parity in transport, accommodation and facilities are the obvious next steps.

But transport discrepancies shouldn't get in the way of what was a huge and symbolic event for both FC St. Pauli and their hosts Clapton Community FC. Rewind just five years and it is highly unlikely that a fixture like this would take place at all – especially with the support and financial backing of the travelling club. It was the first time that Clapton's women's team had faced international opposition but FC St. Pauli 1. Frauen had previously played a friendly game in Austria in 2019 when 3,511 fans witnessed a 3:3 draw against Wiener Sport-Club.

Football is changing – too slowly, yes – but it is changing. The future of football is no longer exclusively in the hands of fusty old white men in suits wandering marble halls. Football – the sport, the concept – may have no gender but I really hope that the future of football is female; that the future of football is non-binary. Why? Because those fusty old white men have fucked it. They have turned it into a monster – a corporate monster. They've done deals with various devils over the years. Selling the game's soul to the highest bidders via Sky, oligarchs and global sports washing. Throw in more than a dash of the misogynistic machismo that sadly still – in 2023 – dominates much of terrace and supporter culture and you can see why men's football remains largely toxic and certainly can't be considered a safe space for anyone except cis males.

The future of football is FLINTA (Female, Lesbian, Intersex, Trans and Agender). *It has to be.* I say that as a cis male. Not because I actively aided and abetted the men's game to go in its current direction, but because I didn't do enough to stop it.

Enough amateur philosophising. Acting as an unofficial guide, I was able to shadow the St. Pauli delegation throughout their stay in London. I didn't serve much useful purpose, aside from occasionally confidently marching the group off in the wrong direction as we did a tour of the sights and sounds of the capital. On the day of the game, the party were up early for another photo-op at the Levi's store on Regent Street before I led them on foot to the German embassy in Belgravia. It might seem most un-St. Pauli-like, considering supporter's views on nationalism and nation states but on these tours, there is always a requirement to press the flesh. For me, as a child of the 1980s, it was a long-awaited chance to attend 'the ambassador's reception' – to be spoilt with a tray of Ferrero Rocher. We met the ambassador in what turned out to be the old East German embassy, as the current German embassy (formerly belonging to West Germany) was being refurbished. There was a very impressive buffet lunch but, sadly, not a single nugget of hazelnutty chocolate wrapped in golden foil in sight. From the reception, the players returned to their hotel in Shoreditch before making their way to the stadium later that afternoon.

By 19:00 there was a celebration going on at the Old Spotted Dog in Forest Gate. A coming together of the clans and – for me – a collision of worlds. Of course, it could never be a perfect synergy. Clapton and St. Pauli are different clubs that exist in very different worlds. FC St. Pauli is a huge professional club with annual turnover that has reached as high as €50 million; Clapton CFC is run by volunteers and is entirely amateur in its football status. Both clubs are vehemently left-wing, although there are key issues on which they hold differing opinions. However, there *is* still a lot that unites us. The clamour for tickets and the sell-out crowd were testament to this. Everywhere you looked it was people either dressed in the iconic Clapton away shirt (the red, purple and yellow honouring the Second Spanish Republic) or the equally iconic Totenkopf hoodies and t-shirts. The bar was doing a roaring trade and the Old Spotted Dog – London's oldest senior football ground – was looking glorious in the summer sunshine. The fact that this game happened was down to the hard work of a core group of volunteers who had been working frantically behind the scenes in the weeks, days and hours leading up to kick-off.

The atmosphere was electric. This was the first international fixture at the Old Spotted Dog since the men of Clapton FC hosted Ajax of Amsterdam in 1927.

There were tifos. There was pyro. There was non-stop singing. St. Pauli striker Rachel Rinast speaking to the *Hamburger Abendblatt* said, "There have been few games in my career where the atmosphere was better" – praise indeed from a veteran of one World Cup and two European Championships.

The game itself was pretty one-sided. FCSP are at Step 3 in Germany compared to CCFC's Step 6 in England and whilst it may be difficult to make accurate comparisons across football pyramids, the 8:1 score line was a clear reflection of St. Pauli's superiority. However, as their FA Cup run highlighted, this Clapton side are not afraid to do battle with higher-ranked teams and despite the final score, they gave a great account of themselves. And, of course, they provided the evening's absolute highlight – Marta Boiro's goal. This was the moment when FC St. Pauli knew why they found themselves in east London. When Marta's penalty crashed against the crossbar, the stadium fell momentarily silent; when she calmly slotted the rebound into the bottom left corner the place exploded. The tin roof of the Scaffold stand – so called because it is constructed entirely from scaffolding – raised at least 10 foot in the air! Subs rushed on to join the celebrations. FCSP coach Jan-Philipp Kalla said to me later that as he turned to watch the Scaffold celebrating, he realised just how much this game mattered. It was a consolation goal for sure but tell that to the Clapton fans as the team rushed to celebrate with the supporters.

There had been some moments of genuine football quality too. Tabea Schütt was a menace upfront for the visitors. I don't think I have ever seen anyone keep Maria Mendonca as quiet as Midou Loubongo did at right back for St. Pauli. And then there was Rachel Rinast. The Swiss international had been signed from Grasshoppers Zürich the previous week and she immediately showed her quality, scoring one absolute screamer in the first half that gave Polly Adams no chance. Before too long she was dancing through the Clapton defence again, hitting the crossbar with another incredible shot before finally doubling her tally with a goal in the second half.

She is going to bring bags of experience to this young St. Pauli side next season – and you can't help but admire a player who discards their shinpads early doors and plays with her socks rolled down. In Rinast there is a St. Pauli legend in the making.

One more word on the penalty. A referee mate of mine pointed out very quickly on social media that Marta Boiro's goal shouldn't have stood. I had no idea why, but apparently because the shot came directly back to her via the crossbar it would count as a 'double touch' akin to taking a free kick to yourself! The ref must've decided to play to the spirit if not the letter of the law. Either that, or the keeper got a touch to divert the ball onto the bar. Regardless, there was no way Marta and this Clapton crowd were going to be denied their moment.

The post-match celebrations were iconic. The two teams jointly doing the call-and-response 'Lo-lo-los' in front of the Scaffold with goalkeeper Polly Adams trying to orchestrate the slightly bemused St. Pauli team during the sitting down part of the chant. The teams thanked fans on all four sides of the pitch with the visitors stopping to do their own call-and-response post-match ritual with the travelling members of the Die üblichen Verdächtigen and Ey, die Hunde fan groups.

Simultaneously, on the other side of the ground the home fans were giving Clapton manager Claudio Gomes an emotional send-off. It is impossible to overstate the influence that Claudio and his coaching staff have had on this team. They've scaled unimaginable heights in the FA Cup, breaking records in the process. They've secured a promotion and more than consolidated themselves in a higher league (leading the table for a prolonged period and nearly bagging another promotion). But more importantly, the team have played some incredible football and grown individually as players. Claudio will be a big miss. My hope is that we see him achieve great things in football, coaching at a much higher level and making a living from the game.

This fixture was a victory for both sides, a celebration of two successful and progressive women's teams and their enthusiastic and dedicated fans. Equally importantly, it provided the opportunity for like-minded football supporters and activists to come together, drink beer, chew the fat and maybe even start dismantling the patriarchy... It was a clear signpost that another football is indeed possible.

And, at the very least, we need to push for parity in the transportation of the men's and women's teams. In an echo of The Redskins album, just as it was neither *Washington nor Moscow* it should be neither *EasyJet nor private jet*. It should be sustainable train travel for all!

From a personal point of view, it had been an emotional day – a day of dream fulfilment. The rest of the 775-sell-out crowd also went home happy. We were probably preaching to the converted, but I hope it got the key message out there: *Football Has No Gender!*

Acknowledgments

Once again there are so many people to thank for their support with this book, that I am sure to forget someone important – so if you've helped in anyway – from a more formal interview through to a casual conversation on a matchday, your input has been invaluable.

I owe the biggest debt of gratitude to Sönke Goldbeck. We first met on the St. Pauli Messageboard back in the early 2000s. Since then I have continued to pester him for assistance with various FCSP-related projects. Sönke and the FC St. Pauli-Museum have been incredibly supportive and encouraging with both Pirates, Punks & Politics and this book. Neither would've happened without their assistance.

The work of FC Lampedusa coaches Hagar and Nico has been an inspiration; they have made a genuine difference to countless young people whose lives have been improved by their presence. Hagar and Nico were, of course, among the original players for FC St. Pauli Frauen back in the 1990s and were part of the generation that began the long fight for equality in football that is still ongoing. The role they played and the prejudice they battled against cannot be underestimated.

St. Pauli international fan groups have also been both a source of friendship and solidarity. Special mentions to everyone at Yorkshire St. Pauli – we've shared some great times together – but even more important is the work they do for refugees through projects like Football For All. Gary and the Glasgow St. Pauli crew have also set the standard for what a fan group should look like, combining fervent support for the team with countless social projects for refugees and other disadvantaged groups in their local community. By extension, pals from Republica Internationale – an organisation that recently celebrate their 40th anniversary –

their 'Ruby Revolution' – remain a blueprint for activist football supporters to follow.

The above people I would describe as activists. People prepared to put in the hard yards who to try and improve lives and change society for the better. These people have my upmost respect and admiration. They also help me recognise my own limitations. I am not an activist; I have learnt over time that my contribution is to try to document the incredible work of these people and in some small way amplify their voices. My contribution is to record and recognise their efforts through both words and pictures. The difference my work makes is marginal; the difference their work makes is vital. This distinction cannot be overstated.

I am also indebted to various friends across the pond. (New York) Shawn and the rest of the East River Pirates have always been supportive and welcoming on trips to the States and the legendary East River Bar. I first met (Canadian) Shawn and Sam from the FC St. Pauli podcast, *Fell In Love With A Girl*, in Detroit back in 2018 and it felt like we had known each other all our lives. Their love for St. Pauli; their dedication and sheer willpower to record (and edit) a podcast for every FCSP game far surpasses the effort of me writing a book; it is also a much loved and vital resource for us English speaking fans of the club. Portland pals Todd Diskin and Joshua R. Duder were incredible hosts when I visited the Pacific Northwest – I hope to return before too long to catch up with them and experience a Thorns game. It is always great to see Zach Rossetto either in the US or at the Millerntor. The importance of the internet in general and Twitter/X in building international relationships can't be underestimated; even with Musk hellbent on its destruction, it remains an important space for us to share ideas and build solidarity.

Trips to Hamburg are always brightened by bumping into friends like Thomas Kozinowski, Dave Doughman, Malte, Caroline and Henk, and Svenja and Pete. Sharing a glass (or bottle) of wine outside the Museum Wine Bar after a game is always a particular highlight.

Since I wrote *Pirates, Punks & Politics* back in 2013, Fanladen St. Pauli has experienced a turnover of staff which makes me feel older than I already am! Stefan and Justus are very much missed, but a continued 'thank you' to everyone at the Fanladen who helps us international fans with tickets – without you St. Pauli's vibrant global fan scene wouldn't have access to the Millerntor.

My daughter Charlotte insists that my 'career' as a photographer is all because I 'ducked under a barrier once' at Clapton Community FC and nobody stopped me from taking photos. From there, I worked with proper photographers like Max, Garry, Rebecca, and George, learning from them and taking their recommendations for equipment. From these humble beginnings, Sven Brux kindly secured me photo accreditation for games at the Millerntor. Photos taken at these games are featured on the front and back cover of this book and via the interactive QR codes at the start of chapters. You might notice a slight improvement in quality of photos over time. This is nothing to do with me as a photographer and everything to do with equipment upgrades.

I have St. Pauli to thank for my discovery of Clapton Community FC. Whilst I still look forward to and plan my trips to the Millerntor months in advance it has been a welcome addition to have a political, antifascist football club a little closer to home. The fact that Clapton and St. Pauli got to play each other at the Old Spotted Dog in June 2023 was one of the absolute highlights of my life.

Christian Prüß was in charge of organising FC St. Pauli 1. Frauen's trip to London. I thank him for letting me be involved and for letting me host the panel discussions in Detroit and New York on the US tours. I also salute Christian and everyone on the tour to London for finding a workaround the last-minute cancellation of their flight from Hamburg to London.

It has also been an honour to be able to speak with Oke Göttlich and Bernd von Geldern who gave up their time to be interviewed for this book. Then there is the irrepressible Ewald Lienen. I'm so glad Ewald and St. Pauli found each other. I'm also grateful for Ewald for chatting to me. Big thanks too to Eddy Dieckow, Annie Kingman, Kim and Schnecke from FC St. Pauli 1. Frauen.

I also need to thank Randall Northam for his support in publishing my previous books with his company SportsBooks Ltd. I hope you enjoy your retirement and keep fighting the Tories on Twitter!

Thank you to long-suffering friends and family. To Mum for believing in this project and for being the first person to read and proof the drafts. To Shaun for always being there. Wayne – my midfield buddy – who left too soon. International rap superstar K Dizzle.

And, of course, the girls, Bess and Charlo who – with minimal and no interest in football respectively – have taken my obsessional tendencies and applied them to the genres of theatre/musical theatre.

Finally, the last few years have been hard on the St. Pauli fan community. We have lost many wonderful people far too soon. Les Rae, Scott Chrystal, John Griffiths, Arthur McCue, Nick Oetjen, Antje Frohmüller – YNWA.

September 2023

Select Bibliography

Backes, Gregory, *With Deutsches Sport greeting Heil Hitler. The FC St. Pauli in National Socialism,* Hoffmann and Campe, 2010

Backes, Gregory, *With A German Sports Greeting: FC St. Pauli under National Socialism,* Unrast Verlag, 2017

Fanladen St. Pauli, *15 Jahre Fanladen St. Pauli, 20 Jahre Politik Im Stadion,* Fanladen St. Pauli, 2005

Fanladen St. Pauli, *30 Jahre Fanladen St. Pauli,* Fanladen St. Pauli, 2020

FC St. Pauli-Museum 1910 e. V., *Football. Escape. Exile. Max Kulik – A Jewish Athlete and Physician from St. Pauli,* FC St. Pauli-Museum 1910 e. V., 2023

Goldblatt, David, *The Age of Football: The Global Game in the Twenty-First Century,* Macmillan, 2019

Goldblatt, David, *The Ball is Round: A Global History of Football,* Penguin, 2007

Hesse-Lichtenberger, Ulrich, *Tor! The Story of German Football,* WSC Books, 2002

Hobsbawm, Eric, *Globalism, Democracy and Terrorism,* Abacus, 2008

Jefferies, Matthew, *Hamburg –A Cultural & Literary History,* Signal Books, 2011

Katzenber, Susanne and Tamm, Olaf, *Millerntor Das alte Satdion,* Braus, 2012

Khun, Gabriel, *Soccer vs. the State,* PM Press, 2011

Kirby, Emma Jane, *The Optician of Lampedusa*, Penguin, 2017

Lowe, Keith, Inferno – *The Devastation of Hamburg, 1943,* Penguin Books, 2007

Mardini, Yusra, *Butterfly: From Refugee to Olympian, My Story of Rescue, Hope and Triumph*, Bluebird, 2018

Martens, René, *Niemand Siegt Am Millerntor,* Verlag Die Werkstatt, 2008

Martens, René, *Wunder Gibt Es Immer Wieder, Die Geschichte Des FC St. Pauli,* Verlag Die Werkstatt, 2007

Nagel, Christoph and Pahl, Michael, *FC St. Pauli. Das Buch.,* Hofffman and Campe Verlag, 2009

Sanderson, Chris, *'Nie wieder Faschismus, Nie wieder Krieg, Nie wieder 3. Liga!' A Social History of FC St. Pauli, 1986-1991,* University of Warwick, 2009

Tate, Tim, *Women's Football – The Secret History,* John Blake Publishing, 2013

Viñas, Carles and Parra, Natxo, *St. Pauli Another Football is Possible*, Pluto Press, 2020

Williams, Jean, *The History of Women's Football,* Pen & Sword History, 2021

Zirin, Dave and Carlos, John, *John Carlos Story: The Sports Moment that Changed the World*, Haymarket Books, 2011

FÜR DEN FC ST. PAULI

"A club like no other deserves a museum like no other"

FC St. Pauli-Museum (or rather its operator 1910 – Museum für den FC St. Pauli e.V.) is a not-for-profit organisation established as a space to celebrate and reflect on the past and future of the club – including both permanent and temporary exhibitions as well as professional archive facilities. The museum has been hosting exhibitions at its 600m² site underneath the Gegengerade stand at the Millerntor Stadion since 2014. It is the biggest project started by volunteers in the club's history.

The author's royalties from this book are being donated to the museum with the specific aim of further developing contributions from (and dialogue between) the club's international fan scene. The hope is that, moving forward, voices can be diversified and amplified to ensure that all members of the community are represented in future exhibitions (both physical and virtual), publications and research. The oral history and personal experiences of a variety of St. Pauli fans from around the globe will play an important part in future generations' understanding of FC St. Pauli's popularity on the world stage. At the same time, the museum will support international supporters' groups, providing them with access to resources (for example: exhibitions are translated into English, accessible by a QR code or available online) that will help develop their understanding of both the club's history and its context in wider society.

Printed in Great Britain
by Amazon

41834253R00215